The Conservative Illusion

M. MORTON AUERBACH

THE
Conservative
Illusion

COLUMBIA UNIVERSITY PRESS

NEW YORK 1959

LIBRARY OF CONGRESS CATALOG CARD NUMBER: 59-10698

COPYRIGHT © 1958, 1959 COLUMBIA UNIVERSITY PRESS
FIRST PUBLISHED IN BOOK FORM 1959

PUBLISHED IN GREAT BRITAIN, CANADA, INDIA, AND PAKISTAN
BY THE OXFORD UNIVERSITY PRESS
LONDON, TORONTO, BOMBAY, AND KARACHI

MANUFACTURED IN THE UNITED STATES OF AMERICA

TO RITA

Preface

A major difficulty of ideological and theoretical debate lies in the frequency with which it is based on contradictory assumptions which never actually clash. The validity of too many ideological critiques depends on the mere assertion of counter-premises, although it is precisely the validity of the premises which is the primary source of disagreement. To avoid this difficulty, I have tried, throughout most of this book, to confine the analysis to arguments which begin with the premises of Conservatism itself. Not until the last few pages of the book have I intended to question the ultimate validity of the fundamental Conservative values. The major criticisms in the study have been focused on the relation between Conservative values and the movement of reality, whether the reality of a single historical period or that of Graeco-Roman and Western civilization as a whole.

My conclusion is a categorical one—Conservatism has no way of making the crucial transition from values to reality, from theory to practice; and in the limited periods of history when it *seemed* to make this transition, it was able to do so only for reasons which contradicted its premises.

But this rejection of Conservatism does not in itself prove the validity of any other single theory, because there are more than two possible theoretical orientations. However, one of the unexamined assumptions of this study (unexamined because it is not essential to the course of the argument) is that the number of known theories, and perhaps the number of possible theories, is not unlimited—that there are, in fact, only four alternative formulations from which one can begin an evaluation of human society. I have referred to these alternatives as Conservatism, Liberalism, radicalism or equalitarianism, and authoritarianism. There are, of course, many more possible combinations of these basic theories, combinations often tailor-made to fit a particular societal customer; and there are historical variations which reflect general changes (sometimes advances) in our knowledge of society. But even within the systems which dominate particular ages—natural law, Newtonian science, Darwinism, positivism, historicism, etc.—the same four alternatives can always be found adapting their premises to the latest findings and techniques of human knowledge.

A full examination of this hypothesis on the nature of theoretical alternatives would, however, require tracing the whole development of each basic alternative, a task obviously outside the scope of this book. Suffice it to say here that if this hypothesis is correct and if the critique of Conservatism presented here is valid, then we must conclude that an adequate theory of society must begin with one of the three remaining assumptions of value. Aside from its relevance to contemporary problems, it is to this larger theoretical conclusion, beyond its own scope, that this book is directed.

The general approach and major themes of this study were originally formulated in a Columbia University doctoral dissertation entitled "Conservatism and Its Contemporary American Advocates." Though a number of revisions have been made in specific formulations, the underlying thesis remains the same. In the preparation of both the dissertation and the book, I am particularly grateful to Professor Herbert A. Deane, whose discerning and trenchant, yet friendly, criticisms made me aware of many difficulties which I would otherwise have missed. I owe a special debt to Professor Franz Neumann, whose untimely and tragic death several years ago did not prevent his influencing my approach to this book in so many ways that I am no longer able to discern with reasonable clarity where that influence begins and ends.

I am indebted for suggested improvements to several learned specialists: to Professor Robert J. Harris of Vanderbilt on the Southern agrarians; to Professor Robert D. Cumming of Columbia on Plato and Burke; and to Professors David B. Truman and Richard Hofstadter of Columbia on American politics and political theory. I am grateful also for their encouragement and for the general suggestions which have improved this book from its original form.

I would like to express my gratitude to Mr. Raymond J. Dixon of Columbia University Press for the inexhaustible energy which he devoted to editing the manuscript and for the generous surrender of his time beyond anything which could reasonably have been expected. To Julius and Elaine Zack, to Jules and Joan Beitler, I offer the thanks of a friend for their ready help in proofreading. To my wife, Rita Auerbach, whose life in recent years has been as intertwined as my own in the writing of this book, an expression of gratitude would border on the superfluous.

I also wish to thank Alfred A. Knopf Inc. for permission to reprint passages from Clinton Rossiter's *Conservatism in America;* Harcourt, Brace & Company for permission to quote from R. H. Tawney's *Religion and the Rise of Capitalism;* and the *American Political Science Review* for allowing me to quote passages from Samuel Huntington's article, "Conservatism as an Ideology."

Beyond these acknowledgments, I submit to the ritual which demands a statement of the obvious—that I alone am responsible for the actual formulations and statements in this book.

M.M.A.

Westfield, N. J.
June, 1959

Contents

The Conservative Illusion

Introduction

Except for fleeting moments of history, no society has ever bridged the chasm which lies between Conservatism and Liberalism. The Conservative seeks harmony and tranquillity, the inner peace which is destroyed by tension. Conservative harmony requires the minimizing of individual desires and the maximizing of affection through a "community," integrated by traditions and institutions handed down from the past. But the Liberal wants freedom, the freedom to satisfy individual desires on the basis of individual ability. Historically, Liberalism has been in quest of progress rather than tradition, competition rather than harmony, individual freedom rather than an integrated community, and restless activity rather than tranquillity.

The American ideal has never been Conservative. Until recently, our only major ideological conflict was between nineteenth-century "Old Guard" Liberalism and twentieth-century "Progressive" Liberalism. But in the past ten years America has shown superficial signs of becoming Conservative. We have developed an intense interest in defining our "traditions." We have "returned to religion" to look for something we lost in one of our yesterdays. The tensions of modern society have sent us in search of psychic tranquillity; and the "need to belong" (what Conservatives call the "sense of community") has become almost a national slogan. Most important of all, a large number of Progressive Liberals have suddenly begun to use Conservative arguments in defense of Liberalism. These trends have provided the historical threads which have been woven into a series of programs now called the "New Conservatism."

This book is an evaluation of Conservatism in general and the New Conservatism in particular. Its conclusion is contained in the title—Conservatism is an illusion which never has been and never will be able to translate its own ideal into reality. But it might seem as though a critique of Conservatism is of little "practical" importance in a country which does not take Conservative ideology seriously. The positive influence of the New Conservatives in American society is extremely limited, and the "programs" which they have been conjuring up are certain to be inconsequential. Such an appraisal of a book on American Conservatism would, however, be wide of the mark. Aside from yielding certain general insights about the whole realm of ideology, a study on American Conservatism is indispensable for understanding the crisis through which American Liberalism is passing.

A recent work[1] has shown that American Liberalism never saw itself in historical perspective, because it did not have a strong Conservative class to force it to self-clarification. America was born without the medieval heritage in which Conservatism has its historical roots; and the "aristocracy" of the Old South, our closest approximation to a Conservative class, was, as we shall see, of a very artificial and dubious brand. The absence of a powerful, Conservative opposition allowed American Liberalism to formulate its ideas in contradictory terms without examining the historical conditions under which the contradictory values were compatible. The result is that we have been left with a legacy in which freedom and authority, equality and traditionalism are thrown together in a vaguely defined recipe which we euphemistically call "Liberalism." It is extremely difficult to understand what this mixture means today, because we are rarely given a meaningful standard by which to test the result. Mixed ideologies cannot be tested by taste, like a tossed salad. The logic of ideological consistency demands historical perspective, and the day when Liberalism could ignore this demand is long past.

In earlier centuries, when medieval traditions were steadily giving way to the new forces of individual freedom, European Liberalism could consistently ally itself with political authority while it hacked away at Conservative traditions, and with Conservatism while it overthrew hostile forms of political authority. In the nineteenth century, when industrialization made the lower middle class and labor into serious contenders for political power, Liberalism became equalitarian and finished the job of sweeping away the old order in favor of a free society. But in the United States, where there was no "old order" to sweep away, Liberalism was, by the middle of the century, so overwhelmingly dominant that it did not have to concern itself much with questions of consistency.

When Progressive Liberalism brought its ideological mixture into the early twentieth century, it was still depending on history to see that the element of freedom remained dominant. But since World War I, political authority has no longer been a reliable junior partner of Liberalism. On the contrary, it has been threatening to become the "Big Brother." The realization that the "organization man," the "other-directed man," the "overadjusted man," and the "man in the grey flannel suit" are all prepared to abandon individual freedom has caused considerable soul-searching among contemporary Liberals. Since all these "men" are products of the new "white-collar" class, and since this is the class which George Orwell saw around Big Brother in his nightmare of *1984,* the pessimistic mood of Liberalism today should cause no surprise. On the other hand, the increase of equality in contemporary society seems to cause an increase in conflict, and conflict is now likely to be an invitation for an increase in authority. For those Liberals who have become sufficiently frightened to abandon the further extension of equality, the only alternative left now is to make an alliance with Conservatism, since Conservatism is the only ideological ally which a frightened Liberalism can still dominate. Being habitually given to crossing ideological lines without looking where it is going, this latest form of Liberalism is having little difficulty imagining itself in that revered American position, the middle of the road—with "some" authority as a traveling companion on one side, "some" tradition on the other, and "some" equality in the back seat.

Unfortunately, the danger of being in the middle of a *real* road is the ease with which one can be hit by cars coming from both directions. Some of the New Conservatives have already tried to add Liberalism to the casualty list. The "New Liberals" have been only too happy to meet this attack, because it enables them to turn away from the real authoritarian danger coming from the opposite direction, perhaps in the hope that it will turn off the road. When the New Liberals do turn to defend themselves against the authoritarian threat, they rely on "American traditions" to bear their standard. Their counterattack against the Conservatives, on the other hand, consists of the charge that Conservatives are not supposed to criticize, but only to defend established traditions, in this case Liberal traditions. This, as we shall see, is the exact opposite of the truth. Conservatism is tenable *only* in criticism, or when it is being used by another ideology which is rising to dominance. But when it is used as a prop by a defensive ideology, it is as empty an illusion as when it tries to stand on its own foundation.

The current Liberal rationalization is that ideological clarity is bad, because it stirs up unnecessary conflict. Even if this were true, it is beneficial only to the winning side in any period of profound change. A defensive Liberalism which closes its ideological eyes while trying to drive in the "middle of the road" is much more likely to commit suicide than to ward off defeat. To push the Conservative crutch out from under the new form of Liberalism is to force it to face its problem squarely. Liberalism can only justify itself if it still has goals to fulfill which are compatible with its own values. If it does not have any such unfinished business left, then no amount of Conservative defense will save it. The only possible direction in which Liberalism can continue to develop is towards increasing equality. If it is incapable of such development, then it has already written its own epitaph: killed in the middle of the road.

A clear evaluation of the problems which Liberalism is facing requires a clear grasp of Liberalism in the perspective of its full historical development. But a historical comprehension of Liberalism still requires a historical comprehension of Conservatism. Since America has never experienced Conservatism, it can only arrive at this understanding intellectually. If the New Conservatives had clarified their own ideology, much of this book would have been unnecessary. But both the New Conservatives and the New Liberals have a strong interest in perpetuating obscurity on the subject of Conservatism, because to understand Conservatism is to understand its impossibility in contemporary America. No such commitment will hamper the evaluation which follows here.

Everyone agrees that Edmund Burke, the intellectual "father" of the British Conservative Party, is the source of modern Conservatism. Many Conservatives are aware, however, that the roots of Conservatism go back beyond Burke to the Middle Ages, and beyond the Middle Ages to the Roman Stoics. But few have admitted the first assumptions of this study—that the original intellectual source of Conservatism was Plato, that Burke's Conservatism can only be understood in terms of its fundamental Platonic values, and that Plato has never been superseded as the Conservative master. It is essential that a work on Conservatism begin with Plato's *Republic*. But a full understanding of Conservative ideology requires insight into all its major historical forms from Plato to the twentieth century.

I

Historical Forms

of Conservatism

An ideology* is a program for organizing the resources, institutions, purposes, and power relations of society. On the one hand, it is based on a transcendent conception of human values throughout history. On the other, it must express these values in changing forms that reflect the historical problems with which it must cope in a particular age and society. A finished ideology must have a "technique" of action, a way of translating its program into practice. But the technique must not be confused with the whole of the ideology. To define Conservatism as the defense of existing institutions is to define it by its most congenial technique but to omit the whole foundation. We shall see that the transcendent value of Conservative ideology is the Platonic idea of harmony and that this conception has assumed a wide variety of historical forms.

If, as is commonly believed today, basic values cannot be disproved, then there is only one comprehensive "test" to which an ideology can be submitted—the test of consistency. Is the program consistent with the values? Are the values consistent with each other? These are the first questions we shall ask of Conservative ideologies, and the historical forms of Conservatism will be delineated in a way which will focus on the answers. It will also be relevant to ask whether the tech-

* This is not the only possible meaning of the term, but it is submitted in this book as the most useful.

niques are consistent with the programs, the "means" with the "ends."

The test of consistency is not a mere logical game, however. It is, in reality, a historical test. Ideological inconsistency reflects insoluble historical dilemmas. The crucial question behind logical consistency is whether the historical movements in a particular age are tending towards or away from the ideological values. On this basis, we shall see that Conservatism has been consistent only in two limited periods during the past two thousand years—the Late Middle Ages when something resembling a Conservative society actually existed, and the Dark Ages, which were the preconditions of the Middle Ages. Only after this test of consistency is applied to Conservative ideologies will we question whether values themselves cannot also be tested. We shall see that an "ideology" becomes a "theory" whose assumptions can be verified only when it places its values within the framework of an explanation of historical change.

Plato: From Utopia to Authoritarian Conservatism

For Plato, as for Edmund Burke, the "good life" is one of harmony and tranquillity. Harmony describes a condition of cohesion in which every part of the whole stays in its proper place, without any outside force. Tranquillity is the "test" of harmony, though the test is a negative one. It is the absence or minimizing of tensions and conflicts, because conflict is the essence of evil for the Conservative.

Plato saw in nature his model for harmony. Behind the movement and flux in nature was a pattern, an "Idea" which kept everything in its relative place. The sun and the moon moved but always circularly back to where they started, as if they were in a state of rest all the time.[1] It is this Idea of harmony, Plato thought, which man must reproduce in his own life and in the life of society.

The characteristically Conservative preconditions of both individual and societal harmony are the minimizing of individual desires (especially material desires) and the maximizing

of love and affection.   If desires are few, there will be few dis-
satisfactions or tensions in the individual and few conflicts in
society.   The key to harmonious personality is therefore the
development of nonrepressive self-control [2]—what Conservatives often call "graciousness"—by proper training from infancy.
Increases in affection, on the other hand, are simultaneously
necessary for the individual and for society; so there is no
reason to limit this need.   The conditions for the internal harmony of both the individual and society are therefore identical,
and there is no necessary conflict between their needs.   "Community," the sense of sharing a common life, is the basis of
happiness for both.   However, since it is society which is the
self-sufficient unit, society must be the starting point for an
understanding of harmony.

Given these premises, Plato's *Republic* is rigidly consistent
in its deductions.   A Conservative society must:

1. Maximize social cohesion by teaching love for the community and the importance of fulfilling moral obligations
above all else.   Morality in turn must be based on confining
individual desires to those which society can permit.

2. Limit the economy to a simple standard which can easily
be maintained, and teach the individual to concentrate on the
skilled performance of a single function.[3]

3. Teach the beauty and rationality of harmony, and stress
the importance of keeping one's "allotted place" in society.
Eliminate all contradictions from the culture, and make it produce a coherent picture of the universe as a harmonious entity to which the harmonies of the individual and society
contribute.[4]

4. Minimize coercive political power, since it is not needed
in a harmonious society, where the happiness of each is also the
happiness of the whole.   The negative function of political
authority is simply to prevent changes which will upset the harmony of society; [5] the positive function is to perfect the over-all
harmony by perfecting the character of the citizens.   If degenerate influences are not permitted to come into the society in

the first place, authority will lead to increasing happiness and will not be felt as repressive at all.

It is a common error to describe Plato as opposed to tradition. Actually, Plato considered tradition to be very important and highly desirable, provided that the tradition did in fact both reflect a harmonious attitude towards the world and support harmonious societal relations.[6] Under such conditions, tradition is the best guide for men and society because it is a noncoercive form of authority, and the use of force is always an admission of conflict and ethical failure. In the *Republic,* his expectation is that all the details of law will evolve "spontaneously" through custom. Political authority is concerned only with the over-all pattern. The use of authority for constant law-making is a sign of conflict and degeneration.[7]

An even worse mistake is to describe the *Republic* as "totalitarian." This ignores the crucial fact that Plato was trying to make the repressive use of political power unnecessary. If the nature of his ideology made "total integration" seem necessary to him, it was only for the purpose of making repression "totally" irrelevant. Besides, neither the Greek city-state of Plato's time nor the later medieval societies made any sharp distinction between the individual and the state. "Totalitarianism" is a purely modern phenomenon which must seek "totality" by continually using coercive power, because it follows the Liberal period when the expectation of individual freedom was greater than ever in history.

Plato's discussions on the distribution of power are equally consistent with his premises:

1. The primary qualifications for all power (except economic power) are the social * qualifications of affection for the

---

* The term "social" refers here specifically to the organized fulfillment of the need for affection, as distinct from "economic"—the need for material goods; "intellectual"—the need for knowledge; and "political"—the need for enforceable decision-making. The term "societal" refers to all these relationships collectively. The social system includes the prestige and status arrangements, the moral rules governing the relations of people to each other, and the institution of the family.

community and fulfillment of its moral rules, as well as the personal capacity for gracious, harmonious self-control, since these are the primary requirements for a harmonious society. Social power (prestige, honor) is due to those who have these qualifications.

2. Strength and force, the bases of political power, are needed only for use against the foreign enemies of a society. For the community itself, the rulers must have only love and affection. Therefore, political power should be rooted in the same social qualifications which merit prestige or honor. The capacity for physical force must coincide with the capacity for communal affection and moral self-discipline.[8] But the highest political offices should go to those who qualify for intellectual power as well.

3. The people who control the culture and philosophic "research" of society must be those who are capable of a rational comprehension of the "Idea" of harmony. It is vital to understand that Plato was not talking about what we would now call "experts," and that the qualification for intellectual power was not only the capacity to learn. The true philosophic knowledge refers specifically to the understanding of harmony and to the capacity for applying this Idea to the problems of society. The first qualifications of the "philosopher-rulers," like those of the "warriors," are the social capacities for communal affection and moral self-control. The intellectual qualifications are additions to the primary ones, not substitutes.[9]

4. Economic power (wealth), on the other hand, must never in itself be the basis for any other form of power, because the pursuit of wealth is the primary cause of conflict and the obstacle to harmony. It is essential to avoid poverty and dire want, but those who seek to expand their wealth are not capable of the maximum degree of harmony.[10] They should be left

---

Morality, in the sense of social rules, should be distinguished from the *capacity* for morality, which is individual and psychological. Plato's test of the capacity for morality is the ability to fulfill the social rules. The social test of communal affection is total devotion to serving the community in the face of temptation, hardship, and sophistry.

to their economic pursuits (within the limits needed to maintain over-all societal harmony), but they should have no access to honor, intellectual controls, or political authority as rewards for wealth.[11] On the other hand, those who are concerned with the welfare of society should be free from productive work.

In such a harmonious society, individual personality would also necessarily be harmonious. Each person would perform for society only those functions which he could easily accomplish without undue tensions, and would expect only rewards that society could actually grant to him. He would view himself as an important element of society and view society as part of the harmony of the universe. Taught harmony from childhood, he would achieve self-control in adulthood with minimum repression. He would therefore be integrated into the world, instead of being alienated from it. He would not, like contemporary man, view both nature and society as forces hostile to him.

Here then is the Conservative ideal: harmonious personality, made possible by a harmonious society in which social cohesion is maximized and economic needs minimized—a society in which coercion is unnecessary because each keeps his place and learns the supreme beauty and rationality of harmony from an integrated cultural tradition, a society in which conflict is minimized because economic power is isolated and all other power is rooted in the social realm of affection and cohesion, where the happiness of the individual and the needs of society coincide. In such a society, the "sense of community" is at a peak, because the sense of conflict is faint. It is this ideal which all Conservatives raise as the hope of mankind.*

It must be pointed out immediately that the historical significance of this ideal lies in the fact that, until the twentieth century, it was applicable only to a society ruled by a landed aristocracy. The middle classes † were never qualified for

* Hereafter when the word "harmony" is used it is this Platonic ideal which is intended.

† The term "middle class" is used throughout this book in its classical sense of the "bourgeoisie" or "capitalist" class. The distinction between "upper"

power by Platonic standards, because they were concerned primarily with making money. The lower classes were disqualified, because they could not fulfill their basic economic necessities and had to spend their lives working. Only aristocracies emphasized morality, "honor," and social "manners" rather than the pursuit of wealth; leisure rather than work; and consumption rather than production. Usually free from an ethic of hard work and economic progress, they were able to foster "gracious" personality as the ideal of a "gentleman," to live by accepted traditions, to have time for the appreciation of the "harmony" of the universe, and to devote their time to "public service." This does not mean that Plato justified all aristocracies. They were really the "best" only if they contributed to societal harmony. For Plato, as for Burke, the aristocratic ideal was fundamentally correct, but the trouble with aristocrats was that they failed too often to understand it or to live up to it.

The historical approximation of Plato's ideal was not simply aristocracy, but aristocracy in a Conservative society, a society in which there was social cohesion because there was little economic expansion, a society in which the rule of the aristocracy was accepted with relatively little conflict. Such a society had existed in the earlier "Homeric Age" of Greece, an age which was, in these respects, roughly similar to the late medieval period of European civilization. Plato sometimes made it seem as though his ideal ran back beyond the Homeric Age to the "Heroic Age" of the Greek tribal societies. But he refused to believe that the tribal period could have been one of continual violence and bloodshed. Therefore, he insisted that all historical evidence of tribal immorality in the Homeric epic poems be purged as "lies," in spite of his reverence for Homer.[12] He frequently referred to the warrior origins of the aristocracy, though he refused to admit that it was originally a

---

and "lower" middle class refers to the upper bourgeoisie of merchants, financiers, and manufacturers on the one hand and the "petite bourgeoisie" of retailers, artisans, and small farmers on the other.

conquering race which imposed its rule on the conquered peoples by force.

The decline of the aristocratic Homeric Age was followed, about the seventh century B.C., by the rise of the classical commercial city-state. Most of Plato's adult life was spent in the fourth century B.C., when the democratized commercial city-state was in its period of decline. This was an age of class conflicts and imperialist wars. The middle class, including the lower middle class, still managed to hold on to some political power, but power was intermittently recaptured by a violent, reactionary aristocracy (which included Plato's own relatives), and democracy was increasingly superseded by a new form of antidemocratic "tyranny." Many of the aristocrats based their claims to power on ancient traditions, but Plato knew that these traditions had been irretrievably abandoned and that they were of no use for the reestablishment of harmony in society. The road to a new Conservative society had to be found through abstract reason or not at all. Plato therefore sought to abstract the basic principles of the earlier age in order to apply them to the city-state of his day. Nevertheless, the dilemma which he never solved was how harmony could be artificially created in society without dependable traditions on the one hand and without the use of coercive political power on the other.

In the *Republic* he "solved" the dilemma only by relegating the work to the realm of Utopia. His technique for initiating the ideal society was to teach Conservative philosophy to a king, who would then convince his subjects to go into voluntary exile, leaving behind them only children under the age of ten. The children would be the nucleus of the new society.[13] This was consistent with his value premises, insofar as the new society was to be launched without repression or conflict. But, as it has turned out in history, a harmonious, Conservative society cannot be artificially created, because the social cohesion on which it depends is an "unconscious" feeling which cannot

be taught but can only evolve through "unconscious" traditions, over a long period of time. Once conflict exists, it cannot be eliminated by explaining to people the need for love
and harmony. This became obvious when Plato was given an
opportunity to put his ideas into practice through Dionysius
II, "tyrant" of Syracuse. He never got past the first step in his
plans. While Dionysius wanted to know how to solve the pressing conflicts of his society, Plato insisted that he must be "conciliatory" while he learned the philosophy of harmony, a long,
complex process of education which was the vital precondition
for the permanent solution. Plato had to leave Syracuse in an
unseemly hurry by the time his relationship with the "tyrant"
had ended.

But the more profound Utopian elements within the *Republic* itself stemmed from the fact that Plato took the claims
of aristocracy at face value and deduced their consequences
with magnificent consistency. Conservative aristocracies have
always claimed that virtue is largely hereditary, in spite of
occasional aberrations. They have always insisted that "honor,"
morality, and the service of society are more precious to them
than wealth. Plato, in effect, took them at their word. If the
surrender of all private wealth in the ruling class is shown to be
essential for its cohesion and for the willing submission of the
ruled classes, then the true aristocracy will be prepared to make
this sacrifice and to derive happiness solely from the honors
which it will receive for serving the community or from the
truths it will learn in the philosophy of harmony. Furthermore, the aristocracy should be prepared to submit the inherited virtues of its children to open competition with the
rest of society in tests of their capacity to love the community
above all else.[14] Normally, the children of the "best" will win,
but if not, they will be dropped from the ruling class in favor
of children from the ruled classes.[15] If private families are
abolished, the aristocracy will not resent this debasement of
some of its offspring, and the competition will increase the willingness of the other classes to defer to the decisions of the

"best," especially since the aristocrats will gain no wealth from their power.

The difficulty with these conclusions is that no aristocracy in history has ever been willing to accept them. Aristocracies have never submitted to any objective tests of their virtues during childhood. Their claims to virtue have always rested on the finished aristocratic product in adulthood. The affirmation that virtue is hereditary has, therefore, never been tested. Furthermore, aristocracies have, during periods of their ascendance, been the wealthiest, not the poorest, class in society; and they have never shared this wealth among themselves. In Conservative periods of history, such as the Late Middle Ages, the aristocracy (including the higher clergy, which was generally of aristocratic origin) had not only most of the wealth in society, but all of the honor, a monopoly on learning, and most of the political power. Since it was an economically stagnant society, which did not expect a general increase in wealth, what was left for them to want? One cannot avoid the suspicion that if aristocrats developed "gracious" personalities, it was not because of their superior capacities for self-denial, but because they did not have to deny themselves anything!

In the actual process of history, the Conservative justification of aristocracy has never rested on proof that the aristocrats were really those "best" able to achieve harmony. In practice, the justification has been possible only in retrospect: the existence of Conservative harmony in a society ruled by aristocrats proves that they are really the "best." This argument has always been used by Conservatives, whether explicitly or implicitly, alongside the reverse reasoning. For the time being, we can accept the argument as tenable, given the Conservative premises. But it should be clear that the program in the *Republic* is based not only on a "pure" type of Conservatism, but that it is so pure that its pattern exists only in "heaven," as Plato himself admitted. His later political "dialogues" were somewhat more realistic, but only at the expense of being less consistent.

In the *Statesman,* Plato changes his technique. He is now prepared to accept coercion, for the citizens' own "good," [16] and he insists that the "good" ruler should not be fettered by bad tradition in setting up a Conservative state. The program also changes in order to adjust Conservative values to the realities of the commercial city-state. He calls for an alliance, through intermarriage, between the aristocracy and the upper middle class.[17] In this way, economic power will at least be neutralized, and his insistence on a common ideal of harmony ensures the ultimate subordination of wealth. This "solution," which Plato sought to achieve through the use of political power, was for Burke the historical reality which had to be "conserved." In fourth-century Athens, however, it was unrealistic, and subsequent attempts by Plato's students to set up a Conservative society ended with their assassinating one another. Plato never explained why the wealthy merchant class should accept the supremacy of Conservative harmony, which rejected the quest for wealth, or how harmony could be achieved with force.

In his last dialogue, the *Laws,* Plato's technique changes again. This time harmony is to be introduced through the promulgation of a comprehensive legal code. But, although he still recognizes that the actual use of repressive force is a measure of failure, he is now willing to make repression a part of his permanent program. His "solution" for the problem of economic power here is to allow only aliens to belong to the middle class,[18] so they are, of course, to have no other power. But the ruling class in the *Laws* is more like a real aristocracy, because its members own property privately, and some are expected to own more than others. To solve the potential problem of conflict within the aristocracy, therefore, Plato proposed a system of "mixed government," based not only on intermarriage and a common Conservative ethic, but also on sharing political power between the wealthier and the "poorer" aristocrats. It is important not to confuse Plato's "mixed government" with Aristotle's "polity" or with American "checks and balances." The system of checks and balances assumes the existence of conflicting interests which are willing to compromise on policy issues. Aristotle's polity assumes conflicting classes which are integrated politically by maintaining a class equilibrium. But the mixed government of Plato (and Burke) is a friendly and harmonious "weaving" of diverse elements through social and ideological, as well as political, means. Its prime purpose is to avoid conflict in the first place, not to use conflict for economic progress, or stabilize it, or encourage "adjustments." In any event, however, this last program was no more successful than the earlier ones, and Plato never solved the contradiction of calling for force to achieve a harmony based on love and affection.

The fundamental concept of harmony in the *Republic* has always remained the basis of Conservative ideology. But Conservatism, like other ideologies, has always had to adjust itself to historical circumstances. We shall see that the difference between Plato's Conservatism and Burke's consisted of the difference in their historical environment, although their fundamental values were identical. But the adaptation to reality made Conservatism increasingly self-contradictory. Plato became inconsistent as soon as he left the realm of Utopia. The inconsistencies grew worse in the periods which followed.

The Stoics: From Authoritarian Conservatism to "Alienated" Conservatism

The history of the city-state ended in Plato's century. It was followed by the expansion of the Macedonian and Roman empires from the fourth century B.C. to the first century A.D. This was an authoritarian period in which both the communal traditions of the city-state and the political participation of its individual citizens were superseded by the laws and military power of world empires. The central importance of force during this period made it clear that the social cohesion on which a Conservative society depends no longer existed. Insofar as Platonism depended on the "unconscious" cohesion of the Greek community, it was now totally out of the question.

Stoicism was the adjustment of Conservatism to these new historical conditions. The Early Stoics, who lived at the end of the fourth and the beginning of the third centuries B.C., made the initial transition by emphasizing that the individual, who was now socially isolated, must look to the world-society, the "brotherhood of man," for his "community." Moreover, since morality could no longer depend on clear social norms, the individual must seek the universal elements of morality— the "natural law"—within his own conscience and reason.[19] The essence of Stoic morality always remained the Conservative code of self-control and self-denial in the interest of human affection and cohesion. But the task admittedly required far greater effort for the Stoics than it would have required in Plato's *Republic,* and the prospects for achieving harmony and tranquillity grew less and less likely with the passing centuries.

The Early Stoa adjusted itself to the acceptance of the "enlightened despotism" of Macedonia, and the adjustment to authoritarianism was carried further by the Middle Stoa, particularly after its introduction to the Romans around the second century B.C. Without ever achieving a consistent ideological integration, the Middle Stoa grafted a justification of coercive political power onto the Platonic ideology of communal cohesion and onto the newer moral doctrines of the Stoic school itself. With this "adjustment," Middle Stoicism became the ideology of the Roman aristocracy in the senatorial class. It lasted until the defeat of the Senate by Caesar Augustus.

The Middle Stoa and Platonism met in the ideology of Cicero. Cicero emphasized the importance of performing well one's function in society, but the highest function was that of statesmanship and political service. Political power was supposed to be legitimized by the consent of the cohesive moral community. But this "consent" did not have to be expressed through election, and popular opinion which contradicted "natural law" was invalid. In accepting Platonic ideas about the primacy of social cohesion, affection, and harmony, Cicero conveniently assumed that these actually existed in Roman society. He therefore saw no problem in superimposing, on this Conservative social foundation, Aristotelian ideas of "mixed government" which reflected a purely political balance of classes. As it turned out Cicero's "mixed government" became an artifice for preserving the dwindling power of the senatorial class. Plato had consistently refused to reason from his Conservative premises to a justification of imperial expansion, under any conditions. Cicero preferred Aristotle's justification of empires which are ruled "in the interest of the governed," and he advocated manipulative and repressive measures to stabilize senatorial power while extending the Roman Empire over "inferior states." [20] He did not ask how coercive power could increase affection and communal harmony, or why coercion was needed in the first place if society was based on a cohesive community which reflected the "brotherhood of man."

The Late Stoa began about the first century A.D., and continued throughout the period of Roman decline. By this time, Stoicism had been adopted by the imperial government, and by the classes which supported it. But in the period of decline, the pretense that harmony actually existed was no longer possible. This was an age of almost total moral degeneration. Conflict was at a peak; the older traditions had disappeared; and the older moral norms could neither be obeyed nor ignored without causing tensions and unhappiness. In such a world there was obviously no hope of Conservative success. The Late Stoa was, therefore, a Conservatism of pessimism and resignation, alienated from its own society, no longer hoping even for improvement, let alone the perfections of Plato's *Republic*. The Late Stoics looked at history as a process of continual decay since the "Golden Age" of simple, primitive communities. But, they admitted, the degeneration could not be stopped now.[21] The individual could achieve inner tran-

quillity only by emptying himself of desires, so that no mis-
fortunes or disturbances could touch his soul.[22]   Some sought
a kind of religious consolation for the miseries of life, but
others strove to achieve an indifference to death which was
tantamount to welcoming it as the solution to all problems,
and still others were frank in pointing out that "the door" was
always "open" for those who had enough of the tribulations of
life.[23] The one solution they could not accept was the destruction of their society. Yet this was ultimately the only real
solution possible, even in terms of their own values. Unable
to find any other way out because of their commitment to the
existing society, no matter how evil it was, they made suicide
the final solution to the quest for tranquillity and affection.

St. Augustine: From "Alienated" Conservatism to Radical Conservatism

St. Augustine's Conservatism was a combination of two distinct though interrelated strands. On the one hand, it was a
Conservatism of "alienation," similar to that of the Late Stoics;
on the other, it was a radical Conservatism, based on an expanding, militant Christianity.

In the fifth century A.D., when St. Augustine wrote, the
process of degeneration, which had long been evident, culminated in total collapse. The barbarian victories at the beginning of the century were a foretaste of the final triumph at
its end. But St. Augustine's sense of alienation was reinforced
by his orthodox Christianity, which taught him that man is
fundamentally evil, because of "original sin." Original sin is
the use of reason to destroy the natural harmony of God's universe by asserting man's ego as the center of that universe.[24]
Man is therefore incapable of achieving the Conservative goal,
and the history of the "City of Man" is a cyclical process of the
rise and fall of civilizations, of early virtue in simple, relatively
cohesive societies and later degeneration in corrupt luxury and
continual conflict.[25]

Towards this corruptible society, the "City of Man," the

Augustinian attitude is one of intense criticism. He only hopes that the rulers will consider their authority a heavy burden to be borne in the service of their subjects, while the subjects learn to submit.[26] Yet St. Augustine's criticisms are limited by his preference for any kind of stable society, however evil, over the even worse evil of political disorder. Though the coercive power of the state is ordinarily used for selfish purposes, it is nevertheless God's instrument for a sinful mankind which must be forced to restrain its proclivities towards evil.[27] The individual should never oppose authority, no matter how corrupt it may be.

If St. Augustine had gone no further than this, his position would have been as contradictory as that of the Late Stoics. Though Conservatism can never justify the actual dissolution of a civilization while it is occurring, because this means the end of all cohesion, a consistent Conservatism must recognize that its own cyclical theory * makes the early period of a new civilization superior to the late period of an old one. Therefore, it must admit that in a totally degenerate period opposition to corrupt authority is in itself neither more nor less justifiable than the corrupt authority itself.

But St. Augustine's deification of authority is only part of a wider view in which the function of authority is to prevent the greater evil of dissolution in the immediate present, while the advance towards more positive good occurs in another realm. The solution to the problem of inescapable sin lies in Christianity, which offers man the grace of God to aid him in finding true harmony through the sacrifice of the self to the love of Christ. The concomitant of grace is faith in God, and the effect of grace is to make it possible to overcome sin.[28] Yet, at best the victory over sin is temporary.[29] The individual can live morally and achieve inner peace by submission to God, but the effort must be continually renewed and there is no point of final rest during life. Societies can maximize harmony by directing their affection to God, but not permanently. Final

* See Chapter IX for a full discussion of this cyclical theory.

salvation will occur only in the resurrection at the end of history, and its precondition is the spread of Christianity. Alongside the history of the "City of Man" is the history of the "City of God," which began with the Jews and continues with the struggles of Christian man towards final salvation through divine grace. Each of these processes becomes intensified with time, and the struggle between them is not resolved until the end of history. Even at the last "moment," both good and evil will be at maximum strength, and the final resolution of the conflict will still depend on the grace of God.

At the end of history, with the resurrection of the body, the goals of Conservatism will be realized at last. The "elect" will live an eternal life of perfect tranquillity in which there will be a total absence of conflict, a permanent heavenly peace of perfect order and harmonious enjoyment of God and of one another in God.[30] Man will have reached final bliss, in which there is no material or physical desire and in which none seeks to be what he is not.[31] In the final community, affection will be maximized, material pursuits will be minimized, and there will be no need for power. The similarities to Plato's *Republic* are suggestive.

Through all the changes and conflicts of early Christian doctrine, Christianity remained "radical" in two crucial aspects, as compared with earlier ideologies and religions. First, it offered all men a release from the accumulated sense of guilt in civilization. This implied a momentary wiping clean of the slate of societal rules, a forgiving of past sins. The heavy moral obligations which Christianity imposed after conversion did not alter the fact that conversion itself was initially a psychological rejection of the earlier norms of society. Secondly, it was equalitarian in attaching no strings of societal status to salvation. The addition by the Fathers of the Church of the concept of the "elect," who were predestined for individual salvation by God, did not alter the fact that "election" was not related to status (at least not until much later). The release from guilt and the equalitarian concept of salvation were radical aspects of Christian doctrine.

The vision of the "City of God" advancing through the process of history also implied the adoption of an aggressive technique in seeking constant expansion of Christian influence on the centers of societal power. If St. Augustine, like all the early Church Fathers, does not face the problem of a possible conflict between the Church and political authority, the position of Christians in later history was that the Church could assert the superiority of Christian doctrine over secular authority.

Nevertheless, the foundations of orthodox Christianity remained Conservative. In the first place, its ultimate goals were attractive only by Conservative standards. Men holding Liberal values in St. Augustine's time might have sought a hedonistic Utopia or found escape in some form of Epicureanism. Radicals might have had apocalyptic visions of impending equalitarian deliverance from all oppression. Authoritarians might have hoped for a Machiavellian "prince" who would weld society together by means of political power. But only a Conservative could have conceptualized salvation as the renunciation of egoistic and material desires. Secondly, the differences in conceptions of ultimate salvation are simultaneously differences in the conceptions of evil. For the Liberal, self-assertion and escape from "natural harmonies" of the past define progress and "good" rather than "evil." For the radical, evil lies in the power relationships of society, while the authoritarian considers power relationships to be the instrument of human salvation and progress. Only for a Conservative could man's capacity for disrupting God's conflict-less, harmonious order be the essence of original sin. Finally, the immediate societal aspirations towards which Christianity led men such as St. Augustine are clearly Conservative. The pursuit of wealth makes the achievement of virtue difficult. Prosperity is for him the harbinger of evil,[32] and even his occasional concession that the man of "moderate wealth" may also be able to achieve inner peace is coupled with a criticism of those whose major purpose is to increase their wealth.[33] His economic values are therefore closest to those of a Conservative aristocracy, and they tend to exclude the ethic of middle classes like those of ancient Greece or modern Europe. The abnegation of the narcissistic self and the absorption in the love of God are profoundly Conservative. Men whose lives are preoccupied with the love of God in the Augustinian sense would have little incentive for economic expansion or technological progress.

St. Augustine's hope was that Christianity would regenerate the Roman Empire without the prior need of total dissolution. But if he could not bring himself to recognize that it might be as justifiable by his own standards to reject the Empire as to defend it, later orthodox Christians had no difficulty in transferring their allegiance to the new societies which followed the destruction of Rome. If Christianity always retained a sense of alienation from existing society, this sense was less and less sharp in the centuries following the breakup of the Empire, as the number of Christians and the influence of Christianity grew.

Even with his Christian doctrine, therefore, St. Augustine's position was historically contradictory, because the dissolution of the Roman Empire and of ancient civilization was the precondition of the advance of Christianity. This was obscured by the later pretense that Christian civilization was merely the continuation of the Roman Empire. But without the barbarian tribes, who had begun to come into the Empire during the early period of decline and who carried Roman influences over into the new civilization which they ultimately built, there is no historical reason to believe that orthodox Christianity and Roman civilization would not have perished together. Besides, in the face of the changing conditions of history, no one has ever been able to maintain consistently that the justification of political authority in itself demands acquiescence to those who hold power at a given moment.

Not only was St. Augustine's view of political authority historically contradictory, but his willingness to use authority in the repression of "heresy" necessitated the assertion of premises which were not inherent in the original Christian doctrines. When Reinhold Niebuhr, the outstanding Augustinian of contemporary America, looks back to this problem, he can only see in it "the first example of the perennial inclination of the religious community to make itself odious by its pretensions of righteousness." [34]

The new civilization of Europe, like that of ancient Greece, began with tribal societies. But if they were less corrupt and more cohesive than the late Roman Empire, Conservatives could find a maximum degree of harmony in these societies only by doing what Plato wanted to do—obliterate the records of their history. The European tribal kingdoms were engaged in perpetual wars and internal contests for power; and the bewildering multiplicity of customs and traditions from both the tribes and the Roman Empire showed that blind adherence to custom could itself be a source of discord. The early stages of feudalism frequently tended to a state of near anarchy rather than Conservative harmony. If the growth of Christianity during this period was often due to its superior religious appeal, it was too often due also to its superior swordsmanship. Still, from the point of view of Conservative ideology and orthodox Christianity, it was better than the late Roman Empire. Above all, the "Dark Ages" constituted the precondition of the Conservative society of the Late Middle Ages. In this sense—that history was finally moving in a Conservative direction—the Conservatism of orthodox Christianity after St. Augustine had an underlying consistency in spite of the difficulties in some of its specific formulations.

John of Salisbury: "Pure" Conservatism at Last

It was only after many centuries of conflict that the actual conditions for a harmonious, Conservative society reappeared. By the twelfth century, when John of Salisbury wrote the *Policraticus*, feudalism had developed into a relatively stabilized and institutionalized system, based on personal loyalties and services. The aristocratic class had acquired hereditary political privileges and authority to match its socio-economic power, and the code of chivalry had softened its warrior ethic. The degree of social cohesion was high and class conflict reasonably minimal. A relatively coherent set of traditions had evolved and was to be further stabilized by the revival of Roman law. Social classes had been clearly delineated into "estates" with more or less explicit privileges and duties. The economy was primarily agricultural and relatively stagnant. Towns had begun to develop, but, within the towns, the economic activities were strictly regulated by customary concepts of "just" prices and wages; and control of this economy was largely in the hands of highly institutionalized guilds. The Church guided the moral welfare of the whole Christian community and drew its ethics from an ideology of "natural law," based on the conception of a harmonious universe. In purely societal terms, the role of the Church was similar to that which Plato had sought for his intellectual elite. On the one hand, it had close ties to the aristocracy from whom its leadership was chosen. On the other hand, its function was to lead the aristocracy, not to follow it. It provided the aristocracy, as well as the whole society, with a coherent, articulate conception of their proper goals and functions. It therefore prevented "timocracy," that uncultured rule by the warrior class which, for Plato, was so inferior to the optimum Conservative ideal. Each man in society had his "allotted" place and few expected to change it.

Here was that period to which later Conservatives were to point as their ideological model, made historically real. In John of Salisbury we come to a Conservative ideologist whose goal is already largely accomplished. Yet in the twelfth century new influences had already begun to appear which were ultimately destined to destroy the medieval world. Accordingly, John of Salisbury is already critical of the corrupting influences of the cities and the moral degeneration of the English fighting man.[35] Even in the period which was to become the later Conservatives' model for harmony, the Conservative looked backward for inspiration. Nevertheless John's criticisms are relatively limited, compared with those of Plato, the Late Stoics, St. Augustine, and even Burke. Unlike Plato, he is not concerned with gaining the centers of authority or changing existing institutions in order to achieve his goals. Unlike St. Augustine, he spends little time on the future consolations of eternity, because earthly life is not really unbearable to him. And unlike Burke, he does not feel it necessary to defend the existing Conservative institutions, because he sees little serious danger to them, except from within.

Since his evaluation of society is really favorable, it is less necessary for John of Salisbury than for Plato to work out in objective rational terms the implications of his Conservative premises. He relies more on analogy than rational insight; his analysis is more fragmentary and less incisive than Plato's. But the essential elements are there, nevertheless. His concepts of morality and tradition are linked to societal and natural harmony in which each "part" keeps its allotted place.[36] He seeks the minimizing of material desires,[37] the intensifying of communal cohesion, and the intellectual binding of the whole society through the "higher law" which teaches each his obligations and relations to the societal and universal totality. Personal morality, in the orthodox Christian sense, and the capacity to preserve societal harmony become qualifications for the holding of political power (though John of Salisbury offers no way of enforcing these qualifications). He is critical of both the aristocracy and the clergy on grounds of frivolity, moral corruption, and a proclivity for discord, but he never suggests that they should not remain the centers of power. On the contrary, he agrees that noble birth has the advantage of "imposing the necessity of probity," [38] presumably because of the sensitivity of nobles to "honor," which in turn should be reserved only for virtue. He places the authority of the Church, that is of the "intellectual" aristocracy, over that of government, though he does not specify how this is to

be carried out.   The middle class, on the other hand, is left
entirely out of his societal structure, and it is obvious that he
would accept no ascendancy of economic over political power.

In view of the fact that John of Salisbury's Conservatism
was a "pure" type, in the sense that his historical environment
did not force him to combine it with other values, the problems which he saw in his society are of some interest.   There
were three major difficulties with which he was concerned: the
apparently widespread corruption in political society; the existence of continuing jurisdictional conflicts; and the increasing
frequency of "tyranny," that is, of rule by force and in violation of the "higher law."   For the problem of corruption his
only solution was moral exhortation, and he doubted that this
would do any good.   For the conflicts between spiritual and
secular authority, and over the standards of succession for em-
perors and popes, he recommended only adherence to the
"higher law," [39] and this did not in fact do any good.   For the
problem of tyranny, his solution was private tyrannicide,[40] a
procedure which could only have destroyed any political society.   It is interesting that later Conservatives, who often referred to the medieval society of John of Salisbury's time as
their model, usually did not bother to mention the insolubility
of these problems or their importance for Conservative ideology itself.   The omission is not really surprising, for if the
"Golden Age" of Conservatism could not solve the supremely
important problems of morality, conflict, and adherence to an
intellectual tradition of harmony, what hope is there for any
other age?   Yet, if his ideological values forced John of Salisbury to criticize his society and seek improvements, this is no
more than any honest ideologist must do.   Reality cannot be
perfect in terms of values, no matter what the ideology.   Conservatives can point out that, though there is no perfect harmony in history, there are nevertheless degrees of societal and
psychological harmony, that if there is no absolute good, there
are at least such things as better and worse.   By this standard,
medieval society was "better," and the relative mildness of

John of Salisbury's criticisms of his age, compared to earlier and later Conservatives, makes it plausible for us to refer to him as a "pure" Conservative.

Nevertheless, the fact that even John of Salisbury looks backward rather than forward for his standards of "better" makes one suspect that the Conservative may have to find his highest point of harmonious human life among the primeval horde, and the irrelevance of John's solutions to medieval problems suggests that for the Conservative "the future" may always be bleak. We shall see that there is nothing in the history of Conservatism to contradict either of these suspicions.

Throughout the entire period from Plato to John of Salisbury, the essence of Conservatism remained the same—a quest for communal harmony founded on "unconscious" ties of affection and a denial of economic expansion. Without these roots, the argument ran, political power is only an instrument of oppression which must be imposed by force. But if this ideal had been approximated in the Homeric Age of aristocracy, it could, by Plato's time, exist only in the world of hope. The reality of the commercial city-state had legitimized the quest for wealth, and even Plato found himself forced to adjust to that reality. But the fact that economic expansion was destroying the "natural" cohesion of society, as Plato himself admitted, meant that the concessions could not be consistently reconciled with his values. The later adjustment of the Middle Stoics and Cicero to an authoritarian age fared no better. Not only was their advocacy of coercion logically incompatible with the concepts of affection and cohesion, but the actual use of coercion was accompanied by the continued disintegration of earlier cohesiveness, and it was followed by increasing conflict and authority rather than harmony and affection. The alienation of the Late Stoa was the final admission of the break between Conservatism and reality.

It was only the beginning of a new civilization which made it possible for Conservatism to return from heaven to earth. But if there was a sense in which the Conservatism of orthodox

Christianity was consistent during the formative period of the Dark Ages, it was only because the period culminated in medieval society—the sole Conservative period in the history of Western civilization.   Since the breakdown of that "Utopia," Conservatism has resumed its weary and frustrating journey back to purgatory.   Its first major readjustment was to the Liberal society which followed the Middle Ages.   The classic reformulation of Conservatism was the work of Edmund Burke.

II

Edmund Burke: the

Contradictions of

Liberal Conservatism

Great Britain was admirably prepared for the development of a strong middle class and of the modern nation-state which the middle class needed in order to destroy the medieval system. It rapidly became what Hegel called the "world-historical" nation of the modern era, because it contained in purest form the prerequisites for a modern society. It had achieved early political centralization, as a result of the Norman Conquest, and had developed a centralized common law out of the earlier chaos of custom. Its insular position had minimized the concern for security and had facilitated the emergence of a tradition of resistance to authority. The same insular position gave it a great advantage in developing as a naval power, as well as in trade and colonization. Because the Wars of the Roses had virtually destroyed the medieval nobility, the nation began the modern period with a largely new aristocracy composed of former members of the upper middle class who had bought their titles with new wealth. Against this background, the British tradition of passing the inheritance of estates to the eldest son led to the further tradition of "setting the younger sons up in business." Family ties, therefore, served as a bridge between the two classes and prevented strong aristocratic resistance to the further progress of the upper middle class. The early break with the papacy and the transition to Protestantism prevented moral and religious resistance to changes. Empiricism and a scientific attitude developed early. Finally a strong, popular monarchy aided the development of the idea of sovereignty, which made it possible to effect political transitions with both clarity and continuity, except for the seventeenth-century Civil War.

It is worth noting, however, that once commercial expansion began, the British nation-state took much longer than the Athenian city-state to develop political democracy. The difference may have been due to the fact that colonization, which began in Greece long *before* the age of democracy, *coincided* in Britain with the lower middle-class bid for political equality in the seventeenth century. As a result, the New World colonies greatly relieved the internal pressure for political democracy, and may have made possible the "oligarchic" Whig settlement which ended the conflicts of the seventeenth century. This settlement signaled the failure of the bid for democracy. It is suggestive that the renewal of democratic pressures in Britain coincided with the American Revolution, which closed the period of colonization (as distinct from the subsequent period of imperialism).

Throughout these changes the position of the Conservative clergy and aristocracy (new and old) varied with the prevailing conditions. By the early sixteenth century, the "pure" Conservative had already been isolated, and his world was left behind in the Platonic and medieval Utopia of the Catholic Sir Thomas More. By the end of the century, Conservatives like Sir Thomas Smith had already accepted the nation-state rather than the Christian commonwealth of Europe as the focus of Conservatism and had half-consciously embraced some of the emerging Liberalism. In the seventeenth century, many Conservative aristocrats stood with the king in the early conflicts, but a number had shifted to an alliance with the upper middle class by the end of the century. In the eighteenth century, upper middle-class Liberalism became "conservative" in the traditionalist sense that it now wanted to preserve the existing institutions, which had already been modified so that they were compatible with its own values, and to prevent further advance toward democracy. But Conservatism had steadily been liberalized, and the class ties had facilitated its acceptance of much of Liberal ideology. By Burke's time, the threat to established institutions came primarily from an aggressive king, George III. Conservatives and Liberals* now found themselves in active political alliance against the royal court, though their respective ideological paths to this alliance were fundamentally different.

The relative smoothness of the process of liberalization in England had made possible the preservation of many of the Conservative medieval institutions and values. But under the impact of authoritarian royal pressure, and, more important, the renewed bid of the middle classes, towards the end of the eighteenth century, to break free entirely from medieval influence, Conservatism was forced to begin to articulate its own ideological premises. It is from this period that the very term "Conservatism" dates, † and its intellectual progenitor is Edmund Burke. In Burke we find a new formulation, one that had not been possible for the Stoics or St. Augustine, and one that had not been necessary for John of Salisbury. It is liberal Conservatism that Burke is expounding. Though it bears some resemblance to Plato's position in the *Statesman,* the fundamental difference is that for Burke the society itself seems to

---

* "Conservatives" and "Liberals" are not here equivalents for "Tories" and "Whigs." The "Toryism" of the lesser gentry who supported a strong independent monarch was authoritarian, not Conservative. Similarly, the Whigs whose fortunes were made through political power (the "nabobs" of the East India Company, for example) were likely to be "Court Whigs." During this time Pitt's Tories and Rockingham's Whigs were the Conservatives; Fox's Whigs were the Liberals.

† Technically, this makes the application of the word "Conservatism" to pre-Burkean ideology incorrect. But it is used in this book to describe the whole ideological tradition from Plato through Burke, because any alternative term ("Idealism" or "communalism," for example) would be far more misleading. For similar reasons, the term "Liberal" is sometimes applied here to the Greek city-state.

be liberal Conservative. He can therefore rely on the congenial Conservative technique of defending the existing traditions while calling for some improvements, instead of relying on political authority to effect sweeping changes. For Plato, the age of possible aristocratic-mercantile alliance has already been superseded by Liberal democracy. For Burke, democracy is a threat, not a reality. It is only in the early Liberal period, before the advent of democracy, that Conservatism really has anything to conserve.

In spite of the fact that almost all of Burke's writings were directed to specific historical problems, they are interspersed with general formulations which can be put together to form a coherent ideology. But there were two stages in the development of his ideological position. From the time he became active in Parliamentary politics until the French Revolution, his major concern was opposition to the power of the royal court of George III, and his assumption was that some Liberalism was compatible with Conservatism. It was in this period that he formulated his characteristic ideology. After the French Revolution, he still tried to adhere to this position, but it became increasingly difficult; and he felt more and more compelled to choose between Liberal and Conservative values. In each case he made it clear that his first values had always remained Conservative.

Moral and Aesthetic Assumptions

Burke's first publication [1] contains few of his real ideological assumptions. It is a satire, designed to prove that too close a rational inquiry into the nature of authority is dangerous, because the oppressiveness of political power is an easy target for criticism. But to say that one should not reason about the nature of power is pointless when there is no serious challenge to existing authorities, and it is valueless when there is such a challenge. Though Burke would have preferred to move no further than this, he was repeatedly forced, during his political career, to make his ideological values more explicit. It is therefore highly misleading to identify Burke's Conservatism with this empty argument.

In his early work on aesthetics, however, Burke does begin to make some of his basic values clear. He distinguishes beauty, sublimity, and proportion as the basic elements of art, but he refers repeatedly to tranquillity or "indifference" as the essential concomitant of the other elements. Without using the Freudian term, he describes beauty as sublimated sexuality. But the crucial effect of artistic beauty, besides its sexual appeal, is an inner sense of "languor and relaxation," [2] and this effect is heightened by "gracefulness," a state in which "no feeling of difficulty is conveyed in posture or motion," a state in which there is only "a small inflection in one part and composure in the rest." [3] The "delight" produced by the sublime results from qualities which suggest fear but whose effect of sublimated "pain" is followed by tranquillity, because the "pain" is not real. The appeal of artistic proportion lies in the rational restraints which it places on emotions, but Burke adds that correct proportion also produces "indifference." [4] The relation here between artistic "gracefulness" and the "graciousness" of the Conservative aristocrat is obvious. True art is not only emotionally satisfying and rationally restraining, it is tranquillizing as well. Burke emphasizes that it is not tranquillity alone which is desirable, for the state of rest itself is too closely related to death,[5] but beauty requires simultaneously the fulfillment of the need for "love" and the minimizing of tensions. The Conservative themes of tranquillity, harmonious proportion, love, and affection, which first appear in his aesthetics, are recurrent throughout his writings, and he applies these themes to society as well as to art.

Though he satirized the notion that primitive, "natural" man was happy [6] because his needs were simple, Burke was Conservative enough to praise those whose wants were few. But he found that in modern society the satisfaction of increased material desires had become both possible and necessary.[7] This concern for material prosperity led him, as it had led the Liberals, to insist on personal freedom as a key moral value, and to emphasize the relation between freedom and increased wealth.[8]   In his disputes with the court during the earlier part of his political career, he rarely found it necessary to state his choice between societal tranquillity and "prosperous liberty," since he was affirming both against the king's party.   Nor was he troubled by the inconsistency of advocating both "prosperous freedom" and a tranquillity which depended on the control of desires.   It seemed to him that eighteenth-century Britain had somehow achieved both.   It was the French Revolution which forced him to recognize that the two values might be incompatible.   His final stand was for harmonious tranquillity rather than freedom.   He never really held any other position throughout his life.

Social and Economic Ideology

Burke's definition of society [9] has often been quoted.   It is, he said,

a partnership in all science . . . in all art . . . in every virtue. . . . It becomes a partnership between those who are living . . . those who are dead and those who are to be born. . . .   It is but a clause . . . according to a fixed compact . . . which hold all physical and moral natures each in their appointed place. . . .   To this compact man must be obedient . . . for if he is not, Nature is disobeyed and the rebellious are . . . cast forth . . . from this world of reason, order, peace and virtue . . . into the antagonist world of madness, discord, vice, and confusion.[10]

But this conception is not self-explanatory unless the key words are understood in terms of Conservative values.   When we know that harmony and tranquillity are Burke's standards of art and virtue, that a world harmony which holds things in their appointed places describes the Platonic-medieval concept of nature, that discord is the essence of Conservative evil, and that Conservatism links generations with tradition, then the entire definition becomes intelligible as a single consistent idea. But when he applied this conception to the actual society of his time, he combined it with Liberalism.

In economics, Burke was an enthusiastic advocate of Liberal capitalism. He held private property to be essential to freedom,[11] and he accepted the Lockean "natural right" to the fruits of one's labor as the moral basis of property.[12] He even wrote a special pamphlet to justify the profit and market systems. In this work the capitalist ideology of Adam Smith seems to become a part of the "natural order" of Edmund Burke.[13]

But Burke always assumed that Liberal capitalist economics could be kept subordinate to the Conservative social ethic. After the French Revolution, he spelled out this social ethic. He emphasized the aristocratic code of honor and the heritage of chivalry, which had "harmonized and softened the whole" with "pleasing illusions" that made power "gentle." [14] He insisted that the standards of honor must be kept constant if men were not to be changeable "like summer flies," [15] and it was the medieval aristocratic tradition which set his standards for constancy. Throughout his early political career, when he repeatedly stressed that reputation is a man's most precious possession [16] and that "fame" is more intimately tied to virtue than "interest," [17] he was always referring to this same aristocratic code of honor.

Furthermore, Burke insisted on the need for hereditary aristocracy in the societal order, to serve as the center of social prestige and political authority. Nobility is, he said, "an incitement to virtuous action" as well as the "chain that connects generations," [18] and the producer of true culture. He always considered that original titles were given for actual virtuous public service, but when he emphasized that *only* virtue and wisdom were entitled to "human place and honor," he meant simply that authority and "distinction" should not be *confined* to "blood, names and titles," and that men of "obscure condition" should be allowed (without undue ease) to rise to eminence, if they deserved it. Under ordinary conditions, he was prepared to accept a "presumptive" relation between an inherited title of nobility and actual virtue.[19] Yet he never specifically accepted the Platonic thesis that virtue is, for the most part, hereditary. His position seemed to be that aristocracy provides the proper environmental conditions for the transmission of virtue through good upbringing and education. This is the clear assumption in his description of "natural" aristocrats, who obviously could come from nowhere but the existing aristocratic or upper middle-class families. They are, he said, (1) well-bred; (2) not accustomed to sordid surroundings; (3) taught self-respect and courage in pursuit of honor and duty, and taught how to serve as moral examples for others; (4) used to public inspection, a large view of society, leisure, access to the wise, command and obedience in armies, service in government or culture; and (5) accustomed to being among rich traders who have the virtues of diligence, order, and constancy.[20]

Burke's inclusion of rich, virtuous traders in his "natural aristocracy" is typical of his liberal Conservatism. He felt that one of the primary reasons for the superiority of the British aristocracy was its ties to the upper middle class. How miserable, he said, is the land where these classes are separated.[21] His position thus resembled Plato's in the *Statesman*. The good society required the harmonious combination of the courageous aristocracy with the temperate upper middle class, linked together by intermarriage and a common Conservatism. But unlike Plato, he did not have to examine in detail the ideological and moral foundations of his position, because he did not have to promote the combination. In England it was already an existent fact.

Like all proponents of aristocracy, however, Burke failed to follow Plato's lead in allowing for some "circulation" *from* as well as *to* the aristocracy. Yet he did not hesitate to criticize actual aristocracies and aristocrats.[22] He was well aware that there could be no guarantee of continued aristocratic virtue, but he proposed no solution for the problem.

Burke's view of religion should also be mentioned. Aside from his personal devoutness, he considered religion to be the basis of society, because it helps people empty themselves of selfish will and provides a "balm to gnawing cares and anxieties." On these grounds even superstition is better than agnosticism, because superstition is the "religion of feeble minds," [23] that is, of the lower classes. This is clearly a Conservative view of religion, which sees it as an instrument for minimizing desires and tensions.

But the "father of Conservatism" never examined the contradiction between his Conservative premises and his acceptance of Liberal capitalism, perhaps because, on the surface, the self-regulating market economy appeared to be a natural extension of Conservative harmony. A deeper probing would have revealed, however, that Liberal capitalism was, in fact, the antithesis of Conservatism. In the first place, while the essence of Conservative harmony is the minimizing of desires, the capitalist market economy is predicated on the opposite ethic of seeking to maximize satisfactions. The whole foundation of Conservatism is negated if one accepts the thesis that desires may be increased without upsetting tranquillity and happiness. In the second place, Conservatism depends on the idea of "keeping one's allotted place," because widespread attempts to move out of one's class cause unforeseen changes, tensions, and conflicts. But the market system assumes precisely such striving to "get ahead," to rise above one's present conditions. In the third place, the laissez-faire ethic, in spite of its use of natural law terminology, makes the conscious individual choice of the consumer the cornerstone of its rationale. This may be compatible with a Liberal concept of individual "utility" but contradicts the Conservative ideal of objective harmonious relationships which are supposed to govern the society. Finally, economic competition does not seek to prevent conflicts but to mitigate them by rational self-restraint and to channel them through the process of adjustment in the profit and market systems. The Conservative ideology assumes that happiness consists of avoiding such conflicts altogether, not of adjusting them.

The ideological contradictions eventually became an irreconcilable historical conflict, even in England. Burke was able to retain Liberal economics only because it did not at the time seem to conflict with his Conservatism.   But in the nineteenth century, such conflict actually occurred and culminated in the fight over the repeal of the Corn Laws, which had protected the landed aristocracy.   By then English Conservatism had split, one branch throwing off laissez-faire economics in favor of a return to medieval ideas, and another abandoning the medieval ethic almost completely in favor of capitalism.   It is this historical shifting which makes it so essential to distinguish the transcendent values of Conservatism from its formal variations.

Even during Burke's lifetime the contradiction between Conservatism and Liberal capitalism became historically explosive, though in France, not in England; and the French Revolution forced him to choose between them.   He had always assumed the superiority of the medieval social heritage over modern commercial achievements, but he now stated it in no uncertain terms.[24]   Like Plato, he had always meant aristocracy to be the senior partner in the alliance with the upper middle class, but he now exclaimed that where there is a crown and a hereditary nobility, new wealth cannot rank first or even near the first.[25]   The worst consequences follow when the middle class is separated from the aristocracy and bids for power by itself.   He spoke now of the virtues of inherited wealth as contrasted with the "upstart insolence" of first acquisition and with the tendency of money towards adventure and novelty.   He was particularly bitter about the lower middle class, whose only talent was for causing conflicts.[26] Burke's liberal Conservatism thus depended on the erroneous assumption that Liberal capitalism was subordinate to the medieval social tradition and that the upper middle class was subordinate to the landed aristocracy.

Tradition

Like all Conservatives, Burke was primarily concerned with preserving and strengthening the sense of "community," the unconscious cohesive forces that hold society together.   Like all Conservatives, he felt that the most important of these forces was social. He repeatedly stresses the importance of affection, reverence, and veneration; and he criticizes those governments which weaken them.[27] Besides its social base, the community also rests on the sense of common economic interests in the society (though Burke never elaborated this conception). But it is his emphasis on the importance of tradition that is most often cited in describing his Conservatism.

Burke justified tradition because it embodied the wisdom of "the ages" rather than present opinion and the wisdom of the "species" rather than the individual.[28] But these ideological justifications of tradition tell us nothing, unless we know what "wisdom" means. We can learn much more about his view of tradition by going to his early work on art. There he states that the distinguishing characteristic of custom and habit is that it produces tranquillity or "indifference."[29] Repeated usage in itself promotes tranquillity—that is the negative justification of tradition. The positive value, he later implied, is that it takes time to cement a "union of minds" and to build "contending principles into a consistent whole."[30] The true purpose of tradition is thus to transform societal conflicts into a harmonious whole. The "wisdom" of the "species" (that is, of the community) is based on the fact that harmony is a communal and not an individual achievement. But this does not mean that all traditions are Conservative. They can be justified by Conservative standards only to the extent that they actually promote harmony. The individual can love his society, Burke emphasized, only if it is "lovely."[31]

One of Burke's most difficult problems was to reconcile his view of tradition with his acceptance of individual freedom. In the early part of his political career he occasionally seemed to accept the Liberal view of "natural rights" as the basis of freedom. He once said with unmistakable clarity that the Liberal position on "taxation and representation" in the English Revolution of 1689 was based on true "theory," not on mere "ancient parchments" or "blind usages," and that the "theory" was correct whether the "old records" agreed or not.[32]

At the same time, he often referred to liberties and rights as traditional, especially when speaking of the contemporary situation. For example, he often supported the arguments of the American colonies in terms of the "rights of Englishmen."

But when the French Revolution revealed the relation between individual freedom and the destruction of Conservative aristocratic values, he insisted that freedom is something to be defended, never something to be actively sought.[33]   This forced him to drop his earlier acceptance of the Whig Revolution on Liberal ideological grounds and to explain it solely as the defense of traditional rights.   We shall see later the gross misinterpretations of history which were necessitated by this attempt to absorb freedom into tradition.   The attempt did, however, reflect Burke's liberal Conservatism.

Before we leave this subject, it is extremely important to distinguish between "tradition" as part of Conservative ideology and "traditionalism" as a political technique.   Burke's justification of traditions which promote harmony and his attempt to combine these traditions with freedom are a part of his ideology, because they are based on his Conservative values. "Traditionalism," however, is not an ideology but a political technique, which consists of a defense of *any* existing traditions and institutions.   Since existing traditions are not necessarily Conservative, traditionalism is not synonymous with Conservatism. Plato justified the Conservative concept of tradition but his political technique was not traditionalist.   Pericles, on the other hand, was a traditionalist in his praise of fifth-century Athenian society, but the traditions which he praised were democratic, not Conservative.   Burke was both a Conservative and a traditionalist, but only because he thought he was defending liberal Conservative traditions.

Political Ideology

THE STATE.   Burke denied that a nation is governed primarily by laws and coercion.[34]   On the contrary, he underscored what he considered to be the essential harmony of the state. He insisted that the tie which holds the state together is a "chain," in which each man must play the part assigned to him by God.[35] The chain consists of the class divisions of society, and each class must have its hereditary privileges protected against the potential conflicts of diverse interests.[36] The most vital class is the "natural aristocracy," which is the "soul" of the political community. The deciding voice should be with these "natural" leaders, because otherwise this "national harmony," this "beautiful order," becomes a collection of "mere vagabonds."[37] Since the community exists before any agreement about freedom or equality, the cohesion of the community itself is superior to any claims of political natural rights. This is the reasoning behind his conclusion that, while the consent of the community to government decisions is desirable so that authority will be based on obedience rather than force, consent need not be actually expressed. The people may be presumed to consent to "whatever benefits them,"[38] and actual consent is void if it is contrary to the "order of God."[39] While some freedom is desirable, it must be subordinate to higher needs,[40] especially those which serve Conservative purposes ("wisdom," "virtue," "justice," etc.).

This general concept of the harmonious nature of the state underlay his evaluation of specific constitutional forms. In his early satire on "natural society," he presented the reader with arguments against various forms of government, presumably with tongue in cheek. He "denounced," under the heading of "despotism," all forms of pure monarchy, because power corrupts and leads to war and repression.[41] "Aristocracy" (which referred here especially to oligarchies of wealth, such as that of Venice) is even worse, because there is a much better chance of a single good ruler turning up in a monarchy than of aristocratic despots either reforming simultaneously or producing good sons simultaneously.[42] Democracy is worst of all, not only because it is a collective despotism but because its tendency towards constant change necessitates constant force.[43] He even pretended to reject "mixed government" on the grounds that a political balance is easily upset, that in a mixed government each branch continues to pursue class interests and this causes frequent "cabals," corruptions, and revolutions.[44] What is curious about these supposedly satirical criticisms, which he presented with surprising vigor, is that they were not very different from the views which he held seriously. He always remained critical of pure monarchies, which he considered to be tyrannical. In this category he included the Tudors, the Stuarts, Cromwell, and the early French kings through Louis XIV. The only monarchies he defended were the British "balanced" monarchy and the "mild" French kings, both of the eighteenth century. He rejected aristocracy "in the usual sense," and democracy in almost any sense. The masses do not have the leisure to acquire "wisdom"; and in democracy, even honor becomes leveled, because each man tends to honor himself and thus both true honor and shame disappear. Like Plato, he was aware that actual aristocracies can fall far short of his Conservative values, and in his time he thought they usually did. (Nevertheless, again like Plato, only aristocratic leadership could potentially sustain the good Conservative society.) During the French Revolution he was still insisting that monarchy was the best of these "corrupt" forms of government, on the grounds that it could most easily be transformed into the truly best form of government, which he called "balanced government." [45] It was on this basis that he defended the "mild" French monarch.

On the crucial question of what he meant by "mixed" or "balanced" government, his satire is useful because it helps to highlight the difference between Platonic and Aristotelian, "mixed government." The arguments which he finds it easiest to direct against mixed government, even if apparently in jest, are those which assume that the "mixture" is purely political. He would therefore find it easy to reject both the later American conception of compromise within political checks and balances and the Aristotelian conception of a political class equilibrium. The "mixed" or "balanced" government which he seriously accepts, on the other hand, is similar to the harmonious cohesion of Platonic mixed government, rooted in social and ideological unity, in family "connections," and common "principles."

The British balance, he said, is composed of the crown, which represents the aristocracy, and the House of Commons, which represents both the aristocracy and the upper middle class. But each of these elements keeps its place, for though each rests on different grounds, they form one harmonious body.[46] Variety is reconciled into a whole,[47] and the parts become accommodated to each other over a long period of time.[48] He once seemed to approach the Liberal conception when he said that it is the "opposition of interests" which draws the "harmony of the universe" out of discordant parts and necessitates deliberation, moderation, and compromise.[49] But to the extent that he accepted this view, it was always subordinate to Conservative cohesion. The British system, he said soon afterwards, is both a balance of opposing interests and their connection as "friends" (that is through social unity), but the latter is paramount because without it all would be confusion.[50]

When he turned his attention to France he found the Estates-General to be a better aristocratic institution than the House of Lords, but doubted that the French middle class could develop within it as good an institution as the House of Commons. Therefore, only the king could bring them into a "just balance," provided the clergy acted as the "connecting link." But the French king would need rather more power than the British monarch if he was to bring the three orders into proper and "harmonious relations."[51] He summarized the British Constitution as a monarchy, directed by laws and balanced by the "wealth and dignity" of the realm, as well as by "reason" and "the feeling of the people." The system he advocated for France was a strong monarchy with a venerated clergy, a spirited nobility "to lead virtue," a "liberal commons" "to emulate and recruit nobility," and a satisfied people taught to recognize the happiness implicit in virtue.[52]

It was a "balanced government" of harmony which Burke sought to preserve or create, not one of conflict. But if ques-

tions of the distribution of authority should arise, at least in
England, it was aristocracy which was of supreme importance
in maintaining over-all harmony in the society. He never examined the contradiction in his insistence that the king establish the "balance" in France. The very reliance on political
authority meant that social harmony did not exist.

Burke's attitude towards constitutional change was also
clearly Conservative. A constitution should not be interpreted
in opposition to the "privileges it was meant to support." [53]
Once it is formed, no change can be made in it without the
consent of all parties or unless the constitutional "contract"
has been broken.[54] But since he does not define breach of
contract here, only unanimity remains as the basis for constitutional change. The only other situations in which he explicitly allows for constitutional change are in periods of "profound tranquillity" or ones of "profound confusion," but he
emphasizes elsewhere that the purpose of revolutionary change
is to "reach the quiet shore of tranquil and prosperous liberty."
This is interesting because it implies that change could be
made during a period such as the Late Middle Ages by men
like John of Salisbury or during fourth-century Greece by men
like Plato. At any rate, he claimed that neither "profound
confusion" nor "profound tranquillity" was characteristic of
his own age. In France "rash counsel" had arbitrarily started
an unnecessary upheaval in time of "profound peace." [55]

To sum up, Burke's concept of the state rested on the cohesion of the political community, perpetuated through an acceptance of aristocratic leadership and the ethical norm that
political authority must not violate harmony by infringing on
established privileges. In the eighteenth century, the best
constitution was a harmoniously "balanced government,"
rooted in the social cohesion of the society and of its ruling
classes.

THE PROBLEM OF POLITICAL CONFLICT. Though Burke's
ideal was a harmonious political society based on social cohesion, the realities of the eighteenth-century British society con-

tained a fair amount of political conflict, based on Whig conceptions of the predominantly economic basis of political power. This was an age when government authority became largely a commercial product which could be bought and sold in the open market.

Burke accepted the important role of economic power in politics. We cannot, he said, separate property from the franchise, because men of wealth are important individually while the "poor and middling" are powerful only if they can act collectively.[56] Furthermore, independent wealth is the prerequisite to an independent mind.[57] The category of property owners, of course, included both the upper middle class and the landed aristocracy, and he accepted both as legitimate centers of power. What disturbed him during his early career was that the wealth of the king was being used to upset the political harmony. He was quick to point out that if elections were held more frequently in England, not only would "violent popular spirits" be aroused, but power would pass increasingly to the court, because the high cost of election expenses and corruption could be met most easily with the large financial resources which the crown had made available (unconstitutionally) for purely political purposes.[58] His greatest worry later, however, was that the French Revolution had opened the possibility of a cleavage between the economic power of the middle classes and that of the aristocracy. In such a conflict, he feared, the weight of power is on the side of the middle classes. Country people act as individuals, while city classes can more easily sustain collective action. What is more important, rural families have less money than those of the city, and their need for more money only throws them into the hands of the financiers and the rest of the middle class.[59]

He had been aware throughout his parliamentary career that economic power could destroy harmony. Therefore, he always insisted on the supremacy of social power (prestige, honor, reputation) over economic power, for this supremacy was the foundation of political tranquillity. It was, of course, specifically the prestige of the landed aristocracy that he wanted to retain as paramount. Political power must, Burke insisted, be accountable to society as a "trust." [60] Therefore the "intermediaries" between the crown and society should be men of both "great natural interest and reputation." But reputation is the more important, because it is essential to entrust power only to men who are trusted both by the public and by other men of authority.[61] He repeated this theme again and again. "Evil" men must be kept out of power, in favor of men of high prestige who are trusted and have influence among the landed and commercial interests. Not only is honor the basis of public trust, but "duty" must always be superior to "interest." [62] The voter should not expect detailed perfection in his representative, but should consider his general conduct in politics and keep those in power to whom honor is paramount.[63] The wisdom to rule depends on habitual leisure, and power should follow "virtue." [64] Within the realm of economic power, it is essential to understand that *landed* property is the basis of stable government, because it is the "least inclined to sedition." Even the existence of freedom in Britain is due to continuing aristocratic leadership and prosperity.[65]

Burke made it clear that he considered the purpose of a political campaign to be the moral self-justification of the candidate, not a partisan or ideological attack on his opponents. His withdrawal from the last Bristol campaign in order to avoid arousing bitter disputes made it clear that he wanted conflict to be minimized even during election campaigns. A proper party contest, he emphasized, is a "generous and honorable contention for authority," not a factional fight for self-interest or power.[66]

This brings us to Burke's definition of political parties, one of his most frequently misinterpreted ideas. "A party," he said, "is a body of men united for promoting by their joint endeavors the national interest, based upon some particular principle in which they are all agreed." [67] It is often assumed that this conception can be applied to the contemporary party system. But Burke would never have considered his definition to be applicable to present democracies, in Britain or anywhere else, because these systems accept the supremacy of private interests, the power of numbers, public opinion, or even the capacity for manipulation as the legitimate basis for political power. Burke rejected every one of these. Again it is interesting to note his early satire, where he said sarcastically that parties are always bad, because they are based on self-interest and ambition.[68] This was not as far from his true position as one might suppose. He merely used a different term to describe the same phenomenon. To political groupings based on ambition and self-interest he applied the names "cabal" or "faction." The term "party" was reserved for a very special type of political group. It was precisely the growing power of "faction" (that is, of the court "faction") which necessitated the existence of a "party," because "when bad men combine, good men must associate." The "generous and honorable contentions" of parties are not the same as factional striving for "interest and power." [69] But even parties are not normally desirable. One is needed now because this is a "critical emergency," because "if we do not act now, we will find ourselves soon conspiring instead of consulting." [70]

The characterization of Burke as the first to understand the true nature of modern political parties is thus completely untrue. He had no intention of accepting them as permanent institutions. The "principles" on which parties were to be based cannot be interpreted in the modern sense of conflicting political ideologies, without making his acceptance of parties totally incompatible with the rest of his own ideology. The only "principles" which he accepted were those based on the supremacy of the ethic of harmony.

Insofar as parties may be based on interest, it should be the "common interest" and "accompanied by common affection." Party discipline is needed to resist evil effectively, but it must be based on "concord" and the "proper spirit" [71] as well as "mutual confidence." [72]   This idea of "mutual confidence" must be understood against the background of his concept of "honor," "public trust," and the aristocratic creed.   For Burke the trustworthy man who merits confidence is the man to whom prestige is supreme, that is, the aristocrat, and the "proper spirit" can only be the spirit of gentlemen.   He could hardly have accepted party discussion based on rank-and-file deliberation or the modern type of discipline under professional leaders and ideologists.

Most revealing was his statement that parties should not be outlawed as long as they encouraged "healing coalitions." [73] There are two implications in this: first, that the real purpose of parties is to promote "healing coalitions," and second, that they might legitimately be outlawed if they did not.   Historically, he said, the dissensions of Whigs and Tories have often distracted the kingdom; their union once saved it; and their collision and mutual resistance have helped preserve the variety of the Constitution in its unity.   But these parties were now "nearly extinct." [74]   He rejected those Tories who had lent themselves to the intrigues of the court, and his post-Revolutionary denunciation of Fox and the Liberal wing of the Whig Party amounted to virtual charges of treason and subversion.[75]   This left only the Rockingham wing of the Whigs and the Pitt wing of the Tories, and these were to become the core of the nineteenth-century Conservative Party.   A strict interpretation of the Burkean conception of parties would conclude that only the Conservative Party fits the definition in England.   It does not imply acceptance of a democratic system of conflicting parties, either of the European or the American variety.

The role of the king is also important in Burke's ideology of politics.   The personal interest of the monarch is in "repose of mind" above all, and he cannot attain it if the community is distracted by conflict.[76]   This is the reason he must use his power to promote the harmony of "balanced government." Similarly, Burke's justification for insisting that succession to the crown should be by heredity rather than election was that this also helps preserve the "quiet and security," the "unity and tranquillity" of the realm.[77]

Burke's ideology of politics thus sought to maintain the supremacy of Conservative aristocratic social power. The economic power of the middle classes, the physical manpower of the lower classes, and the authoritarian as well as the economic power of the royal court were to be kept subordinate. The harmonious unity of the landed aristocracy and the upper middle class depended ultimately on the seniority of aristocracy. It was, to repeat, the second "solution" of Plato applied to the modern, commercial, capitalist era of history.

THE ORGANIZATION OF GOVERNMENT. Burke rejects the Liberal idea that legislative representatives are primarily delegates of particular interests, or that they reflect the shifting current of "opinion." His ideal is "virtual representation," which rests on both community of interests and "sympathy of feelings" between constituents and representatives.[78] Parliament is not a congress of hostile interests but the deliberative assembly of a single nation, seeking the reconciliation of conflicting interests and the "general good" rather than "local prejudices." [79] Above all, Parliament is the "image of the nation's feelings," [80] and it should, of course, be remembered that these "feelings" were rooted in ancient traditions. As new problems arise, the people express their wants and sufferings "in the gross" (that is, as a "community"). Parliament must find the causes and remedies.[81] His concept of representation only makes sense in terms of his fundamental Conservative ideology. Legislative representation is legitimate when it lies with the two classes which represent the economic interests of the community—land and trade. But it must be based on aristocracy, which is the true representative of the community's "feeling" for unity and harmonious tradition. Furthermore, Burke occasionally links "virtual representation" with the "virtuous" character of the representative, and there is no doubt where true virtue is to be found. When he insists that the representative must never sacrifice his "judgment" to the interests of his constituents,[82] he is not talking about any kind of judgment but judgment based on proper values. When he justifies the inequality of representation for different constituencies (from which the cities suffered most) on the ground that it does not imply inequality of protection,[83] the argument is intelligible only if it is Conservative harmony rather than a special interest which is being protected.

Burke wanted to retain the king's veto on legislation, but during his early career he was more concerned with the Liberal problem of ensuring executive responsibility to Parliament. He criticized the court cabals because they tried to separate power from responsibility.[84] Parliament, he felt, should use its power to vote "no confidence" when the king forgets his personal interest in maintaining tranquillity. Administration was not yet highly developed in Burke's day, and he was not concerned with problems of bureaucracy. But he did not think much of permanent administrative boards in general, and the Board of Plantations and Trade in particular, since he considered administrators to be always less informed than parliamentary committees. He felt it especially important to have the decisions of administrative bodies subject to review by the courts [85] and to safeguard the independence of the courts themselves.

Burke had no concept of judicial review for the British system of "balanced government." He accepted the ideas of the legal sovereignty of Parliament and the prerogative powers of the king, on the grounds that law cannot bind the lawmaker, and that the king is the "keystone" which "binds the arch of the Constitution." [86] But though there is no legal check on sovereignty, there are superior ethical principles. The monarch *should not* violate law or use his discretionary power to promote court intrigues or court policies instead of promoting "principle." Parliament *should* be aware of the fact that there is a practical limitation on how seriously it can violate the "feelings of the community"; and it *should* be guided by "reason, equity, and the general sense of mankind." [87] Apparently, then, Burke does distinguish constitutional sovereignty from ethical principle, unlike medieval Conservatives such as John of Salisbury. But, since his definition of terms such as "principle" and "reason" is always Conservative, he still asserts the supremacy of Conservative values over sovereignty.

It is, to conclude, a mistake to think that Burke foreshadowed the modern idea of responsible Parliamentary government. His acceptance of the sovereignty of Parliament was the Liberal element of his concept of government organization. But it was neutralized by his conception of Parliament itself, a conception in which the clarification of responsibility was specifically attuned to "honorable" Conservative gentlemen, whose task it was to apply the ideology of harmony and tranquillity to the problems of the day.

GOVERNMENTAL POLICY. It is not surprising that Burke advocated a laissez-faire policy for government in relation to the economy. Government must not and cannot provide people with economic necessities, he insisted, for its general function is to prevent evil, and it can do little positive good.[88] Tampering with trade is "always dangerous," and affected pity for workers only tends to dissatisfy them instead of making them properly dependent on their own resources. Work is a task imposed by God, and government cannot remove the burden.[89]

His social policy always upheld the traditional views on marriage and the family. But he held that "mere failure to be completely moral" must be borne, unless such moral failure should "strike at the root of order."[90] One of the most important positive functions of government, however, is to make proper rewards (both financial and honorific) for public service, since these rewards are the bases of noble families, which are in turn the foundations of government.[91]

After the French Revolution he cautioned that care should be taken in the books which people, especially young people, were allowed to read,[92] but he made no specific recommendations on the subject. It was, of course, essential for government to support the Established Church, but he also said that it would be absurd to allow individual Church leaders to teach what they pleased.[93]   He advocated toleration for Catholics and Protestant Dissenters but not for Unitarians, because he considered that they were allied with the Jacobins and were seeking to subvert Church and State.   He generalized that the only valid ground for withholding toleration was "raising faction." [94]   But he never advocated toleration for Jews, a term he frequently used as a synonym for unscrupulous bourgeois.

The basic guide of Burke's political policy was the Conservative norm that tranquillity is "good" and that discord and conflict are the essence of "evil."   The promotion of "prosperous freedom" was a secondary "good."   Therefore he denied that nations are ruled primarily by force.[95]   The use of force was for him as for Plato an admission of discord and hence of failure.   His praise of the Rockingham administration was based not only on its having restored prosperous colonial trade and British "reputation," but also on the restoration of "tranquillity" in American colonial relations.[96]   He considered that the earlier harmonious relations had been upset by the policy of the court, and called for resumption of the Rockingham policy to recover the "natural repose" of imperial relations.[97]   He offered Ireland and Wales as models for achieving harmony through admission to the British system.[98]   He raised the same problems and set the same goals when Irish relations later deteriorated.   He rejected Hastings' use of force in India on the grounds that it would have been unnecessary if he had dealt fairly with the Indians and adhered to the British Constitution on the one hand and Indian traditions on the other.[99]

Burke described the natural, "ancient" state of colonial relations as one of "unsuspecting confidence" in the mother country, the true center of gravity around which all "the parts are at rest," the remover of difficulties, and the reconciler of contradictions.[100]   In his domestic criticism of the policies of the royal court, he stressed not only that its cabals were seeking power but that they were seeking it by fostering disunion.[101] His summary of current discontents charged that the court had "disturbed tranquillity" and "weakened the Empire." The only good effect of the aggravated imperial problems after 1776 was that they had put an end to "civil distractions." [102]   When he announced that he would not put up a fight for his Bristol seat, his official reason was unwillingness to start a contest which could only lead to disunity.[103]   He justified his previous actions as the representative from Bristol by saying that he conceived his task to be "giving quiet" to property and conscience, peace to families, and reconciliation to kings and subjects; loosening foreign holdings; and teaching citizens to look to law for protection and to good will for comfort.[104]

Political Technique: Traditionalism, "Concreteness," and Conciliation

The major element of Burke's political technique was traditionalism, that is, the defense of existing traditions and institutions.   But Burke's traditionalism was related to his whole ideology.   He accepted a presumption in favor of existing institutions which "have been tolerable for ages," [105] because his position was that these generally contained an acceptable blend of freedom and Conservative harmony, with the latter ascendant.   To the extent that reality did not promote liberal Conservative values, however, Burke was quite prepared to see it changed.

He was well aware that a defense of the *status quo,* simply on the ground that it exists, was meaningless nonsense.   He insisted that only general principles—never merely the prevailing standards—could be the basis for evaluating an art [106] (and he considered government to be an art).   Besides, he readily admitted that traditions were contradictory and often "extremely difficult" to ascertain.[107]   Until the French Revolution he was frequently engaged in opposing some of the existing traditions and institutions.   He criticized certain features of the jury system.[108]   He attacked the East India Company because it was corrupted by the spirit of "cabal." [109]   He opposed discriminatory religious laws, debtor laws, and colonial slavery; and the list could easily be extended. Only after the Revolution did he begin to use traditionalism as a systematic rationalization, and even then he often rejected traditions, even medieval and aristocratic traditions, when they defeated Conservative purposes.

The subsidiary element of his technique was an emphasis on the importance of understanding "concrete" reality. Sometimes this was simply another way of defending existing traditions. But when this was not his meaning, he was referring to the fact that there were many new historical problems for which there were no precedents, and that for these problems, traditions were no longer relevant. Therefore, one had to look to new concrete developments as they emerged.[110] But this did not mean that reality itself sets the standards of value. The exclusion of abstract ideas and "principles," he said, would leave only a confused jumble of particular facts.[111] He still insisted on applying his liberal Conservative values to reality, but he knew that once he could no longer rely on traditions, the task of maintaining the proper blend became extremely difficult. Hence his insistence that government is an "art" for which he emphatically rejected any hope of "perfection." His rejection of perfectionism was not equivalent simply to drifting with the tide, however. It meant only that since government is not an exact science, one should not lose the attainable levels of "contentment and tranquillity" while seeking "perfect harmony." [112]

This attitude does not for a moment imply alteration of his fundamental political ideology. He was suspicious of the use of force and always rejected equality. His goal remained harmony, tempered with some freedom. But his "concreteness" led him to advocate conciliation and compromise, though within limits, as the safest technique for new developments. If reforms must be made, he said, they should be consummated early, because then they can be done calmly, whereas late reforms are too often "inflammatory." [113] When formulating proposed general policies for the revision of American taxation, he said it was important that the distinctions involved should not be made too clear, for this might only stir up additional conflicts.   He warned against making the choice of American freedom or Parliamentary sovereignty too sharp, because it would only force total conflict.[114]   When the conflict had already reached the breaking point, he called for conciliation of the colonies, because it was wise to yield from a position of superior power, since it could then be done with "honor and safety" and would be attributed to magnanimity.[115]   Kindness by government, he generalized, produces esteem by the governed.[116]   But he did not confuse political technique with underlying realities.   When discussing the discrimination against Irish Catholics, he reminded his reader that "mildness in the exercise of absolute power does not alter its absoluteness." [117]   The only time he agreed to the use of repressive force was when it was directed against the French revolutionaries.   In such a situation, honest men must act decisively on the assumption that evil men are capable of any evil.[118]   But when it came to projected policy after an assumed counterrevolutionary victory in France, he again returned to his advocacy of moderation.[119]

It should by now be clear how misleading it is to take either Burke's traditionalism or his "concreteness" out of their ideological context and use them to describe his essential position, or even independent elements of his position.   It is especially ironical to see this done with the technique of "concreteness" which, abstracted from Burke's ideology, means simply an empirical or a realistic approach to facts.   The empirical tradition, especially when linked with "compromise," is not Conservative but Liberal; and political realism in itself can be found as clearly in Lenin as in Burke.   When Burke denounced the French Liberals for not being "concrete," he meant that they were not traditionalists, which was true enough but, in itself, pointless.   Burke's own ideology stands or falls on the basis of its values, not its technique.   Many commentators take both contrasting elements of his technique and say that Burke's

Conservatism consists of the thesis that existing institutions and traditions should be defended, unless change is warranted by the "concrete facts." But this is only to burden Burke with a position that is so vague as to be unintelligible. Yet we shall see that it is one of the most common conceptions among both Conservatives and Liberals in contemporary America. The only tenable explanation of Burke's position, however, is that he was simply trying to maintain Conservative values in an essentially uncongenial, changing Liberal world.

Beneath the adaptation to that Liberal world, his basic values were the same as Plato's. If we "subtract" prosperous freedom from his value postulates, personal tranquillity and societal harmony remain. Without the Whig modifications, the Conservative medieval tradition remains. Even with his acceptance of capitalism and a friendly upper middle class, the medieval social ethic and aristocratic social power are superior to the new economy and to economic power in general. The maximizing of communal cohesion is more important than the maximizing of wealth, and his latent preference was to minimize the pursuit of material objectives. Even with the capitalist system, it is still essential that everyone learn to fulfill the obligations of his "allotted place," and inherited property, especially in land, is superior to "first acquisition." Political power should rest above all on "honor" and aristocracy, for aristocrats are "gracious," leisured, and "natural" servants of the community. If Burke had to accept middle-class institutions in the constitutional system, he nevertheless insisted that harmony itself was the key "constitutional" rule. If he had to accept the complex structure of modern government, he nevertheless insisted that political responsibility be kept clear in that structure, not because responsibility would facilitate popular power or rational discussion among citizens, but because it was the concomitant of "honor" and would enhance the rule of Conservative "natural" aristocrats.

The Burkean values were, therefore, essentially Platonic, though unlike Plato he did not think that a sweeping process of reeducation or coercive political authority was necessary to restore a lost harmony. Like John of Salisbury's, his Conservatism still seemed to be objectified in the actual traditions of his society. But his Liberal historical environment modified his Conservatism, and sent him on a lifelong search for the reconciliation of the original Conservatism with the Liberal modifications. This historical difference, and not their attitudes towards "totalitarianism," was the difference between Burke and Plato.

This does not mean that Burke consciously drew his Conservatism from Plato. He occasionally cited Cicero with approval, and referred even less frequently to Aristotle. But he picked from these sources only the particular argument that he needed at a given moment. There was never any attempt to make clear the relations between his total ideology and earlier formulations. The usual explanation for this is that he was interested more in "concrete reality" than an "abstract theory," but it should be obvious by now that this explanation is untenable. On the rare occasion when Burke mentioned Plato, his criticism was that perfect harmony is impossible, or he implied that Plato's "philosopher-king" was a despot. A much more important reason for his steering clear of Plato, however, was the fact that Rousseau, his ideological archenemy, had already drawn revolutionary conclusions from Plato. The real source for Burke's Conservatism was, in any event, the medieval tradition of harmony. But his plea for toleration of Catholics did not prevent him from rejecting "Popery" as a form of "tyranny," and he never accepted Catholic natural law formulations. Augustinianism and Late Stoicism were much too pessimistic for his purposes. This forced him to go back to Cicero occasionally, though Cicero's ideology was largely a modified form of Platonism. But when he wanted to emphasize the importance of "interests" in politics, he found Aristotle more to the point. Nowhere in Conservative history, however, could he find any combination with the concept of freedom and commercial prosperity. His lack of interest in earlier Conservatism was the natural result of the fact that none of it was relevant to his problems.

The Contradictions of Burkean Conservatism

Burke once said that lifelong consistency had been his highest virtue.[120] If this means that his "programs" and techniques were generally consistent with his value premises, there is some truth in the claim. But his premises themselves are certainly not consistent, and the contradictions between them forced him to conclusions which were contradictory in terms of historical reality. The assumptions that commercial capitalism was compatible with Conservatism, that the middle class could accept aristocratic supremacy, that the party and parliamentary systems were fundamentally Conservative—these were the fallacious premises of Burke's ideology. All were manifestations of the inescapable historical truths that individual freedom and Conservative harmony were not compatible but antithetical, and that the movement of history was not towards greater harmony but towards more freedom. The conditions which made Burke's liberal Conservatism seem feasible were ephemeral, and he interpreted those conditions upside down, so to speak. It was the Liberal values which were dominant, even in his day. The reality was a conservative Liberalism, not the reverse.

The French Revolution showed with unmistakable clarity the superiority, as well as the anti-Conservatism, of Liberal forces, and it sent Burke into an ideological tailspin from which he never pulled out. His problems centered around the question of revolution itself, and he moved frantically from one formulation to another in order to stabilize his position, but never succeeded. By purely Conservative standards, violent revolution can never consistently be justified, because violent upheaval is the final contradiction of Conservative harmony. Burke was aware that the Conservative medieval society of England had been founded in conquest. But he cared more about the fact that after "many centuries," the Normans became "softened into the English," the "conquerors" "blended with the conquered." [121]   He did not deny that the whole system of feudal landed property had also begun with force and conquest.   But he emphasized that the acceptance of this settlement over a long period of time had produced a mild authority based on tradition.[122]   While force, perhaps even revolutionary force, might eventually lead to a Conservative system, it could be justified only in historical retrospect, never in the immediate present.

Yet Burke could not simply stop with a Conservative criticism of the French Revolution.   He had to defend the English Whig Revolution of 1689 simultaneously.   For this purpose, he claimed that revolution is only legitimate if it is recognizable as "just" and if its settlements are expected to "mellow" into "prescription" through long usage.[123]   But this is an impossible criterion except *after* "long usage," especially if "just" means "harmonious."   His most frequent argument was that the Whig Revolution was "necessary," because it sought to preserve "ancient" law, or to deliver England from the "despotism" of the Stuarts.[124]   But aside from the fact that this argument ignored the real Liberal revolution which occurred earlier in the seventeenth century (the Civil War), it contradicted his own earlier statements about the ideological truth of the Liberal position regardless of "ancient parchments." Furthermore, it merely accepted the shallowest seventeenth-century Liberal ideology at face value.   The Stuart kings had had at least as much justification for their actions as the Liberal parliamentary forces, if adherence to constitutional traditions of the preceding century was the only "test."   Hence the seventeenth-century Liberal shift backwards to medieval "tradition," which they reinterpreted to fit the Liberal case (the misinterpretation of Magna Carta as a Liberal document was an outstanding example).   Burke admitted that hardly any parliament in English history knew how to limit its own authority, though he used the argument for satire.[125]   If, on the other hand, "despotism" is defined in ideological terms of Liberal freedom, then the justification of the English Revolution was no different from that of the French. At any rate, Burke continually shifted his ground, justifying the Whig Revolution because it delivered England from "Popery" (why was this not applicable to France?), because it was the only way out of a "great and pressing evil" or "anarchy," or because it was based on "self-preservation" [126] (whatever these terms mean in a revolutionary situation).

His untenable position forced Burke into one contradiction after another. He condemned the French Revolution for confiscating Church lands, but he accepted similar Tudor confiscations in sixteenth-century England, as well as English confiscations of Irish lands, on the ground that these had become "prescriptive" [127] (that is, they had occurred in the past). He defended the Whig shift in the succession to the crown as a mere "exception" which must be distinguished from the "real principles" of the Revolution.[128] But elsewhere he cried out that "the last prescription eats up all the former," like a son devouring a father,[129] which is to say that "prescriptions" of any kind are irrelevant as arguments against a revolution and that the English are quite capable of ignoring them in an actual revolution.

We shall see later that Burke was at times cognizant of some of the basic historical differences between France and England, and of the fact that it was these differences which accounted for the differences between the French and English Revolutions. But he could not bring himself to accept the necessary conclusion that, in terms of Liberal values, the two revolutions were fundamentally similar, because this would have destroyed the basis of his whole ideology. Fortunately for him, he did not live long enough to learn that in England too the forces of Liberalism were to destroy the Conservative hangovers from the Middle Ages. In this respect, the French Revolution was a preview of things to come.

But Burke's occasional criticism of actual aristocracies raises the crucial question of the conditions under which an aristocracy can no longer be defended at all on the basis of Conservative values. Neither Burke nor any other Conservative ideologist ever claimed that aristocracy infallibly produces morally superior children, and all have been ready to admit that aristocracy degenerates sooner or later. Yet none has ever been prepared to follow Plato in providing for social demotion of inferior children. How does one know, under these circumstances, when an aristocracy has reached the point of degeneration? Certainly not by an analysis of the personal characteristics of aristocracy, because these are too susceptible to rationalization. What an aristocrat calls "graciousness," a "commoner" may call pompousness. What the aristocrat calls "prestige" or "honor" may appear to others as an empty deference, enforced only by repression. Conversely, while many may consider the *philosophes* to have been the most cultured men of mid-eighteenth century France, they were mere upstarts and agitators in the eyes of the aristocracy. Most important, the minimizing of desires to the point of easy, or at least feasible, satisfaction is much simpler for an aristocrat in a Conservative society than for the rest in such a society, not necessarily because he is capable of greater self-control but because the satisfactions which he must deny himself are relatively fewer. An aristocracy may therefore display highly harmonious, tensionless, and graceful personalities but may have no interest in devoting itself to perpetuating these characteristics in society. Yet the power of aristocrats in society can be justified only by their actual Conservative contributions to the society, not merely by their personal characters.

Plato was aware of this problem of the potential conflict between individual harmony and societal harmony. In the *Republic* the true philosopher (who is capable of sublime personal happiness) is the man who should hold political power. But such a man, Plato says, has no need for power, which becomes a mere burden on him. The problem is to persuade him to take office. Plato's "solution" is simply to assume that he will consent because he is just and understands his duty.[130]

The same problem arises in the discussion of a possible incompatibility between the happiness of the devoted guardian class and the happiness of the whole society. In the perfect Republic there can, of course, be no such contradiction, but if there were, Plato makes it clear that the happiness of society must come first.[131] The difficulty, however, is that individual and societal harmony may not coincide in an actual aristocracy. In such a case, according to Plato, we are dealing with a "timocracy," and "timocracy" not only causes conflict but also sets off a chain of events which leads ultimately to complete degeneration.   John of Salisbury's criticisms of aristocracy are also directed against the concentration on private as opposed to societal happiness and harmony. There is a recurrent ambivalence in aristocratic apologetics between describing aristocracy in terms of personal graciousness and describing it in terms of public service. When such a divergence occurs, we may expect the aristocracy itself to emphasize graciousness while the Conservative intellectuals or clergymen stress service. We shall see that a difference similar to this separates "Northern" from "Southern" Conservatism in America.

This brings us back to our earlier question on aristocracy: how can we know when an aristocracy has failed to perform its societal functions?   In other words, how can Conservative ideology ever be used to criticize aristocracy in a concrete situation and not simply in the abstract? What is there in Conservative ideology to distinguish it from crass rationalization? The answer to this question is implicit rather than explicit in Conservative ideology. *The existence of conflict itself is the measure of aristocratic failure.* If the Conservative ideology is feasible, then a properly functioning aristocracy will *prevent* conflict, for it will create or maintain a harmonious society. If conflict exists under an aristocracy, then either the leadership has failed or Conservative ideology is fundamentally false and it is not possible to institutionalize harmony. But if Conservative theory is false then the whole justification for aristocracy disappears. The criterion of conflict to distinguish true from false aristocracy is clearly implicit in Plato. In the *Republic* it is the overbearing attitude of the "timocracy" which first stirs up conflict with the upper middle class, and it is this conflict which leads to all the rest.[132] For John of Salisbury the disputes for power within Church or government, or between the two, can be avoided, if the leaders follow divine law. Hence if there is conflict, it must be because of the moral failure of the leaders. In an early formulation, Burke specifically says that popular discontent is a sign of defect in the constitution or government.[133] Even when he later denounces European aristocracies or "monarchies," such as those of Spain or Rome, it is in the context of their vulnerability to the revolutionary challenges emerging from France.[134]

But the Conservatives are never explicit on this point and it is not difficult to understand why. The reason is that each of them sooner or later abandons the ideology for rationalization, and a clear statement of the criterion of conflict makes such a transition dangerously difficult. In the *Laws*, when Plato lapses into calling for obedience to *any* tradition or law, he has abandoned his own values. John of Salisbury has least need of rationalization because he sees no serious challenge to the existing leadership, but his passing statement that nobility "at least" imposes the necessity for probity could easily provide the framework for a blind defense of aristocracy. The clearest transformation of all is to be found in Burke's Conservatism after the French Revolution. The sudden overemphasis on traditionalism and the defense of the French aristocracy are untenable, on Conservative grounds, against a successful revolution.

All of the grounds on which Burke defended the French aristocracy were rationalizations which he acquired by rummaging through Conservative and Liberal values, picking those which were useful and ignoring those which were not. This was especially true of one of his major arguments in the *Reflections on the Revolution in France,* namely, that France under monarchic and aristocratic leadership could not have been really evil, since it still had considerable wealth, a high level of culture, an expanding population, etc.[135] (as if these were not also true of seventeenth-century England before its revolutions). He quickly dropped his earlier criticism that the French Revolution was not, like the English Revolution, followed by increased prosperity and international power.[136] This was obviously a dangerous criterion to apply to the expanding post-Revolutionary France   Not once did he ask whether the existence of revolution did not itself indicate the failure of aristocracy to provide that "chain" of subordination which knits the community together, that "beautiful order" which keeps "each in his allotted place." The truth is that while the Conservative can never justify an imminent or existing revolution by his values, he can never argue against one that has already occurred. He can only lament the degeneration of society or "sink in adoration" before the "inscrutable" will of God. Burke finally did both.

Conservative Confusions after the French Revolution

In the post-Revolutionary period there could be no doubt that in Western Europe there had been a total rejection of aristocratic leadership, and in the face of violent and successful social revolution it was absurd to ask whether the aristocracy had properly performed its Conservative functions. It is not surprising, therefore, that in the nineteenth century Conservatism was broken into a bewildering variety of ideological fragments. In Britain some Conservatives like Coleridge and Scott became complete reactionaries, looking wistfully back to the "pure" Conservatism of the Middle Ages. Others, like the radical Tory preachers Oastler and Sadler or the Christian Socialists, allied themselves to the labor class and developed a new kind of radical Conservatism, calling for equalitarian economic and political changes. The mainstream of British Conservatism, however, merely adjusted itself to changing realities, adopting more and more of Liberal values and industrial imperatives, until only a few bones were left of the Burkean skeleton which they had inherited.

In France and Germany, there had been no Conservative link to Liberalism, as there was in Great Britain. Therefore, the French and German defenders of Conservative aristocracy tended to seek authoritarian, rather than Liberal or middle-class support. Almost all of them were reactionaries, whose concrete standards were based on a past which no longer existed. Some, however, sought a solution in "corporatism," which was at least a rational attempt to develop a new societal harmony for industrial society and which implicitly admitted that the old aristocracy was no longer a feasible instrument for Conservative harmony.

During the nineteenth century, there was a continual tendency for Conservative arguments to be cut loose from Conservative values, and therefore subject to rationalizing manipulations. Conservatives produced involved analyses of the "organic" (that is, the "naturally" cohesive) nature of society, in order to reject the Liberal demands for change. Society, the argument ran, is an interdependent entity, analogous to a biological organism, in which conscious changes inevitably produce unforeseen consequences that contradict the original intentions. But this argument never explained why the consequences of "unconscious" change should be any less contradictory or unforeseen, and it constantly neglected the fact that "organic" concepts could be and were, used indiscriminately to justify aristocracy, Liberalism, hereditary monarchy, or democracy.[137] The "organic" argument would have been tenable on Conservative grounds only if it were used to defend a Conservative society. Since the existing society was no longer Conservative, Conservatives should have concentrated on programs for producing Conservative harmony in the future. This is what the "corporatists" and the Christian Socialists did. But most of the Conservatives wanted only to restore aristocracy or to protect what was left of it. They therefore shifted the argument away from Conservative values, and said, in effect, that all current attempts at change upset social cohesion and are, therefore, evil. The argument conveniently ignored the fact that cohesion had already been upset by the failure of the aristocracy and the kings to fulfill the needs of their societies.

A related argument was the deification of tradition as the "silent working" of the "folk spirit." The obvious objections to this are that the "folk spirit" speaks with many dissonant voices, and that in the revolutionary changes on which later traditions are based, the "spirit" is anything but "silent." But the real fallacy was the failure to recognize that Liberalism itself could become the new tradition and, therefore, impregnable to traditionalist arguments. The underlying error of aristocratic Conservatives, however, was their refusal to follow Plato in his admission that the original Conservative sin of a useless aristocracy is the first cause of all subsequent conflict. Even worse was the usual failure to examine the question of whether an enforced restoration of the *ancien régime* would not bring still greater conflicts and tensions than those which the Conservatives found in Liberalism or democracy. At any rate, it was these aristocratic Conservatives and their arguments which served as the stereotypes of Conservatism for the contemporary world, in spite of the crucial fact that the societies they sought to save or restore were no longer Conservative at all.

The adjustment of Conservatism to Liberal society was a failure, and the failure was reflected in its contradictions. The adaptation to the industrial society which began in the nineteenth century has only widened the contradictions. At this point, however, we must shift our focus to the United States, the "world-historical" nation of the industrial age.

III

Conservatism

in America

If European Conservatism faced a new crisis in the nineteenth century, the difficulties of Conservatism in the United States were insuperable. It has frequently been pointed out that America was born a Liberal nation and did not, like Europe, have to fight its way to Liberalism against a medieval past. In addition, an overwhelming array of historical forces pointed in the Liberal direction. Economically, Liberalism was promoted by the abundance of land and resources, the chronic labor shortages and the impetus they gave to mechanization, the need for immigrants and the growing market they provided, and the continual over-all expansion of wealth. The near universality of the middle class meant that severe class conflict was minimal, the most serious cleavage being only that which lay within the middle class itself. Socially, the ubiquitous frontier promoted individualist equality rather than deference; westward geographic mobility made traditionalist roots tenuous; social mobility between and within classes made a settled system of "manners" seem impudent and artificial; and large-scale immigration insured a continual class fluidity even when geographic movement began to slow down. Contrary to the claims of contemporary Conservatives, not even the rural areas developed a Conservative sense of "community," since the farms were too isolated and the area too sparsely populated [1] for anything but an ethic of self-reliance and purely utilitarian cooperation. Even in an area such as upstate New York, where the large estates provided the economic basis for a kind of aristocracy, there was little of the social deference needed to make such a society Conservative.

Only a Liberal political system could have been built on this socio-economic foundation. The frontier areas were too primitive, the country too large, and its geography too diverse for a strong, centralized state. Even more important, the absence of feudalism made it unnecessary to repeat the European process of building a strong state in order to destroy the feudal classes and restrictions.[2] Without a strong, class-conscious aristocracy, there was neither need nor likelihood of class-conscious middle and lower classes.[3] The emphasis was primarily on conflicts of economic interest within the overwhelmingly dominant middle class; and geographic diversity multiplied these conflicts. This created well-nigh perfect conditions for Liberal politics of compromise within conflict, because on the one hand there were obvious divergences of interest, and on the other none was serious enough to disrupt the society. It is significant that in the one civil conflict which did reach serious proportions, something resembling a real class cleavage coincided with sectionalism. But except for this single case, the Civil War, American politics seemed to offer classic support for the Liberal position that conflict and competition could encourage over-all progress without seriously upsetting the society.

The institutional framework needed to encourage a system of political compromise was adequately provided by the governmental process of checks and balances, and the natural policy of such a government was to do little except provide some aid for the over-all economic expansion of the country. It could be claimed without serious distortion of the facts that the system was constantly providing increased satisfactions for the desires of its citizens, and that the distribution of these satisfactions according to economic "merit" left "something for everyone." The Liberal justification of American society was therefore very strong, and there was relatively little challenge of the Liberal values themselves. If there were other ideologies they were nevertheless so strongly influenced by Liberalism as to have virtually surrendered the battle, and the lines separating one ideology from another were often so blurred as to be almost indistinguishable. Liberalism pervaded almost all thinking and controversies tended to center on means and details rather than fundamental values. Hence the acceptance of a Supreme Court empowered to interpret law according to a "self-evident" value system.

American Conservatism in the Nineteenth Century

Aside from all the forces which added to the strength of American Liberalism, there were ideological factors which insured the weakness of American Conservatism. America never had a medieval Conservative tradition, just as it never had a feudal history; and the dominant ideology of the colonists was Puritan and Lockean Liberalism. The paradoxical result was to separate Conservatism from traditionalism. In Europe, where tradition meant medieval tradition, the Conservative could defend "ancient" tradition and Conservative values at the same time. But since the American tradition was Liberal from the beginning, tradition and Conservatism became contradictory terms here.

It was a foregone conclusion that Conservatism in America would be liberal Conservatism; but while Burke's Conservatism was only tempered by Liberalism, American Conservatism was overwhelmed by it. Burke could remain Conservative because he thought that the Conservative social ethic still dominated British society. But in America there was no Conservative social ethic to assert over Liberal capitalist economics. The Conservative could not offer prestige plus wealth as against "mere" wealth in his bid for political power, because prestige in America had little to do with moral self-control or community service, and the relations grew ever more tenuous as time went on. Indeed, one may say that the Conservatives tended to be those who did *not* receive the deference which they felt to be their due and those who found themselves losing status because they could not keep pace with the rapid increase of wealth. In England, Conservatism rested on two classes: the landed aristocracy and the upper middle-class mercantile families. In America the vestiges of a feudal land system were easily abolished by the end of the Revolution, and within a short time large landowners had become land speculators rather than aristocratic rentiers. Even the New York land system eventually succumbed. Without a Conservative landed class as ally, the New England merchants turned easily to a more congenial Liberal orientation. The absence of both a Conservative class base and a Conservative social ethic compounded the confusions which resulted from the separation of tradition from Conservative values. The result was the disintegration of Conservative ideology throughout the nineteenth century.

To these generalizations there was one obvious exception. The Old South did have something that resembled an aristocracy, a real Conservative ideology, and the beginning of a Conservative tradition. But the Conservative society of the Old South lasted only for one or two generations, and it was, in several crucial respects, a very spurious kind of Conservatism.

In a physical sense, the colonial South of the seventeenth century was only half-Conservative. The coastal area was dominated by a kind of planter "aristocracy," which shared its prestige and power with the merchants and manufacturers. This seaboard society, like that of England, held both Conservative and Liberal values. In Burke's terms, it combined "tranquillity" and "prosperous liberty." But the inland piedmont area was not Conservative at all, and it was recurrently at odds with the tidewater strip.[4] For the piedmont aristocrat, leadership was possible only if it was Liberal leadership, as the career of Thomas Jefferson reveals. Taken as a whole, then, the colonial South was *not* Conservative, because a society cannot be half harmonious, as the history of England indicates. The growing strength of the inland middle-class farmer made it evident that the historical trend in the South, even more than in England, was towards increased Liberalism.

What made the later ante-bellum South seem Conservative was that in the eighteenth century the trend towards Liberalism seemed to become reversed, and the antipathy between farmer and planter seemed to disappear. Underlying this apparent reversal was the invention of the cotton gin just before the turn of the century. The consequent expansion of the plantation system westward was of vital importance in changing the nature of Southern society. But this westward migration did not really get under way until after 1820. The rough delineation of class lines throughout the South did not occur until about 1840, however; and while sectional conflict began as early as 1820, it did not produce real political solidarity among Southerners until the 1850's.[5] Therefore, the Southern "Conservatism" which died in 1865, with the victory of Northern armies, was only one generation old, two at the most. Still more important, there are at least five reasons for insisting that, even within this limited period, Southern Conservatism was extremely artificial and unstable, which is to say that it was of questionable Conservative value.

In the first place, the Southern plantocracy not only originated in the middle class, it never really severed its middle-class roots. The powerful historical factors which promoted land speculation and economic expansionism in nineteenth-century America affected the Southern planters as profoundly as any group in the country.[6] No amount of self-sufficiency on the plantations could immunize them from the fluctuations of the capitalist cotton market, with all the potential instability implicit in such involvement. The expansion into new western cotton areas not only kept planters on the move but it also was a major cause of the conflict which led to the Civil War. In a sense this combination of "aristocratic" Conservatism and a Liberal capitalist outlook which emphasized individualism, freedom, and economic expansion was not unlike the liberal

Conservatism which in England had produced the ideology of Burke. But the Southern brand of Conservatism was based on the ambiguous combination of capitalism and "aristocracy" in a single class rather than in two classes, as in England. It had no permanent agricultural roots because of its migratory characters. Its capitalist roots predated the "aristocratic" addition, the reverse of the English sequence, and it continued to be completely dependent on and sensitive to the market system of international commerce. Such an unstable Conservative compound depended on very special conditions for its continued existence, especially the continuation of imperialist expansion into new cotton areas.* When this expansion was stopped by the Civil war, the aristocratic veneer disintegrated; and industrialization easily completed the process of restoring a middle-class South.

In the second place, even at its height, the plantation system was responsible for perpetuating an extremely backward society along the entire frontier region, especially in the mountain areas. The land system, the relatively static economy (whose prosperity depended on conditions outside its control), and slavery discouraged immigration, which in turn prevented economic development.[7] The frequently condescending planter attitude towards trade and industry (as distinct from its commercial attitude towards agriculture) spread throughout the society and also retarded economic progress.[8] The inadequate transportation system linking the sparse Southern population with the rest of the country left the frontier region economically primitive and its farmers impoverished.[9] For the South as a whole, the expansion of agricultural production, caused by a short-term rise in the prices of farm commodities, could not compensate for the relative decline in industrial expansion.[10]

---

* Without land expansion, a South which refused to industrialize would have become steadily more impoverished and unstable as world cotton prices fell and foreign competition increased. Under these conditions, the continuation of Conservative harmony in the South would have been highly unlikely. If it turned to industrialization, its Conservatism would have been destroyed anyway, as its actual history shows. In any event, the South had no Conservative future unless it could continue to absorb more land.

From a purely Conservative viewpoint there is, of course, nothing wrong with economic stagnation in itself. On the contrary, it is actually desirable in order to maintain social cohesion. But Southern Conservatism always remained liberal Conservatism, and a liberal Conservatism has no defense against stagnation, because its primary assumption is that freedom and economic progress can be compatible with Conservative values. Burke was very proud of the improved economic conditions in England, but Southern Conservatives could only concentrate on blaming "Northern exploitation" for its economic problems.* The liberal Conservatism of the Old South was thus neither truly Conservative nor successfully Liberal. It remained in a state of economic limbo, suspended in historical mid-air.

Thirdly, the Old South had a highly ambivalent moral code. On the one hand, it developed a hedonistic ethic which was superimposed on the rugged individualism of the frontier. Short seasonal work periods and ease of subsistence in the sparsely populated rural areas, coinciding with the effect of the climate, meant considerable leisure for all classes. The existence of slavery encouraged loose sexual mores, and a relatively unrestrained pursuit of pleasure was characteristic of all free men.[11] But there was simultaneously a strong strain of Puritanism which was carried over from the frontier. The result of this curious tension between hedonism and Puritanism was to perpetuate the frontier tendency to private violence, in which the peculiarly Southern sense of guilt found periodic

---

* Clear evidence that Northern merchants were generally unscrupulous does not seem to be available. The economic advantages which the North derived from cotton trade and manufacturing were due to its superior economy. Southern capital did not go into commerce or industry, because it was being invested in land and slaves. (See, for example, Eaton, *A History of the Old South*, pp. 399–400, 404, 407.) Therefore, the economic weakness of the South was really caused by the same agrarianism which was the source of its Conservative strength. A society which is prepared to abandon Conservatism may argue that outside exploitation prevents it from industrializing and expanding. But it is sophistry for an ideology to acclaim the Conservative virtue of social cohesion over "materialism" and simultaneously to blame others for the economic weakness of the society which it dominates.

outlet.[12] The combination of hedonism (which becomes "graciousness" in an aristocracy) and a strong religious sense of moral
self-denial is not necessarily destructive of a Conservative
society in itself.   A kind of aristocratic hedonism existed in the
Middle Ages, alongside the religious morality fostered by the
clergy. The morality of the Middle Ages, however, was much
less repressive than the later Puritanism.   But to combine both
hedonism and a repressive Puritanism in the same people is apt
to produce precisely this oscillation between guilt and violence
which actually existed in the Old South.   Guilt is a clear indication of Conservative failure, since Conservatism seeks to
avoid guilt by adherence to morality. Violence is equally anti-
Conservative.   It is true that private violence and lawlessness
were characteristic of early feudalism, but feudalism did not
really become Conservative until private force had been subjected to a considerable measure of control.   Certainly by the
nineteenth century a Conservative society in which violence
was still rather common was of questionable merit.   Burke
found nothing desirable in the feudal predilection for force
until it had become transformed into the code of chivalry.

The fourth, and most telling, weakness of Old South Conservatism was that it depended to a major extent on the continued existence of Negro slavery. The conflict between the
planters and the yeomen farmers began to disappear only after
the extension of the plantation system and slavery.   Even during the Civil War the farmers in the mountain region still rejected planter leadership. To the extent that social solidarity
did develop, it depended largely on the existence of an alien
labor class in relation to which even the poorest white man
had a superior social status. The Northern opposition to
slavery, which arose over the question of which social system
would dominate the West, reinforced the sense of Southern
white solidarity.[13] Since the development of slavery had caused
the emergence of the Conservative social cohesion and the acceptance of the "aristocratic" ethic in the first place, it is clear

that slavery was the social cornerstone on which the whole Conservative structure of the Old South rested.

Conservative apologists in the twentieth century like to cite the argument that slavery would have disappeared by itself, without Northern opposition, because they assume that Southern Conservatism could have existed without the social cohesion provided by racism. But, had the plantation system depended on white labor, the entire history of the South would have been different, since there would have been no motivation for accepting social fixation, economic stagnation, and planter leadership without conflict. Until slavery spread westward social cohesion did not exist. Furthermore, when the apologists say that slavery would have disappeared without Northern intervention, they do not add that racism would have or should have disappeared. Racism performed the same role of sustaining artificial social cohesion after the Civil War that slavery had performed before. The postwar Populist revolt in the South was a clear indication of the kind of conflict which would have existed had military defeat and Reconstruction not made it possible to use race hatred for neutralizing the conflict. Most important, the apologists' position assumes that the Negroes could have been expected to continue indefinitely submitting to racial inferiority. But even a "foreign" race, accustomed to enforced submission, must eventually refuse to accept such inferior status in a country which was changing rapidly because of industrialization.* The Conservatives simply write their apologetics in a historical vacuum. In the "real world," the entire Southern system of social cohesion had to be revealed as artificial and not "organic" at all.

The crucial point, however, is that slavery must be considered immoral by any nineteenth- or twentieth-century Conservative in Western civilization. The fact that Plato accepted

* This applies also to the occasional speculation that the South might have industrialized with slave labor. The assumption that slave status would have been acceptable to workers with the skills and education necessary for industrial labor is unsupportable.

slavery as part of his system is completely irrelevant, since any modern Christian (or non-Christian for that matter) must reject many features of ancient society, especially slavery. To cite the patristic acceptance of slavery and the early Christian concept of purely moral equality before God is a very thin defense. The patristic doctrine viewed slavery as a consequence of original sin. This did not mean that slavery was a part of God's divine order for the world, as Southern Conservatives often argued. It was simply one of the sins that could be expected from corrupt mankind, and one of the possible punishments for sin itself. Therefore no attempt was made to abolish the institution at a time when it was still widespread in Western civilization. But to defend it in the nineteenth century when it had disappeared from virtually the entire world demanded the grossest rationalizations. The idea of moral equality under God does not prohibit actual equality of condition in society. One can only say that the second kind of equality does not *necessarily* follow from the first as a matter of abstract reasoning. The abolition of slavery has, however, followed the Christian concept of moral equality as a matter of historical fact. Moreover, the Old South itself had earlier rejected slavery as immoral. It abandoned this position only when the cotton gin transformed the economy, and it began its positive defense of slavery only in reaction to Northern criticisms. So the Southern Conservatives were themselves aware of the immorality of their position. This forced them to circumvent the whole Christian medieval tradition and look to ancient Greek sources for their model. Conservatives have always looked to earlier societies as models, but only for the general theme of social cohesion, never for a specific institution or moral code. Plato retained all the moral advances of the city-state; the medieval theorists kept the advances of Christianity; and Burke did not surrender the improvements of modern society, least of all the abolition of slavery and serfdom. To have regressed to ancient society from the nineteenth century in order to justify slavery was a totally indefensible rationalization, for Conservatives no less than others.*

The major positive argument of the Conservatives in the Old South was to cite the virtues of Conservative society as a justification of slavery. Southern cohesion and lack of class conflict, it was held, made the treatment of slaves more humane than Northern treatment of industrial labor.[14] But even if this were true, it was a reversal of the actual historical sequence. Slavery had made Southern Conservatism possible; now Conservatism was being used to justify slavery. Yet if slavery was itself immoral in the nineteenth century, then Southern Conservatism was an immoral historical freak. Rather than defend slavery because Southern society was Conservative, Southern Conservatism should have been rejected because it depended on slavery. That this was not done was a measure of the artificial and unstable nature of that Conservatism. Moral self-control based on affection and the avoidance of conflict are twin pillars of Conservatism, which is as effectively negated by violating one as by violating the other. The Southerner's inability to honor the Conservative moral conscience was just as anti-Conservative as the Continental aristocrat's inability to avoid conflict.

The fifth and final difficulty which Conservatives of the Old South had to face arose from the sectional conflict which precipitated the crisis over slavery and ultimately destroyed Southern Conservatism. The South was, of course, not a separate society but part of a predominantly Liberal country. Until the 1820's there was little sense of sectionalism in the South. Loyalty was primarily to the individual state.[15] Political self-consciousness, including Conservatism itself, developed only under the impact of sectional conflict, just as

---

* The tendency of contemporary historians to insist that the abolitionist bill of particulars against slavery was exaggerated is understandable only as it reflects a desire for historical accuracy. No amount of empirical evidence alters the impossibility of justifying Southern slavery on either Conservative or Liberal grounds. The question of justification is an ideological, not an empirical, problem.

social solidarity developed in reaction to the attack on slavery. Even the conclusion that the South attained the Conservative goal of avoiding conflict depends largely on the assumption that the South was, or should have been, an independent society. Since it was not a separate society (and not even the most rabid Southern Conservative would now hold that it should have been), then its aristocracy was responsible for avoiding conflict with other parts of the country. Therefore the part which Southern leadership played in precipitating the Civil War (and it was certainly considerable) was a measure of its failure to perform a proper Conservative role. The argument by some historians that the Civil war was avoidable or "repressible" is irrelevant here. The point is that the Southern plantocracy, like the European aristocracy, is vulnerable to the charge that the very existence of conflict proved Conservative failure. The use of the Liberal argument that conflict could have been avoided by a compromise of interests is of no value in defending a South whose major justifications were Conservative. Since the days of John C. Calhoun, a Conservative defense of Southern society has never been compatible with a Liberal defense of sectionalism or states' rights.*

Once defeat occurred, the weaknesses of Southern Conservatism became rapidly apparent. The upper class was quickly transformed back into the Liberal, commercial capitalist class [16] it had been in the beginning. Economic backwardness easily lent itself to new exploitation. The hedonistic-Puritan ambivalence led to an extremely unstable religious fundamentalism; and the tradition of violence continued,[17] with periodic force being used to prolong the social inferiority of the Negro. Finally, the clear decision that the South was part of the larger United States opened the way to industrialization, and in the face of this new force, little of the old Conservatism could long survive. If isolated traits like Southern "hospitality" and "good manners" survived, these did not add up to Conserv-

---

* See Chapter IV, under the subheading "Agrarian Illusions and Dilemmas," for a further discussion of Calhoun's inconsistency.

atism; and the nostalgic "plantation legend" was often promoted by the same people who advocated industrialization.[18]

It is useless to ask whether Southern or "Northern" Conservatism came closer to embracing the Conservative ideal.   In
America only liberal Conservatism was possible, but it was
hopelessly fragmented between an aristocratic hedonism in the
South and a Conservative moralism in the North.   This split
reflected Plato's distinction between the "timocratic" aristocracy which rejects the control of "philosophers" and the true
"guardian" class which accepts it.   It was the recurrent medieval cleavage between noble and priest, king and bishop, em-
peror and pope.   When Oswald Spengler wrote, in the
twentieth century, his Conservative history of *The Decline of
the West,* it was his preference for the aristocratic affirmation of
the sex instinct through "race" and "blood" against "priestly"
self-denials in the name of morality which endeared him to the
Nazis.*   In nineteenth-century America the conflict between
the hedonistic Southern Conservatives and the moralistic
Northern Conservatives was this same ancient Conservative
conflict of aristocrat and priest-intellectual.

This was only one of several Conservative conflicts.   If
Southern liberal Conservatives were aristocrats who wanted
more wealth from commerce, Northern liberal Conservatives
were men of commercial wealth who wanted to be aristocrats.
If the Southerners were never really aristocrats, the Northerners were never really men of wealth.   If the Southerners
defended slavery in the name of "organic" cohesion, the
Northerners (the Adams family, for example) denounced
slavery in the name of morality.   If the Southerners wanted to
avoid sectional conflict in order to preserve Southern cohesion,
they nevertheless had to face conflict in order to preserve the
slave base of that cohesion.   If the Northerners were prepared

---

* Spengler's rejection of morality was simultaneously a rejection of reason
and of any coherent standards of evaluation, and this enabled him to affirm in
the name of aristocracy not only "blood and race" but also what in Conservative
ideology becomes their contradictions unless controlled by reason and morality
—conquest and power.

to see sectional conflict in order to further morality, the real victory went to Liberalism and industry, not to Conservatism of any kind. If the Southerners could not develop a rational Conservative ideology because of the South's artificial "aristocratic" social base and Conservative "traditions," the Northerners could not develop one because the North had no aristocracy or Conservative traditions at all. Put Southern and Northern Conservatism together and you have a potentially complete liberal Conservatism. But it was of the essence of the situation that they were separate entities, and there was no way outside the realm of fantasy that they could have been joined. One need not cite economic factors to demonstrate this, especially since Conservatism will deny that economics are primary anyway. The moral and social cleavages, even within the Conservative "world outlook," were themselves irreconcilable.

By the last quarter of the nineteenth century there was virtually nothing left of American Conservatism. There was no longer a Conservative landed class in the North. The Southern plantocracy had been destroyed by the Civil War and its industrial aftermath. The Northern upper middle class was solidly Liberal capitalist. Only the Conservative New England "brahmins" were left, and their Conservatism was so esoteric in the American environment that it could be said of the intelligibility of their values as well as of their social exclusiveness, "The Lowells talk only to the Adamses, and the Adamses talk only to God." * Insofar as the New England Conservatives remained active in politics, as leaders of the Mugwump reformers, it was at the expense of their Conservative values. They had already accepted Liberal capitalist economics, now obviously part of the American tradition. Without a concrete means for linking a Conservative social ethic to society, they had already become "moralizers," preachers of abstract morality and "community" in a society which interpreted both morals and community by Liberal definitions. Instead of concern with the fundamental Conservative idea of preventing in-

* The Adamses are more relevant for our purposes than the Cabots.

dividual and societal tensions, they had tended to accept the Liberal ideas that tensions may be economically progressive and that conflicts need only be tempered. Political reform, especially of the civil service, now became the Conservative road to a moral community. The ironical fact that professionalized bureaucracy has become one of the most powerful anti-Conservative forces of the twentieth century only underscores the fact that American Conservatism can become politically active only at the cost of completing its own self-destruction.

The absorption of Conservatism by laissez-faire and political reform, however, meant the absence of the kind of critical insights for which Conservatives should have been equipped. Louis Hartz, among others, suggests incisively that while the energies released by American society were tremendous, the psychic tensions must have been proportionately intense. Especially towards the end of the nineteenth century, when the westward movement was coming to a halt and industrialization was bringing new dimensions to the universal success ethic, the continual emphasis on competition and "getting ahead" exacted a heavy toll. For those who failed in the race the ideological identification of success and merit could only imply a corresponding identification of failure and guilt.[19] But even those who succeeded could find no rest from continuing competition, because there was no fixed social status which could be attained by the man on the top. Nor was there a compensatory status for the man on the bottom,[20] and, of course, no outlet for guilt through radical hostility or class conflict, as there was in European society.[21] The absence of radical release for guilt is of no interest for a Conservative, but the problems of psychic tensions and the absence of "status cushions" are Conservative problems of prime importance, and a strong American Conservatism would have insisted on airing them continually. But there was no American Conservatism, and the term "conservatism" in America became a description only of political technique, of attitude towards change irrespective

of the values which were being defended. In the twentieth
century, therefore, it has been fixed in the American vocabu-
lary as a synonym for "laissez-faire Liberal," the very opposite
of its valuative meaning in Europe.

Historical Problems of Twentieth-Century Conservatism

Conservatives since Plato have insisted that an individualist
rejection of Conservative morality and the Conservative community could only result in a new social organization based
on conscious, artificial reason and imposed by repressive political power. This was also Burke's warning against the consequences of democratic Liberalism. Contemporary Conservatives lean heavily on the indications that the warnings have
turned out to be correct. During the nineteenth century,
democratic Liberalism and industrialization developed together
in Western civilization, and, especially in America, it was common among Liberals to assume they would continue to develop compatibly. But the twentieth century has produced
an ever-mounting mass of evidence which indicates that industrialization, whose essential characteristics are organization,
discipline, control, and authority, is the antithesis of Liberalism, whose center of value lies in individualism and freedom.
During the past fifty years, Liberalism has repeatedly been
forced to reformulations of its ideology, in order to make its
values and industrialization more compatible with each other.
Yet after each reformulation, the organizational imperatives of
industry have grown stronger while Liberals have retreated
from their "Progressive" reformulations to more defensive pos-
tures and attempts to understand what has gone wrong.

This does not mean, however, that the Conservatives have an
adequate explanation of the history of the twentieth century
(or any other century, for that matter). Least of all does it
mean that a Conservative society is any more feasible in the
twentieth century than it could have been in the nineteenth.
On the contrary, industrialization is even more anti-Conservative than Liberalism, and the twentieth century is undoubtedly

the least congenial period in the history of Western civilization for Conservative ideals. Conservatism seeks "community," tradition, harmony, and quiescence. In this century, it has found organization, violence, political power, and revolutionary upheaval.

If America has largely escaped the disasters, she has perhaps had more than her share of the tensions which have accompanied industrialization. And if Freud was correct in concluding that violence and hostility are the easiest outlets for tensions, then the absence of physical upheavals here may only have compounded the psychic tensions. Industrialization has brought a fantastically high standard of living in America. But if tensions are the result of unsatisfied desires and hence purely relative, as the Conservatives among others assert, then material progress has not necessarily brought greater psychological satisfaction. Advertising and the increasing emphasis on a consumption ethic have continually kept expectations far ahead of actual satisfactions. Since Conservatism depends on willingness to minimize desires, the contemporary ethic could not be more diametrically anti-Conservative than it is. But since industrialism carries with it an inherent promise of unlimited expansion, there is no foreseeable future in which men are likely to stop expecting some fulfillment of that promise. Besides the problems of consumption, industrialization has multiplied the conflicts of economic interest. The fantastically complicated scope of industrial organization may favor hierarchy and clear lines of authority, but conflicts over how these lines are to be drawn are likely to continue throughout the century.

Whatever the eventual implications of industrialization for social relations, its effects thus far have been completely upsetting and anti-Conservative. Revolutionary changes have occurred in the nature of the family, which has been increasingly displaced as the major agent of socialization. The mores of society have become fluid and uncertain, and the whole system of social prestige has undergone radical transformation.

This produces another major Conservative problem. Aside from the nonsatisfaction of desires, the major source of tension is guilt. Guilt is a result of the failure to fulfill moral norms. But when mores are rapidly changing, the fulfillment of traditional norms becomes increasingly difficult and the potentialities for guilt increase proportionately. Since virtually all contemporary Conservatives insist on holding to traditional moral codes, they become trapped between Scylla and Charybdis. On the one hand it becomes more and more difficult to be both moral and psychologically harmonious. Hence the proclivity of twentieth-century Conservatives (especially of the reactionary group) towards crotchetiness and pessimism rather than the graciousness to which they may still lay claim. But even if their psychic constitutions were strong enough to escape this problem, they would still be impaled on the other horn of the social dilemma—the traditional moralist is unlikely to be rewarded with the high prestige which he seeks above all societal goods. For the Conservative this is the cruelest cut of all, and the long, venerable history of this second problem in America goes far towards explaining the grumpiness of American Conservatives even before the twentieth century.

The intellectual problems are correspondingly difficult for the Conservatives. Obviously the traditional aristocracies are now irrelevant, especially in America. From whatever source the new "natural" aristocrats are to be drawn, it is clear that the need for their intellectual preparation is greater than ever. To be equipped for Conservative leadership, in the twentieth century, they must master not only technical knowledge in all fields but they must also be taught Conservative values through a conscious intellectual process rather than by reliance on unconscious traditions. At the same time, they must teach the community to accept Conservative values and leadership. But the processes of both leadership training and communal education presuppose control of the media of education and mass communications. Actually, many ideologies compete for such control and, particularly in America, this competition requires conscious propaganda and symbol manipulation. Conservative ideologists who participate in the process are forced to appeal to prevailing values and prejudices, no matter how anti-Conservative the prejudices may be (and they usually are just that), if they are to make an actual bid for intellectual leadership. If they adopt such practices they dilute their Conservatism; if they do not they become superfluous. Besides, there is the obvious problem that the Conservatives are not in fact serious contenders for control of either the universities or the mass media in America. For the most part American culture and American intellectuals have always been Liberal, and if that Liberalism has been changing in the twentieth century, the changes have certainly not been in the direction of a real Conservatism.

The political changes in twentieth-century society are equally as anti-Conservative as the social, economic, and intellectual. The fact that these changes have also caused recurrent anguish to Liberals does not alter their incompatibility with Conservatism. In the realm of government organization, the center of gravity has been shifting from the legislature to the executive and administrative authorities. The growth of administrative law has been phenomenal. Political parties have put new technologies and large-scale organization to work in the service of political manipulation, and pressure groups have developed as independent centers of power alongside the political parties. In this crucial area of political power, Conservatives have indulged in typical feats of rationalization in order to prove that Burke's ideology still has meaning for the twentieth century. One of the earliest of these attempts was made by Woodrow Wilson in formulating what has been called "the doctrine of responsible party politics." [22] At the end of the nineteenth century, before he entered politics, Wilson was a kind of Burkean, though he combined Burke with the optimistic Liberal doctrine of progress to such an extent that his "Conservatism" was of a highly doubtful variety. Concerned with the need for men of honor as public leaders, he stressed the con-

cept of clear political responsibility. Responsibility was to be
the product of disciplined parties, composed of men who devoted themselves to public service and who adhered to common
principles on public policies. Responsible parties were to be
the alternative to bosses and machines. It is worth pausing
here to consider in some detail whether any modern doctrine
of responsible parties, though ostensibly based on Burke, can
possibly be Conservative.

It should be recalled immediately that Burke never really
defended a party *system* at all. It was only a Conservative
party he was justifying. The farthest one can go is to say that
he accepted a system of competition between a Conservative
landed party and a Conservative commercial party. Under
these conditions Whig-Tory competition would have been acceptable. Not once did he ever indicate that there would be
anything desirable in a permanent contest between Conservatives and the king's men, or between Conservatives and Foxite
Whigs. The conflict was an emergency which necessitated the
formation of a single Conservative party in order to preserve
a harmonious Britain, nothing more. Without the "emergency," Burke's tendency would have been much closer to a
"no-party" system, a term which Maurice Duverger uses to describe older Conservative societies, than to any modern party
system.

To this it may be objected that Burke's party analysis is not
relevant, and that we should begin with the Conservative attitude under modern conditions. But there are four reasons for
insisting that Burke's analysis is relevant. The first is the continuing persistence within Conservative parties of the traits
which Burke wanted to see in his party as well as in the state
as a whole.

In his recent study of political parties Duverger has noted a
striking relation between party structure and political ideology.[23] Authoritarian parties tend to adopt authoritarian organization; socialist parties favor democratic organization; etc.
Political parties generally reproduce within themselves the

kind of political relations which they would institute in the society as a whole if they had permanent power. Conservative parties tend to have narrow socio-economic bases for their local units, centering especially around large landowners, manufacturers, bankers, and churchmen. The purpose of these party units is to recruit leaders rather than mass membership, and they tend to be active only during elections rather than as permanent institutions. The units operate by personal and customary relationships more than by formalized rules. Overall party structure tends to be decentralized, but the lower units are relatively inarticulate in transmitting their opinions to the national leadership. Real leadership is therefore exercised by the parliamentary representatives, not by party officials or ideologists. But the natural bent even of the national leaders is toward personal loyalties and clique formations rather than formalized organization or other types of leadership relations, and there is relatively greater resistance to party discipline among them. Historical circumstances cause variations in these characteristics among Conservative parties of different countires. The long history of centralization in England, connected with the early emergence of state sovereignty, has caused its Conservative Party to develop a high degree of centralization and party discipline. But this is exceptional and even the English Conservative Party is a "cadre" party with relatively weak "articulation" from below, rather than a "mass" party.

For Burke also the purpose of a party was to bring honorable leaders rather than masses together; policy was to be left to the discretion of the parliamentary party, and agreements were to be reached in the deliberations of all the gentlemen-representatives rather than in the workings of a formalized party hierarchy. Burke also had no concept of permanent local party organization. Furthermore, he stressed party discipline only defensively because of the exigencies of political conflict. The persistence of these predilections among Conservative parties is of considerable interest.

The second point to note is that contemporary Conservatives have no more succeeded in reconciling democratic suffrage with Conservative ideology than Burke did. Historically, modern democracy resulted from the demand for political power by the lower middle and labor classes. The arguments which were used to justify democracy were based on typical Liberal or radical values: the natural right of men to share in political power; the right to protect one's private interests; the right of the majority to transform an oppressive society; the use of political equality as the instrument of social or economic equality, etc. These are arguments which no Conservative can really accept. But political democracy is an overwhelmingly powerful force in the twentieth century. Certainly no American Conservative could hope to gain a hearing by advocating its abolition. The Conservative has therefore had to reinterpret democracy to make it compatible with his own values.

For this purpose, most Conservatives have chosen to present democracy as a system of moral self-development which places on the citizen the burden of fulfilling the moral "law," contributing to communal cohesion, and selecting morally superior leaders who will maximize the harmony of society, all on the basis of free individual choice. The illusion behind this conception is easily discernible. The Conservative task of selecting superior leadership can be entrusted to the whole of a people only under very limited conditions. The society itself must be so traditionalist that there is a single standard of morality by which to judge its leaders. It must be so harmonious that all the people are prepared to give the fulfillment of morality first place in the criteria by which they choose their political leaders. And it must be so Conservative that all accept harmony as the supreme value of the society. This is patently untrue of twentieth-century societies, including America, even by the analyses of the Conservatives themselves, if indeed such admissions are needed. Burke at least honestly felt that these characteristics had some relation to the British electors of his time. Modern Conservatives can only say that the people show good sense when they elect Conservatives, and poor judgment when they do not. But they cannot justify the universal franchise itself; they can only resign themselves to it as an unavoidable concession. They may (and do) formulate generalities about the capacity of the people to recognize moral excellence when they see it, but this is mere propaganda which becomes transparent when they criticize particular electoral choices, and is a measure of the extent to which Conservatives have had to surrender their values to the peculiarities of modern communications. Burke's rejection of democracy is far more relevant to Conservative ideology than any contemporary adaptation to it, the more so since the adaptations are often grudgingly made

The third point is that nothing has changed the incompatibility, which was clear in Burke's ideology, between Conservatism and the party system. The mere fact that what Burke thought was a temporary "emergency" has turned out to be relatively permanent is besides the point, except to underscore the inadequacy of Burke's analysis. To say that the party system is a means of settling conflicts without violence is not to say that it is a system of Conservative harmony, for it does not prevent conflicts; it only settles them. The European party conflicts are between directly contradictory ideologies and values, even in England. In the United States there are no major ideological cleavages because both parties have traditionally used Liberal arguments, but there are actual conflicts between shifting coalitions of economic and social interest groups. None of these systems is compatible with Conservatism. Other ideologies are in a position to develop justifications of the party system and even of majority rule because they accept conflict as inevitable, even as desirable. Liberals may argue that modern democracy facilitates compromise among conflicting interests or that such competition promotes progress. Authoritarians may argue that democracy tells the political leaders where power lies and hence what is and is not politically feasible, or that it provides a harmless safety valve for discontent while allowing a small number of competing oligarchies to hold relatively stable political power. Radicals may argue that it is an instrument of peaceful social revolution. But what can the Conservatives say? Certainly not that it actually prevents conflicts or that it elevates Conservative moral leaders. When Conservatives say that democracy is primarily a system of moral self-development, they are stating a hope, not a fact. This may be the aspiration of a Conservative party; it is certainly not a tenable Conservative justification of the modern party system.

The fourth point follows from the first three. Any attempt to take Burke's pronouncements on parties out of context and apply them to the contemporary party system can only result in a misinterpretation of both Burke and Conservatism. Proposals for a responsible party system, in the context of American politics, might lead to parties based on varying interpretations of Liberalism or to some vague kind of Conservative-Liberal dichotomy with all the advantages weighted on the side of Liberalism. In the context of European politics the doctrine might justify a clear choice from the full range of ideologies as the maximum political freedom available to the individual citizen. But under no modern conditions can it produce a Conservative system. Burke's definition of parties, torn out of context, becomes the opposite of its original purpose. Early in the twentieth century, Oswald Spengler observed that Conservative aristocracy is comfortable only in "estates" and in cliques based on personal loyalties. Political parties were originally Liberal institutions in which Conservatives have never been comfortable.[24] Nothing that has happened since Spengler offered this observation has made it any less true.

The Social Base of American Conservatism

The primary characteristic of a Conservative class is its avowed preference for social over economic goods. A Con-

servative ruling class must devote itself to community service
and morality in preference to economic activity and must pro-
fess to be more interested in prestige than in wealth.   These
are still the traits claimed by continental European aristocracies which have medieval roots or by classes in some way related to them, though the aristocrats are by now largely thread-
bare caricatures of their ancestors.

   In the United States, however, the absence of a medieval history and of an aristocracy have made the feasibility of both a
Conservative ruling class and Conservative "follower classes"
remote.   The closest approximation in twentieth-century
America to a Conservative leadership class is the local business
elite of the American city or town, particularly that group
which represents "old wealth."   The major economic activities of old wealth are real estate and finance,[25] the former sug-
gesting a kind of rough urban approximation to a landed gentry and the latter to the old Whig merchant-financiers.   Since
we have never had the "real thing," old wealth is as close as
America has ever come to a Conservative ruling class outside
the Old South, and it has been the source of most of American
Conservatism from John Adams to Henry Adams and beyond.

   Old wealth has several of the characteristics of a Conservative aristocracy.   It appears to be relatively content to enjoy
its wealth, rather than attempt constantly to break new economic or technological barriers.   As a result, it tends to emphasize prestige or status plus wealth rather than wealth
alone.[26]   Its moral code is closer to the traditional one, and it
has something of an ethic of community service.   It is conscious of family ties, good breeding, manners, and gentlemanly
graces.   Thus, although not comparable to European standards
of aristocracy, American old wealth, considered abstractly,
might be viewed as a reasonable substitute.   The major problem for American Conservatism is, of course, that the society
in which this group functions is not Conservative at all.   But
an equally difficult problem for Conservatism is that old

wealth in America has not in fact been even traditionalist in its politics. It has, on the contrary, continually adjusted itself to the prevailing currents of political change.

It has already been noted that Conservatives adjusted to laissez-faire at the end of the nineteenth century, and that some of them participated in political reform movements of that period. But far more interesting was their role in the Progressive movement of the early twentieth century. Richard Hofstadter points out that the "Mugwump type" became Progressive not because of economic loss but because his status declined as industrial corporations and the new class of national wealth overshadowed all other centers of prestige.[27] Although the ethical leadership of these Mugwump Progressives was still centered in New England, the group included local old wealth elites in New York and the Midwest,[28] as well as local professionals, especially lawyers, and some of the clergy. Thus, after having adjusted itself to the prevailing industrial laissez-faire in the late nineteenth century, old wealth adjusted itself to the prevailing Progressive sentiment of the middle classes in the early twentieth century, and even took over much of the new leadership. It was not traditionalist and certainly not Conservative in politics, except for a small segment which kept it uneasily aware of its own contradictions.

The division in the Adams family was itself a kind of microcosmic reflection of the ambivalence of old wealth, which sometimes oscillated between a backward-looking, alienated Conservatism and a Conservatism of adjustment, however grudging, to the prevailing drift of society. Henry Adams was the traditionalist whose unwillingness to adjust drove him ever further backward into history until he finally came to rest in the Middle Ages. But this process, as his autobiography shows, served increasingly to isolate and alienate him even from his own class. Much closer to the process of reality was his brother Brooks Adams, who looked forward to a new form of human organization, centralized by a powerful state and a dedicated aristocratic bureaucracy superimposed upon industrial society.

Though Brooks went much further in the direction of authoritarianism than the Mugwump Progressives, he was far closer to this group than Henry. The "new look" of old wealth was represented by Theodore Roosevelt and, as Hofstadter says, it produced the beginning of modern statism, although this was not really its intention.[29] Old wealth continued to be the bearer of the old New England Protestant morality, but in politics it shifted sharply in abandoning laissez-faire and in embracing democracy for the first time.[30]

Most important in understanding the dilemmas of American Conservatives is the fact that old wealth cannot play the role of national leadership in twentieth-century America. It is not only that the class has lost its relative preeminence in wealth to the *nouveau riche* and the corporations. More essential for a Conservative class is the fact that it has lost prestige and social status because of its failure to keep up with the pace of wealth accumulation in a country where prestige tends to follow wealth. Both Hofstadter and C. Wright Mills agree that the local elites of old wealth have been continually losing status. Mills notes that prestige has not only been transferred to corporation leaders, but perhaps even more to mass culture celebrities such as movie stars, crooners, and athletes. Under these circumstances, this potentially Conservative class lacks its prime counterclaim against wealth—public honor—and without a status of honor it has no independent channel to political power. The result has been that old wealth has been a follower, an adjuster to changing sentiment, rather than a leader; and its role in the Progressive movement was probably closer to real political leadership than any role it is ever likely to play again.

The question of a proper class base for societal leadership continues to be one of the insuperable problems of twentieth-century Conservatives. They often talk in vague terms about "natural aristocracy" or about a "democratic elite" recruited from all classes, and sometimes they even cling to the absurdly unrealistic hope that this new "elite" will play the part of a

Platonic guardian class, sacrificing all material comfort in its devotion to social service.[31]   All of these solutions are too far-fetched to require detailed criticism; we need only ask who will select the "elite" and where we are to find leaders with truly Conservative characteristics.   The recurrent assumption of the Conservative intellectuals is that they, like Plato's philosophers, can somehow create a Conservative society out of nothing.   All they need is the right start, but somehow this start never materializes.   In the meantime, the Conservatives repeat Burkean phrases about the need to be "practical" and to avoid "Liberal abstractions" which are not rooted in society. Some Conservatives have, however, cut the Gordian knot and have transferred their hopes for Conservatism to the corporate owning and managerial classes.   There will be occasion later to consider the feasibility of this "solution."

American Conservatism in the Twentieth Century

The differences in the proposals and the detailed analyses of twentieth-century American Conservatives have been appallingly numerous.   This is not, as the Conservatives are wont to claim, due to the fertility of their thought, any furrow of which would yield a ripe harvest of Conservatism.   Rather it is due to the bewildering confusions which are the natural fruits of their historical dilemmas.   There are, however, several distinctions which should be made on the basis of historical and ideological categories.   Until recently, the most important distinction has been between what we may call "reactionary Conservatives" and "adjusted Conservatives."   The reactionaries are liberal Conservatives who are bitterly hostile towards the fundamental changes which have come with industrialization and democracy in twentieth-century America, changes which have destroyed the only world in which they could feel at home.   In their critiques of these changes they have reverted to theoretical standards much closer to the essential Conservative themes of inner harmony as the prime basis of human happiness and maximum communal cohesion as the goal of society. As a result, their criticisms have tended to be more incisive and more relevant to the historical problems of twentieth-century Conservatism. But when they turn to making positive proposals for societal harmony in order to promote individual happiness, their only standards are those of a lost historical past. They are consequently reduced either to advocating the repressive use of political power in a society where they have no political power, or to vague hopes for a "moral regeneration" which they do not really expect. Unlike the reactionary Conservatives of nineteenth- and early twentieth-century Europe, the American reactionaries have not been at all dangerous. They are therefore almost as close to an "alienated" Conservatism which has openly surrendered all hope of improvement and is confined only to criticism as they are to liberal Conservatism.

The "adjusted Conservatives," on the other hand, are much more at home in the twentieth century, though they are also critical in varying lesser degrees. The elements of Conservative theory are relatively weak and blurred in this group, and their acceptance of democratic Liberalism and industrialization much stronger. They are generally more optimistic in tone and more apparently "realistic" because they demand fewer difficult changes, and they are therefore better prepared for a practical appraisal of the actual possibilities of change. Not only has their acceptance of Liberalism been far-reaching; they have followed Liberalism wherever it has led—from laissez-faire to Progressivism, back to laissez-faire, and through the New Deal to postwar traditionalism. In this respect they probably reflect more adequately the attitudes of a partially Conservative group like "old wealth." The reactionary Conservatives, on the other hand, tend to be alienated intellectuals with highly colored representations of the people for whom they claim to speak. The reactionary Conservatives remain in the Burkean tradition because their Liberalism is distinctly subordinate to their Conservatism. The "adjusted" Conservatives, however, although they begin with liberal Conservative prem-

ises, have gone so far in their acceptance of both Liberalism
and industrialization that they shade easily into modern Liberalism itself.   But like most Liberals, they have also adjusted
to the increased scope of political authority.   In this latter respect, adjusted Conservatism is a kind of modern Middle Stoa,
especially since the acceptance of some Liberal elements is by
now common to all forms of American Conservatism.   Two new
forms of American Conservatism appeared during the 1920's.
These two forms are corporatism and neo-orthodoxy.   The first
is a sort of Platonic program for building a new, "purely" Conservative society within the framework of the industrial corporation.   The second is a revival of Augustinianism.

Henry Adams symbolizes the sudden shift of American Conservatism from Mugwump laissez-faire and political reformism
in the late nineteenth century to sweeping criticism in the
twentieth century.   As the new age unfolded before him he
seemed suddenly to realize the widening incompatibility between historical reality and the Conservative values which he
and his friends had long held without seriously examining
them.   Forced now to look elsewhere for a more congenial
world, he "discovered" the natural Conservative haven of the
late Middle Ages, a period which had not previously served as
an American Conservative ideal.   The material backwardness
of medieval society he found to be inconsequential compared
with the profound tranquillity which he ascribed to the unifying love symbol of the Virgin.   Since this Golden Age, history
had been a process of steady dissipation of human energy, of
degeneration of societal harmony, and of growing unhappiness.
In the twentieth century the nadir of this process has been
reached, because the effect of the machine, the new value symbol, is not harmonious unity but fragmentation, chaos, and
conflict.   Apparently overwhelmed by the magnitude of the
Conservative problems which he perceived, he made very little
attempt to suggest remedies.   It was clear to him that the old
"aristocracies" were totally unequipped for the new world.   It
was also clear that there could be no reversal of industrialization or of the greater material satisfactions which it promised.

Except for vague hints about a new Conservative intellectual elite, he could therefore fruitfully concern himself only with trying to understand the scope of the problems themselves. Adams is the matrix for at least two different forms of twentieth-century Conservatism. The reactionaries have continued his criticisms of industrialization and the corporatists have worked from his insistence that industrialization is here to stay. But a totally alienated Conservatism of the future can accept both of these positions simultaneously and draw the obvious conclusion that there is no hope.

The tendency of old wealth to adjust to both the democratic Liberalism and the industrialism of the Progressive movement is evident in the writings of A. Lawrence Lowell, representative simultaneously of old wealth and adjusted Conservatism. Lowell was an adherent of laissez-faire, but it was not the kind of laissez-faire that had been advocated in the late nineteenth century. Rather, Lowell retained all the changes which had occurred in Mugwump opinion. He wanted some government regulation of business; he was suspicious of large corporations; and he accepted the framework of political democracy, though the acceptance was at times a qualified one. On the other hand, he also retained the old elements of American Conservatism: moralism, a critique of "excessive materialism," a desire to avoid conflicts of interest, and attraction to traditionalism. But the combination of democracy and traditionalism produced a political Conservatism of adjustment. He understood the difficulty of determining what was traditional and what was not, especially on the national level. The function of political parties, as he saw it, was therefore to act as opinion brokers, mediators between conflicting interpretations of tradition (not between conflicting *interests*), and thereby create new traditions where the existing ones were not clear. Naturally this proper function depended upon statesmanship and leadership by the "best men" rather than upon bosses and manipulators.[32] In Lowell's analysis the distinction between Conservatism and Liberalism is confined to one of attitudes to-

wards change. Both Liberal and Conservatives he said are
"contented," but the Liberal is optimistic about change while
the Conservative is not.[33] What is interesting about this definition is that it virtually removes all ideological differences between the two.   Lowell's own real preferences, which he obscured only with difficulty, were for a traditionalist, harmonious, aristocratic society.   But he had adjusted himself to accepting a society in which none of these was to be found.   The
task he set himself was really to find the way back to a society
approximating his true ideal through changes in the existing
society.   He was cautious about changing basic political institutions, but he nevertheless retained a faith in progress,[34]
though the progress he sought was primarily moral.   His categories were well suited to cover the ambiguities in his own
Conservatism by obscuring the real differences between ideologies.   After rejecting all meaningful ideological categories
and focusing merely on attitudes towards changes, he could
conclude that in the 1920's Liberals had become Conservatives.
He might also have added that by the same process Conservatives like himself had become Liberals.

The reaction to the New Deal of representatives of old
wealth such as Lowell was mixed.   He favored new regulatory
commissions like the Securities and Exchange Commission, but
he was appalled at the growth in the power of unions and of
the Federal government, including its use of deficit spending
as an instrument of "pump priming." [35]   While his group may
have been anti-New Deal, at least after 1935, it is likely that
this has changed since World War II.   In view of the adjustability of the group to the twentieth century and in view of
the fact that it is often given positions of prestige in corporations or new businesses,[36] old wealth is probably much more
susceptible to the argument of the latest "adjusted" Conservatives that the New Deal has produced new harmonies in a
changing America than it is to the reactionary Conservative
argument that the New Deal program has been destroying
America's oldest traditions.

Henry Adams died in 1918, and in the 1920's the "new humanists," Paul Elmer More and Irving Babbitt, developed the reactionary line of Adams' thought. These "new humanists," like Adams, were generally alienated from their societal environment, but they still had hope for a Conservatism that could resist democracy and industrialization. The essence of civilization, they found lay in an inner moral "check," embodied in conscience and based on a moral source above the individual. Spiritual peace, and hence happiness, can come only from obedience to this "inner check." Paul Elmer More considered the best moral code to be the one institutionalized in the Anglican Church. Babbitt was less clear about institutionalization, religious or otherwise. Both thought that society should be based on the offering of deference and the entrusting of public office to those who most perfectly lived according to a moral code whose essence was self-restraint and service to the community. Both felt their ideals to be almost nonexistent in contemporary American society, and neither could find any clear social base for the future success of those ideals. Their proposed solution was the building of an intellectual elite trained in the universities or churches, presumably under their Conservative tutelage. The "humanist" criticisms of twentieth-century America followed generally the same lines as those of Adams, but they were more moralistic and Puritanical and less impersonal than his. Babbitt in particular found industrial machinery in the form of the automobile to be personally upsetting to his psychic equanimity, and he was more pointed in his charges that American democracy lacked proper (Conservative) leadership. But he insisted on retaining the more traditional features of American constitutionalism such as judicial review to prevent further degeneration.

Both Adams and the humanists were associated with Harvard University, symbol of the status position of old wealth in New England. But the humanists' anti-industrialism linked them also to the small farmer class, a class which was losing both status and economic security in the twentieth century. It may thus have been more than coincidence that Babbitt's childhood was spent on a farm.   During the depression of the 1930's, however, a specifically agricultural brand of reactionary Conservatism developed with the revival of Southern agrarianism.   The appeal to the small farmer was extended to the urban lower middle class also, and this class base was adopted as well by non-Southern reactionary Conservatives.   Southern agrarianism became part of the ideological movement known as "distributism," a reactionary Conservatism which had originated in the late 1920's with Gilbert Keith Chesterton and Hilaire Belloc in England and Father John A. Ryan, a Catholic clergyman, in America.

While distributism was based on predominately Conservative values, it sought to appeal to the whole lower middle class in advocating the widest possible distribution of small property, and its Conservative doctrine was qualified with the Liberal language of freedom, individualism, and "true" capitalism. Ralph Adams Cram was a kind of link between the New England humanists and the distributists of the 1930's.   He had been a student of Henry Adams and he repeated Adams' general criticisms of contemporary society.   Cram was also friendly with the "humanists" and had, in 1917, written a thin book emphasizing the inadequacy of democratic political leadership and the lack of "honor" in public life.   But in the 1930's he wrote a book based largely on the program of the distributists. His political proposals, however, were uniquely his own.   He called for the building of a new moral aristocracy, complete with titles and ceremonial trappings; a Senate composed of "aristocratic" representatives of various functional "guilds" elected for life terms; a lifetime President-king empowered to choose a prime minister and dissolve the House of Representatives in case of failure to support the prime minister; and a Supreme Court with curbed powers of obstruction.   Little comment is needed on the absurdity of these proposals, which compound the vagaries of an "aristocracy" that has no clear

social base with the unreality of an artificial constitutional upheaval, made even more dubious by proposing actual aristocratic and medieval paraphernalia to a twentieth-century
America.

Thus all five major historical forms of Conservatism have
reappeared in our age, though under new auspices. We shall
soon see that all of them exist simultaneously within the New
Conservatism of the present day. Before we examine this New
Conservatism, however, it is worth pausing here, for several
reasons, to consider in some detail the nature of Southern
agrarianism. In the first place, this was the only reactionary
Conservative attempt in the twentieth century to formulate a
political program for the "restoration" of a Conservative society, and its failure is instructive. Secondly, several of the
agrarians are still writing today, and their postwar metamor-
phosis is a good indication of the reactionary tendency to shift
either to an "alienated" or to an "adjusted" Conservatism.
Thirdly, this was the last manifestation of the difference between
Southern and "Northern" Conservatism. But most important,
agrarianism makes it clear what the nature of reactionary Conservatism would have been if it had ever wielded any real
power in twentieth-century America.

IV

The Illusion of

a Southern Conservative

Revival

The continued industrialization of the South in the twentieth century steadily destroyed more and more of the traces of its former Conservatism. Agriculture declined in relative importance as industry grew. The old planter class became largely transformed or displaced, part of it going into industry, part going into bankruptcy and selling out to small farmers or new men of wealth, part moving to the city to become absentee landowners.[1] The ethic of *noblesse oblige*, such as it was, was increasingly replaced by the older doctrines of laisscz-faire and states' rights. More than ever the South became sensitive to a market economy. Urbanization progressed rapidly at the expense of the countryside. A fairly strong middle class, followed by the new white-collar class, emerged. Individualism became for a time as strong as it had ever been. The dwindling segment of the plantocracy which still took its old role seriously became obsessed with a hollow sense of social rank and tended to withdraw into ever more profound seclusion. The shell of social solidarity remained but it was filled with an oppressive caste system which frequently spawned racial violence and a characteristically Southern demagoguery. That planters often became leaders in Negro-baiting was only another measure of their decline, since this was a diversion they had eschewed in their "best days." [2]

However one might describe twentieth-century Southern politics, it is certainly not correct to call it Conservative. Even the Byrd "machine" in Virginia, whose reputation for honesty and devotion to public service might have qualified it for Conservative leadership, has been linked more to laissez-faire Liberalism[3] than to Conservatism. Furthermore, signs of the organization's political decline after World War II were followed by its joining the front ranks of extreme segregationists, although it had refrained from any such position throughout its earlier history. One is tempted to view this move, therefore, as a determined bid to hold power through an emotional mass movement, no matter what the cost. It is questionable whether this entitles the Byrd organization to continue claiming even the attributes of integrity and devotion to public service.

But once we go beyond Virginia the disparity between the Conservative ideal and the reality of politics in the South widens markedly. On the one hand there have been serious socio-political conflicts in states such as Alabama, Georgia, Louisiana, and Texas. On the other, an issueless politics of localism has prevailed in Arkansas and Florida, and localism is as far removed from aristocratic leadership, which is supposed to reflect moral superiority, as the ascendancy of industrialists in North Carolina. In South Carolina and Mississippi the worst kind of rabble-rousing and Negro-baiting has been common; and in Tennessee the Crump machine held power for years by manipulating the balance of power and sometimes flirting with violence and illegality.[4] If these varied brands of politics usually left power in the hands of industrialists and other elements of the upper middle class (rarely the plantocracy), there were times when even this class was successfully challenged, as it was by the election of Hugo Black and John Sparkman in Alabama and, even more effectively, by that of

Huey Long in Louisiana.　Except in racial problems, the tendency of Southern congressmen was to vote according to the prevailing economic interests of their constituents, as everyone else did;[5] they did not follow the Burkean concept that legislators should be guided by the permanent interests of the nation as a whole or his view that the legislature should reflect the image of the cohesive feelings of the society.　Again, whatever one may call this pattern of politics, it was certainly not Conservative.　Out of this changing Southern world came one of the strange fantasies of American ideology, a reactionary program conjured up by "rootless" intellectuals in search of a lost Conservative society which had never been securely Conservative.

The Agrarians: Last Stand of Old Southern Conservatism

Southern agrarian Conservatism was born and died during the depression.　Though historical reappraisals of the Old South and the Civil War have been rather common, there appears to have been virtually no serious Southern Conservative analysis of contemporary problems between Reconstruction and the depression.　Apparently the area was changing so markedly and so rapidly that no one seriously considered advocating any reversion to the earlier so-called Conservative society.　The depression hit the Southern textile industries during the late twenties.　The earliest manifestations of the Conservative revival at that time appeared in the literary protests of the Nashville "Fugitive Poets," original core of the agrarians.　It was, however, the national depression of the thirties which turned them to societal analysis.　Capitalist industrialization had apparently failed, and for the first time it seemed that an agrarian program for the restoration of a Conservative society might command an audience.　The depression, the Conservatives thought, had had a "calming" effect on Americans, who were now in search of "roots" like those of the Southerner.[6]

The original literary group included John Crowe Ransom,

Allen Tate, Donald Davidson, Stark Young, and Robert Penn Warren.   In 1930 they contributed, along with Frank Owsley, A. N. Lytle, F. C. Fletcher, and other Southern intellectuals, to a joint publication which they entitled *I'll Take My Stand*. Between 1933 and 1937 they were the main pillars of a Conservative periodical called the *American Review*.   During this period they were joined by a group of distributists, of whom the most important was Herbert Agar of the Louisville *Courier-Journal*.   In 1936 the enlarged group wrote a book called *Who Owns America?*, which emphasized the distributists' economic proposals.   Agar was by far the most noteworthy political author of the group and wrote more than half a dozen volumes, most of them after the 1936 venture.

The agrarians' model for a Conservative society was, of course, the Old South.   They never really denied the anti-Conservative characteristics of Old Southern society, but they made excuses for them.   They admitted Southern economic backwardness, but blamed it more on Northern exploitation than on the nature of the plantation system.   No one defended the morality of slavery, but Ransom repeated the old argument about humane treatment and Owsley sympathized with the fear "naturally" evoked by proposals to free "cannibals." [7] None closed his eyes to the Southern tendency towards violence, but Tate felt that it was due to the disappearance of "feudal" institutions such as the duel[8] and to the lack of an adequate religion in the area.[9]   Owsley admitted that the Civil War was an inevitable clash of fundamentally different societies within an expanding America, though he justified the Southern role in terms of resistance to Northern exploitation and the threat of freeing the "cannibals." [10]   In the group's second book, *Who Owns America?*, the agrarians made no attempt to deny the powerful Liberal and individualist forces which underlay Southern society and plantocracy.   In fact they emphasized Jeffersonian agrarianism as the true Southern ideology.   These excuses did not, of course, refute the thesis that the Old South itself was a highly dubious species of Conserva-

tive society.   But the agrarians preferred to focus their attention on the characteristics which were Conservative.   Lytle
emphasized in *I'll Take My Stand* the social solidarity between
planters and yeomen.[11]   Fletcher thought the superiority of
the Old Southern educational system was proved because it
avoided a technical mélange in order to produce a harmonious
balanced character rooted in society.   Harmony, he agreed
with Confucius, means keeping emotions within limits, and
when perfect it produces a state of tranquillity.[12]   Naturally,
the themes of an organic society and *noblesse oblige* were frequently reiterated in the agrarian appraisal of the Old South.

Industrialization and "radical" democracy, the agrarians
found, have caused continual degeneration from these desirable earlier conditions.   One writer bemoaned the loss of societal harmony, another the disappearance of *noblesse,* still
others the destruction of the family, the community, "true"
leisure, and the moral degradation of women.   The depression
proved to them that industrialism was unstable, that it tended
to fragment the society, to prevent any real enjoyment of work,
to cause unemployment, poverty, oppression, inefficiency, and,
ultimately, fascism.   Art was becoming industrialized; education was being made subordinate to technology; and the artist
was being alienated from his society.   American political
power was considered to be in the hands of a Northern plu-
tocracy and a corrupt Supreme Court which exploited both the
South and the agrarian West.

All were agreed that the only way to solve these problems
in the South was by returning to the "Southern way of life,"
strengthening the sense of religion, promoting true culture,
and reviving the proper social amenities—good manners, good
conversation, and hospitality.[13]   The economic key to the good
society was to be agrarianism, that is, a restoration of agriculture to a position where it would again set the norms of the
whole society.   The individual approaches to the problem of
how to restore a Conservative society varied, though there was
not necessarily any serious incompatibility among them.   Stark

Young was most defiant in defense of the "aristocratic" ethic. He sneered at "middle-class confusion" and "peasant stolidity," and defined aristocracy as the habit of domination with "some degree of arbitrariness," but with major emphasis on honor, leisure, and self-control.[14] Most of the others were less blatant in their attitudes; indeed they tended to obscure their aristocratic bias behind a fervent affection for the yeoman farmer and "agriculture" in general.

The agrarians tried also to obscure their racial prejudices by concentrating on special aspects of race relations. Robert Penn Warren stressed the "natural" need of the Negro to live on the farm or in rural towns.[15] Others confined themselves to the usual remarks: the North freed the Negroes at the expense of enslaving the whites during Reconstruction; the South must keep whatever race relations it considers most feasible; beware the danger that "monopoly capitalism" will stir up race hatred. But occasionally, frank prejudices were unveiled in individual books or articles written after the joint ventures. Davidson could not repress the observation that the racial equalitarians in the North had never lived among the Negroes, so they did not understand the disorders that might arise from "unashamed and happy dirt." [16] Tate took the blunt position that only acceptance of white supremacy could solve the race problem.[17] Agar complained of the urban cynics who were so indifferent to moral principles that they did not care if their wives went to bed with Negroes.[18] (It should be added quickly, however, that Agar clearly abandoned such crude racist gibes later). Little was said by the group about the white labor class, but Ransom offered the reader a hint of what the Conservative Southern attitude would have been without the artificial aid of racism. Though the lower classes should be provided with decent housing, medical care, and "relief from boredom," there is, he observed, nothing romantic about the "smell" of the poor.[19]

The key problem of the agrarians was economic. They readily admitted that the "old families" had become rentiers and absentee owners, and that planter control in the contemporary tenant and sharecropper system had led to serious abuses. But the real villain, of course, was the one-crop system, which was in turn caused by industrialization. Since it was industry which had destroyed the spirit of *noblesse oblige* and produced immorality,[20] the way back to a Conservative society was through agriculture. It was not simply a question of increasing agricultural production, since it was still increasing, except in relation to industrial production. The problem was to restore agriculture as a "way of life," and the class medium for the restoration was to be the yeoman farmer. It was in the 1936 volume that the agrarians took up the championship of the yeoman as resurrector of Conservatism.

The result was a curious kind of liberal Conservatism which tried to weld Jeffersonian Liberalism and Southern Conservatism. The agrarians now accepted the "American dream" of freedom, stability, and equality; and emphasized small property as the best means of attaining that "inner peace which is the mark of a good life." [21] Real freedom, Tate said, presupposed a high degree of control over markets and production and therefore was best fulfilled in a yeoman economy. Individual property was the precondition of individual freedom, and a small farmer economy was based on true use-value rather than exchange-value, which only facilitated exploitation. Small-property systems even solved the problem of political conflict, because they did not lead to expansion or aggression. Besides, the farmer knew that man could not conquer nature and respected its mysterious power without idle or dangerous speculation.[22] The specific proposals for a yeoman system varied among the group, but a major common assumption was that the small farms would have to be as self-sufficient as possible and produce largely for the local market in order to minimize the problems of a market economy. This would also decrease political conflicts over questions like farm subsidies, which "cannot continue indefinitely." [23] A typical suggestion for implementing this agrarian goal was to have the government buy up all corporate and absentee-owned lands and give them to prospective yeomen with the proviso that land ownership could not be transferred to creditors for defaulted debts.[24]   One agrarian estimated that one fourth to one third of the total population should be farmers.[25]

Most of the agrarians conceded that industry should be controlled rather than eliminated.   This would require the decentralization, both regional and local, of as many industries as possible.   Smaller units of production, it was maintained, improved efficiency because they were based on personal contact among all the participants in the industry.   Decentralization was also essential for trade and retail businesses, and chain operations should be rejected in favor of small independent dealers.   Giant industries which could not be decentralized should be nationalized and run by the government as a public service.[26]   The Conservatives eulogized small business as the essence of capitalism and denounced large corporations as dependent on economic and political privilege rather than efficiency.   Some emphasized consumer and marketing cooperatives, and there was occasional talk of encouraging corporations to sell stock to their workers, to pay higher wages, and to charge lower prices.

It was clear that the government would have to play the major role in securing these near-revolutionary changes in the American economy, and the agrarians did not balk at the prospect.   Jeffersonianism, one of them rationalized, means weak government only in an agrarian society.   In a corrupt society, government must be strong to achieve salvation.[27]   Hence they were prepared to advocate discriminatory taxation against chain stores and large corporations, forced resale of foreclosed land, forced dividend distribution, and numerous other measures designed to achieve their agrarian goal, not to mention less unusual proposals such as rural electrification.   There were occasional objections to the concentration of land ownership and proposals for government action, but these concerned commercial corporation farms.   Large plantations devoted to a multi-crop system and a self-sufficient communal economy, especially plantations with a large percentage of renting tenants, did not fall under the ban.[28]

Most of the group seemed to agree with Davidson that American culture must be viewed as primarily regional and that Southern culture must be preserved as a special Conservative product.[29] Furthermore, regionalism seemed to fit the agrarian proposals for economic decentralization. Education, they felt, should also be regional, in order to escape artificial domination by the educational philosophies of other areas, notably New York City, and specifically Columbia University's Teachers College.[30] But Davidson warned against a nonpolitical regionalism. Without political safeguards, he indicated, a Conservative South would have no defense against corrupting economic and cultural influences.[31] In actual fact, anti-Conservative influences from the "outside" have been continually transforming Southern culture. Those agrarians who were simply affirming economic or cultural regionalism were describing a reasonably interesting phenomenon, but the description had no valuative or ideological significance, for they had no defense against the weakening of their regionalism. Davidson, however, insisted on sectionalism (that is, political regionalism); and he rejected administrative regionalisms which take geographic differences into consideration only to make national planning operate more successfully.[32] Instead he insisted that only Calhoun's "concurrent majority" offered the right solution.[33] Calhoun's original proposal had been to give the South a veto on the national government by requiring a "concurrent majority" within each section for major political decisions. But Davidson made no attempt to specify how "concurrent majority" might work in the 1930's.

Herbert Agar provided a rather different political focus for the group. A Southerner and a distributist with agrarian preferences, Agar was, however, primarily interested in the country as a whole rather than in Southern sectionalism. He was by far the most prolific political writer of his company, several of

his books being histories of American politics and political
ideas. Agar is typical of the American Conservative tendency
to obscure its real values behind a fervent concern for "saving"
democracy. But salvation turns out to be Conservatism wear-
ing a democratic mask which never really fits.

Throughout most of his first book [34] Agar sounded like a
Populist Liberal, who was prepared to see great merit in con-
senting to entrust power to the "best-educated" men. Only
agrarian democracy was desirable; industrialization corrupted
everything, especially democracy. [35] Jefferson, John Adams, and
Calhoun were all his heroes.

Only towards the end of the volume did his real assumptions
begin to show through. Industrialism may be powerful, he
admitted, but moral values must be asserted over economic de-
terminism. This, he insisted, can be done only by a religious
ideal like that of the Middle Ages or a "social ideal" like that
of the Old South. Furthermore, he suggested, since democracy
can only succeed in an agrarian, small-business society, it may
be that democracy will have to be saved at the cost of some economic retrogression. This is a typical hitching of a democratic
cart before the Conservative horse. It soon becomes clear that
Agar really wants Conservatism, for which he is willing to pay
the price of accepting democracy, not democracy for the price
of economic simplicity. His final conclusion was that America
must restore "good" leadership (as in the early days of the Republic) [36] along with agrarianism and religion.

In the second book [37] Agar revealed much more of his values.
He again presented agrarianism as the best way to make democracy effective. Social democracy, he found, was best developed in rural areas, while there was no real equality in cities.
But almost immediately he began to clarify what he meant.
The relations between people of different incomes could be
smoothed either by a class system like England's or by social
equality as in rural America. Rural equality was therefore
the American means to social harmony. But this was in no
way superior to the English system in which each "knows his

place and feels protected" by this knowledge. As the analysis proceeded, Agar periodically injected Conservative values as they became necessary for his thesis. Using the terminology of Oswald Spengler, he distinguished "culture," which was based on tradition and faith, from "civilization," which was urban, skeptical, and decadent. He found the worst failing of capitalists to be their lack of *noblesse*. More important, he could not conceal his sympathy for John Adams' view that the right to vote should be restricted to property owners. Society is best when its people are contented with their lot, and, he continued, the worst feature of American society is that it succumbed to the "get-rich-quick" ethic. Unrestrained competition meant that the many failed and were unhappy while only the few succeeded. The ideal society was therefore the kind that existed in the Middle Ages, when men sought wealth commensurate with their social station and when economics was based on morality. He found that the prestige of Protestantism had fallen low in America, but he expected to find a strong ally in the Catholic Church. The old Southern religion at least had the merit of stressing the satisfaction only of necessary wants, thus encouraging leisure for "contemplation," but Northern Puritanism was used to justify capitalism.[38] In the second half of the book, he noted that the essence of well-being is the inner harmony which comes from "being at home in both this world and the next." [39] The good citizen in the good state is the "balanced man" whose inner peace and "mental stability" enable him to "understand reality." [40] This is not a very clear statement of the Conservative postulate but its intention is unmistakable.

The third book was the most revealing. This time he specifically defined democracy as a system based on the need for moral self-development.[41] True equality is the moral equality of souls, and it demands "nobility" and devotion to duty. True freedom is self-discipline and sacrifice in the service of God. The United States has attained only the political machinery of democracy, but not its moral essence. This, Agar found, is the real cause of the failures of American democracy in the twentieth century. He preferred to see policy made by the elected government after intelligent public discussion rather than have decisions made by experts,, demagogues, or disciplined party machines. But the American masses cannot participate in the necessary public discussion because of the weakness of their moral training and because they lack a status system which would protect each man no matter how humble his position. The result is that democracy plays into the hands of the political machines. Political power now depends on popular appeal, and political machines are necessary to prevent democratic politics from degenerating into mere personal and factional squabbles. But on the other hand machines tend to subordinate moral principles to party regularity and discipline. Therefore, the dilemma of the principled leader in modern democracy lies in his inability to preserve his principles and to hold power at the same time. A John Quincy Adams resists the system and becomes politically ineffective; a Henry Clay submits to it and compromises so much as to be morally ineffective. It is true that parties find it politically expedient to preserve at least a semblance of unifying principles, but the corrupting effect of the American convention system tends to lower the moral quality of political leadership.[42]

Given this degenerate form of democracy, Agar, like Davidson, suggested that Calhoun's "concurrent majority" contained the most fruitful possibilities for political salvation. He found that Calhoun's concept had contained two rather different implications: first, that a society of conflicting interests might evolve a structural harmony by giving all major (sectional) interests a positive voice in lawmaking; and second, that if the conflicts persisted, each major interest should have a veto on legislation to protect itself. In contemporary America, however, the major interests were classes as well as sections, and the American pressure group system had produced something akin to the interest vetoes which Calhoun had advocated. But this system at best represented the negative side of Calhoun's thought and at its worst led to serious corruption. To promote the positive goal of a harmony of interests, America needed a body of functional representatives, elected by socio-economic interest groups, and empowered to make decisions on major problems. The existing system had to be tolerated for the time being, but Agar insisted that the veto which Calhoun had in mind was not applicable to the contemporary system, because it was now an oppressive system of industrial exploitation; and an interest-group system which emphasized the veto only entrenched the dominant interest in power.[43]

It should be pointed out here that Agar's analysis of Calhoun's "concurrent majority," partisan though it obviously is, is the only interpretation which makes sense in the context of Calhoun's Conservatism. Since it was a harmony of interests which Calhoun sought, the major justification of the "concurrent majority" had to be that it would promote such harmony. The advocacy of a veto if conflict persisted might be justifiable for Calhoun in order to preserve a Conservative South, but its use to entrench a dominant anti-Conservative interest could only be interpreted as a perversion. The use of "concurrent majority" as the rationale of the contemporary American political system is a complete transformation of Calhoun's meaning, because it has been torn out of the context of his ideology. Yet we shall see that Agar, who clearly saw the nature of the misinterpretation in the 1930's was one of its major proponents in the 1950's. But Agar did not follow through on his proposals for functional representation. He tossed the general idea out as something needed for "the future" and returned to the favorite American Conservative idea of moral reform as the answer to the political problems which he had posed.

In 1941 Agar joined with Reinhold Niebuhr, W. Y. Elliot, Lewis Mumford, Hans Kohn, and a number of others in publishing a brief statement of principles [44] for a wartime America. They denounced modern pragmatism, Liberal "relativism," and the belief in the perfectibility of man. Democracy, they affirmed, must be founded on harmony, not on individual conflict. It must rest on a moral and religious base and not be subject to the will of the momentary majority. The statement called for a decentralized economy based on smaller communities; for the elevating of moral responsibilities over economic goals so as to prevent mass unemployment and achieve social security without a strong state; and for the encouragement of cooperatives. It also denounced the growth of pressure groups, spoke of the need for moral self-restraint in politics as well as a "structural harmony to mediate conflict," and insisted that there must be no undue hamstringing of the executive branch of government.[45]

A year later Agar wrote another book on politics.[46] The war, he found, had made the need for "constructive conservatism" greater than ever. He reaffirmed his principles with only slight variations. The essence of civilization, he said, is restraint on the instincts rather than economic progress, which only tends to destroy inner peace.[47] Society therefore depends on rules and customs, and it degenerates when these are ignored. He hammered away at pressure groups again, adopting the argument that though private groups promote civic interest and prevent a "mass society," their concentration on self-interest fragments American politics, confuses the citizen, and promotes political apathy.

Two shifts in his attitude and approach were, however, fairly clear. In the first place, though he was still unhappy about bosses, machines, and the low moral quality of political conventions, he was now prepared to keep the party system. Apparently taking from *The City of Man* the hint that a stronger executive might be the proper solution to the problem of pressure groups, he now shifted his attention to the subject of government structure. He agreed with Henry Jones Ford that parties were a necessary instrument for counteracting the fragmentation of American politics. The major difficulty in United States government was that checks and balances covered the tendency of Congress to act as the agent for selfish class and sectional interests.[48] Since the voters are more enlightened than their legislative representatives, since they can choose intelligently if offered real policy alternatives, and since they

naturally turn to the President in crises because he is the true
representative of the country as a whole, the solution is to increase the power of the President as policy maker and to transform the government into something resembling the British
cabinet system.[49]   Clear authority means clear responsibility,
and this in turn presumably encourages honorable men to
enter government.   By this line of reasoning a strong executive and a cabinet system should promote Conservatism.

In the second place, he was beginning to adjust himself to
American politics and to be less sweeping in his denunciation
of current trends.   He was more concerned with preserving the
existing condition of agriculture and the existing distribution
of property rather than with restoring either to earlier conditions.   He repeated the definition of equality as "moral equality," but added that this required minimum economic welfare
for everyone and that this minimum was not available for
Negroes, Southerners, or poor people all over the country.
Racial equality was now also included in his values, though he
cautioned against making promises to the Negroes which could
not be kept.   To the acceptance of New Deal social security
programs he added approval also of TVA, which was only
"mildly coercive" and encouraged individual farming.   He now
became interested in labor unions and, though he rejected the
closed shop, found unionism to be an essentially Conservative
force which gives workers a sense of status and participation.
Capitalists still fared badly in his evaluations and he emphasized their moral inferiority to large landowners.   For the first
time he became concerned also with problems of civil liberties
and warned of the dangers from anti-New Deal isolationists.
In this book, therefore, Agar was already making his transition
to the "adjusted Conservatives," a transition which has been
completed in the present day.

Agrarian Illusions and Dilemmas

In 1952, Richard M. Weaver, one of the New Conservatives,
wrote an appraisal of the Southern agrarians.[50]   By then the

agrarians were ready to admit the practical unfeasibility of their program, so there was obviously no point in his trying to defend agrarianism as such. However, he emphasized, the charge that the agrarians were trying to "turn back the clock," a criticism frequently leveled against them, was completely irrelevant. They were affirming timeless moral values, he said, and the particular way they did so was quite beside the point. Whatever truth this evaluation may have for Weaver's own Platonic Conservatism, this is certainly a false analysis of the Southern agrarians. Agrarianism revived the older differences between Southern and non-Southern Conservatism. The Southerners specifically rejected the humanism of such men as Irving Babbitt, on the grounds that the moral "inner check" of the humanists can only result from embodiment in a concrete organic society like that of the Old South.[51] There was frequent mention by the agrarians of the distinction between what Davidson called "Yankee uprightness" and "Rebel relaxation,"[52] a rough approximation of the difference between the Old South aristocratic hedonism and New England moralistic Puritanism. The half-hidden racism of the agrarians and their repeated apologies for slavery in the Old South made it clear that they too valued social cohesion above Conservative morality. The economic aspect of the agrarian program was not incidental, but the essential means of restoring what they themselves insisted was the distinctively Southern brand of Conservatism. It is therefore appropriate to insist that Southern agrarianism be judged on the totality of its original position and to reject attempts at rescuing it from such judgment by absorbing it into the other Conservative wings and pretending that twentieth-century American Conservatism is a simple, unified entity.

When the Southern agrarian program is evaluated in its own terms, it becomes clear that it advocates not only failed to correct the faults of Old South Conservatism, but that they could not approximate, even ideologically, its Conservative virtues. In the first place, Southern solidarity, such as it was, still rested largely on a racial caste system which was almost as difficult to defend morally as slavery had been. At times they were quite explicit about the "impossibility" of having two different races live side by side on an equal basis.[53] But since the 1930's problems of Southern race relations have in a real sense become more serious for Conservatism than slavery had been in the Old South because growing Negro militancy has made it impossible to describe Southern society as socially cohesive. Southern Conservatism has thus lost its major rationale.

Secondly, the suggestion that religion would be the solution to the problem of Southern violence [54] only replaced the problem with hollow rationalization. Aside from the failure to suggest which religion was supposed to solve the problem, the whole idea of "advocating" religion as something which can be artificially injected into a society is contradictory to the idea of natural "organic" development and to the insistence on the integral links between morality and society, both of which the agrarians stressed. If the Old South was an organic society, then its religious weakness was indissolubly linked to the whole nature of the society. If an organic society can be created artificially, then they could as validly have shifted their attention to constructing a Conservative society based on industry as insist on retaining an agrarian base.

Thirdly, the economic position of the agrarians was infinitely weaker than that of the Old South. Their primary economic aim was to attain a maximum number of self-sufficient farms which would avoid the upsetting fluctuations of the market and which would therefore sustain a Conservative culture and social ethic. But in order to have enough farm families to make the agrarian program successful, the vast majority of the farms would have to be small and impoverished by twentieth-century standards, and since the agrarians rejected universal education, the farmers would be illiterate as well. Indeed, given the tremendous expansion of population since the days of the Old South, an agrarian society would be even poorer in 1930 than in 1860, and the problem would grow constantly worse with further population increase. Therefore, the agrarians could not advocate the complete elimination of industry and the agricultural market, and often emphasized that this was not their position in order to answer charges of completely irresponsible romanticism. But since industry and the market were to continue expanding, the Conservative agrarian economy would admittedly be relegated to permanent inferiority. If economic leadership was to come from industry and the city, however, then social and cultural leadership would be supplied by the same sources; and there was no reason to believe they would be Conservative, even if dominated by small business and small industry. The only result of the program would be to perpetuate rural backwardness, the typical economic evil of the Old South, made doubly indefensible within a larger industrial civilization where economic progress might be proceeding at a rapid pace and the contrast becoming constantly more heightened.

Fourthly, agrarians and distributists completely misinterpreted the nature of the American lower middle class. Their false conception of the farmer was part of what Richard Hofstadter has called "the agrarian myth," the myth that the American farmer has always been a Conservative yeoman who sought roots, self-sufficiency, and a placid, moral "way of life." If there was some truth in the conception during early American history, it has, in modern times, really amounted to no more than a nostalgic glance backwards as the exodus from the farms gained momentum during periods of agricultural depression.[55] In reality, the American farmer, at least since about 1860, has been a capitalist, seeking material gain above all, frequently on the move, and up to his neck in market problems, speculation, and borrowing for economic improvements in order to increase his profits.[56] The severity of the depressions to which he became subject was in part the result of his own recklessness. The yeoman myth became especially articulate during the Populist period, when it became intertwined both with a "folkish" ideology of racist, nativist solidarity and a conspiratorial "theory" which blamed a small, predatory, industrial capitalist minority for all societal conflict.[57]

In the twentieth century, farmers rapidly abandoned this pseudo-Conservatism and adopted a more congenial business mentality as the reduction in the number of farmers and a rise in farm prices restored prosperity.[58] During the depression of the 1930's the agrarian myth was revived, though this time it was much weaker than earlier. The Southern agrarian "movement" itself, with its attempt to link Southern and Midwestern farmers, was an expression of this revival. But the farmers had by then learned how to use organizational, pressure group methods to attain economic ends, and agrarianism made only a ripple compared with the main flow of farm support programs designed to keep the farmer in the market. As for the poor farmers in particular, their political allegiance was divided between Progressive Liberal organizations such as the Farmers' Union and reactionary Liberal movements such as isolationism. If there was anything Conservative about either of these, it was at best submerged and secondary. When World War II ended the farm depression, agrarianism disappeared. The Conservatism of the American farmer was thus only skin-deep and ephemeral. Weak as the foundation of Old South Conservatism had been in this respect, it was a veritable Rock of Gibraltar compared to the shifting sands on which the Southern agrarians would have built their restored structure.

The urban lower middle class is no more Conservative than the farmer. Much of "small business" has become an adjunct of the large corporation, though it retains its traditional Liberal ideology. If the small shopkeepers, on the other hand, are dissatisfied with contemporary society, they are much less adequately described as Conservative than by C. Wright Mills' category of "lumpen bourgeoisie." Even if the program of the reactionary Conservatives were realistic, the support which they could expect from the small shopkeepers would be worth next to nothing, and whatever numerical strength they have is constantly being drained off into the white-collar class. But, in any event, the susceptibility of the shopkeeper to guilt feelings for petty tax evasions and economic failure in an ethic where success is often the measure of virtue [59] would hardly make them candidates for a society of harmonious personalities or make them likely to look upon moral and harmonious characters as the natural claimants to respected leadership.

The final dilemma of Southern agrarianism lay in its attempt to revive Calhoun's "concurrent majority," whether on a sectional or national basis. Southern sectionalism originally had to combine the idea of a nonconflicting organic society in the South with the idea of sectional conflict in the United States as a whole. Louis Hartz has pointed to Calhoun's basic inconsistency in trying to combine a Conservative justification of the organic and "divine" order of Southern society with his Liberal arguments about sectional minority rights and the importance of compromise in advocating "concurrent majorities" for national politics.[60] In itself the idea of a political veto power for Conservative leadership (in Calhoun's case, a sectional veto) is not incompatible with Conservatism. But it is subject to the same difficulties as European ideas of aristocratic veto power. As long as such a power was not seriously challenged (in the medieval English Parliament or even in Burke's day, for example), it could be justified as a safeguard against selfish class interests which might occasionally threaten social cohesion. But once such power is seriously threatened by sustained and widespread objection, there can be no illusion of a cohesive society at all. When this happened in Europe, the defense of aristocratic veto privileges became pure rationalization. Calhoun's sectional veto, which was supposed to provide the framework for continual compromise, might have been abstractly compatible with his Conservatism if one assumed that there was indeed no real sectional conflict and that the interests being compromised were fundamentally harmonious. But such an assumption had no basis in reality and, what is perhaps more important, Calhoun himself was aware of this.

He repeatedly warned of the disastrous consequences which would result from sectional conflict, especially for the South. The proposed "concurrent majority" system was not a harmonious political arrangement which would organically reflect a harmonious society. It was for an artificial political system which was to superimpose harmony on an otherwise divided society. This is surely a very questionable Conservative solution. No Conservative can consistently argue that harmony is to be achieved by political power alone when there is conflict in economic interests, social mores, and ideology. Under these circumstances, Calhoun's "concurrent majority" can only be viewed as an inconsistent appeal to a dominant national Liberalism in order to safeguard a subordinate sectional Conservatism. Even less than Burke could he integrate these two divergent elements of his thesis, because Southern Conservatism and American Liberalism were too obviously incompatible. In this context Hartz's observation about Calhoun's inconsistency is irrefutable. The Old South was, in this respect, consistent only when it seceded from the Union.

In the twentieth century, the Southern Conservatives' attempt to revive Calhoun's sectionalism was even less tenable than the original formulation. The agrarians' concern for protecting the "Conservative" features of Southern society was understandable. But to achieve this protection they had to claim new political privileges from the wider American society of which they were a part, and they had to claim them on Liberal grounds, because there were no Conservative justifications for them. In the more inclusive American society the Southern Conservatives performed the roles neither of aristocratic moral leaders nor of the vital links in the chain of social cohesion. Under these circumstances the claim of privilege had no Conservative ethical support and was obviously rationalization (not to mention being absurdly unrealistic). Davidson's frequent references to Jefferson and Owsley's use of Liberal natural rights and "limited government" arguments to justify sectionalism only confused the real issue.

Agar's interpretation of "concurrent majority" to mean functional representation, a favorite idea of European Conservatives, is not much of a solution either. It is true that representation by classes or industries or occupations is congenial to Conservatism. Proposals for such representation are usually based on some fixed apportionment of representatives, and the idea of fixation unaccompanied by a strong center of sovereignty presupposes a high degree of political harmony. There is, in general, an obvious resemblance between functional representation and medieval estate representation. But the crucial difference is that the medieval system reflected a relatively higher degree of actual social and economic harmony, while a modern system of functional representation would have to be superimposed upon socio-economic conflicts. Under these conditions any fixation of political power can only result in breakdown, or more likely, in facilitating the emergence of authoritarianism, the very problem which Conservatives presumably seek to avoid by proposals of functional representation. In a period of socio-economic conflict and change, to adopt a political system which assumes harmony is to create a reality which concludes with the need for repression.

The fact that Conservative aims are defeated when its forms are adopted for a society which is not Conservative applies also to proposals for clarifying political responsibility by focusing on executive power. For Burke political responsibility served the purpose of underscoring the concept of honor. It is pointless to pull the isolated concept of responsibility out of its Conservative Burkean context. In modern democracy, clear responsibility may discourage corruption and dishonesty, but this kind of "honorable" conduct has little to do specifically with Conservatism. The cabinet system and political responsibility in Britain serve a democratic not a Conservative purpose. They facilitate change much more than they entrench Conservative tradition. In America the superimposition of a cabinet system might cause prolonged deadlock; it might cause crises out of which an authoritarian presidency would emerge.

But it could not create a politics of Conservative principles or Conservative honor in a society conscious of multiple conflicts of interests, a society where honor does not go to the moral Conservative. In 1889 the Conservative A. Lawrence Lowell already understood that the party system tended to transform cabinet government into radical political democracy, and this remains true today.

In 1955 Clinton Rossiter, one of the "adjusted" Conservatives, tried to obscure the impossibility of the agrarian distributists' position by claiming that they were well aware of the irreversibility of history and that they wanted only to temper and humanize industrialization.[61] This is untrue. They were not so totally blind as to call for the abolition of industry, but it is perfectly clear that they did want to cut back industrialization, to revert to an earlier economy in which industry and agriculture were more nearly equal, and to reverse artificially the tendency to centralization and physical growth within industry itself. At a time when Negroes were demanding equal rights, the agrarians were still relying on racism to maintain social solidarity. When they were not asking for a Conservative political veto to protect a South which was no longer Conservative at all, they were asking for a political system which would impose Conservative harmony on a national society which was not harmonious. It was precisely a turning back of the clock which they sought, in spite of recent protests to the contrary. Their solution to the problems of the twentieth century was the artificial restoration of the "organic, Conservative" society of the early nineteenth-century South, a society which had not really been either organic or Conservative in the first place. To cover the absurdity of this historical position, they camouflaged the premises of liberal Conservatism with a contrived veneer of "democratic" and individualist ideology. The "natural aristocrat" became a yeoman farmer, and the American lower middle class became "nature's noblemen." Blissfully unconcerned about problems of consistency, they continued, in good Southern Conservative tradition, to sneer at the abstract moralism of New England Conservatism.

To implement their fantastic program, the agrarians offered two methods of action: first, moral exhortation, and then the unabashed use of government repression to accomplish their goals if and when they won political power. Obviously the use of political power to accomplish the extraordinarily wide range of changes which the agrarians advocated was a confession that the program would run into serious problems of conflict. To an outsider it might well seem that the conflict would assume near-revolutionary proportions and that intense and prolonged repression would be required for the success of the agrarian program. Hence the frequent, though incorrect, charges of fascism against the agrarians. But like Oswald Spengler, the German Conservative who unwittingly supplied the Nazis with much of their pseudo-ideology, the agrarians were never bothered by the irrationalism of their position. Fortunately for them (as well as for the rest of the country), there was never the remotest possibility of putting their program into effect. If there had been, they, like Spengler, would have learned that in the twentieth century the political success of a reactionary Conservative program means the destruction of all the values for which the program was designed.

V

The New Conservatism:

From Reaction to Alienation

The impact of industrialization has continued to revolutionize the nature of American society. Since World War II the imperatives of large-scale organization have pervaded every aspect of societal life and the need for integration is becoming the major premise of American thought. The white-collar class, for the first time, is about to include a majority of the total population, if indeed this is not already the case. In every sphere changes which had been occurring gradually and of which we were only half aware have begun to crystallize into qualitative changes whose significance can no longer be ignored. An increasing number of studies have been arriving at the uncomfortable conclusion that, contrary to Liberal assumptions, industrialization may not have been achieving Liberal purposes at all. We are finding that industrialization may follow purposes which are antithetical to Liberal values, and we are beginning to suspect that it is Liberalism which has been serving industrial purposes rather than the reverse. Even without the internal pressure of McCarthyism and the external pressure of Communism, Liberals would probably have become defensive in recent years. But the convergence of all these pressures has turned the attention of even progressive Liberals to their defenses.

In the new defensive pose of Liberalism, its willingness to accept Conservative allies and its readiness to use Conservative arguments have set the stage for what Russell Kirk has hopefully called the "recrudescence of Conservatism." The "New Conservatism" is a phenomenon of the 1950's, but it has revived and expanded almost all the earlier cleavages within Conservatism. The voices of reactionary and "adjusted" Conservatism have multiplied, although the numerical additions have not made them more consistent. Some of the reactionaries have, however, become sufficiently aware of their permanent displacement from society to adopt a tone of total alienation, reminiscent of the Late Stoa and indicative of Conservative trends to come. Corporatist Conservatism has acquired an articulate spokesman in Peter Drucker, and the neo-Augustinianism of Reinhold Niebuhr has become respectable. But few analysts, whether Liberal or Conservative, have dug beneath the obscurantist presentation of Conservative premises to understand the utterly incompatible assumptions which make the New Conservatism an eclectic potpourri rather than a single entity. If the New Conservatism repeats all the earlier divisions, however, each of these divisions has been modified by the altered historical conditions of the third quarter of the century. The change in reactionary Conservatism should be traced first.

The Disappearance of Southern Agrarianism

If Southern agrarianism was reactionary in the 1930's, it has become a historical museum piece since World War II. Industrialization has proceeded so rapidly that, except for a few states, the South is now preponderantly industrial and urban. Even the last strongholds of "deep South" agrarianism (Mississippi, for example) are trying to attract capital and industry. As the new urban classes grow with giant strides, the old Southern "way of life" is left ever further behind. Southern literature is preoccupied with themes such as the total decay and displacement of the "old families," of *noblesse oblige,* of tradition and "manners." Politically the "solid South" is dead, except for the façade which can still be thrown over it by racism. Astute observers such as Samuel Lubell see not a

single political cleavage, but a "three-party South." [1] In the
cities a "normal" party division has developed between the
Democratic lower classes and the Republican middle classes, old
and new. In the small rural towns, especially the county seats,
the merchants must continue to keep the area under local
Democratic control though their national sympathies may be
Republican. But most interesting of all for our purposes, it
was the agrarian areas of the deep South "black belt," the areas
with the strongest vestiges of the old Southern "way of life,"
which became the strongholds of the "Dixiecrat" or "states'
rights" party; and what bound the area together, alienating it
from the leadership of the major parties, was its extremist stand
on the racial issue. Race relations may now be an explosive
question all over the South, and political machines in areas outside the "deep South" may have seized on the issue of segregation to bolster faltering support, but in the postwar period the
issue was first nurtured in the black belt. At a time when almost all traces of Conservatism have disappeared from Southern
society, the one characteristic which remains is that which was
least defensible on Conservative grounds. And in the face of
obviously intense Negro militancy, even the rationalization that
racial castes preserve social cohesion is no longer possible. Yet
this is all there is of the presumed Conservatism that was to be
resurrected on a Southern agrarian base.

    It is therefore hardly surprising that Southern agrarianism
and distributism have disappeared from the American scene.
The swan song of the agrarians appeared in a 1952 article
written by a cross section of the group in response to questions
submitted to them by the literary periodical *Shenandoah*.[2]
They still upheld regionalism, but the regionalism was now
"literary and sociological" rather than political and therefore
subject to all the currents of "outside" influence. Their repeated emphasis on religion implied that they no longer expected salvation through society itself. All felt that they had
exerted "some" good influences on American society. But one
implied that publishers had suppressed their books, which

would otherwise have had greater effect. Another emphasized that the professional interests of each of the group had broken them up, perhaps prematurely. And a third hinted darkly about an industrialists' plot to separate the group by getting them assigned to widely separated universities. Whatever the truth of these charges, the reliance on conspiratorial explanations of failure makes clear the purely intellectual base of the agrarians, in spite of their earlier professions concerning the integral ties between their Conservatism and a concrete society. Actually they were nothing more than a group of ideologists who completely failed, or hardly tried, to understand the nature of the society which they were attempting to "save." The clearest indication of their aims is found in an early complaint by Davidson that only in feudal society could the speculations of intellectuals be translated into action. In modern democracy, he wistfully noted, the process is much more tedious.[3] It was precisely a kind of rule by Conservative intellectuals which the agrarians were seeking. In some mysterious fashion they were looking for a way to revive for themselves the authority of Conservative medieval intellectuals by re-creating a Conservative society virtually *ex nihilo*. The best that can be said for their assumption that the materials were close at hand is that it was wishful thinking.

Most telling of all were their answers to the questions of whether an agrarian society was now more remote than before and of whether they could see any hopeful signs in contemporary society. Ransom answered that there will always be those who love the soil but that the possibility for an agrarian society was now ended. His hope now was that Negro emigration from the South and New Deal "humanization" of the industrial process might enable the country to retain the "European cultural tradition" in spite of the new industrial economy. Davidson admitted the strength of industrialization, but insisted that this does not make it desirable and that strong forces can always be resisted with the proper determination. Somehow he still thought that agricultural property, political

Conservatism, and the sense of community were strong in Southern society, but as if to cover himself against expected future changes, he immediately added that the agrarians had been wrong in putting too much emphasis on economics and not enough on religion. The most hopeful positive sign he saw was the emergence of the states' rights party in the South.

None denied the contemporary remoteness of an agrarian society. John Donald Wade offered no qualifications for his pessimism; nor did Herman Nixon. But the others hastened to make excuses for the group, to shift the focus, or to dissociate themselves from agrarianism. Tate said they had never expected "immediate" success but had sought to create a new society through religion and morality. He himself now understood that their range had been too limited and that the problems must be solved on a scale wider than the South. Lytle said the group should not have emphasized the word "agrarian" but should rather have been concerned with the problems of unrestrained majority. He echoed Henry Adams' charge that modern society has no moral image of love such as the Virgin in whose likeness it might re-create itself, but he remembered that one leader of stature, a Gregory the Great, might bring renewal out of chaos. Owsley emphasized the original divergence among the agrarians over the question of whether to try to restore agriculture or only to achieve better "balance" between agriculture and industry. Their real protests, he said, were against Northern exploitation rather than against industrialism itself, though the depression prompted the group to go further in its proposals than it might otherwise have gone. There is no doubt that the South now needs more industry, he found; the only problem is how to insure that control of the industries remains within the South. He was hopeful of the prosperous conditions of agriculture and because it was now both "profitable and respectable" to be a farmer, but he noted that the connection between these two motives tended to be "too close." The balance between industry and agriculture, however, continues to be a problem, he warned, for if industrialization continues unchecked it can lead too easily to Communism.

Whatever one chooses to take seriously from these comments, it is clear that agrarianism, distributism, "rebel relaxation," and sectionalism as the means of re-creating a Conservative South are dead. A similar death warrant for national distributism was pronounced by Herbert Agar's postwar shift to the "adjusted" Conservatives. The agrarians now concern themselves with literature, religion, and morality, or the achievements of great men, abstractly evaluated out of their historical contexts. Some, like Ransom, have joined Agar in the "adjusted" ranks. Others, like Nixon, have abandoned Conservatism altogether. Most, like Tate, have adopted the new brand of reactionary Conservatism, which, no longer specifically Southern, relies entirely on abstract moralism and religion and is already preparing the ground for a Conservatism of total alienation—the Late Stoa of Western civilization. Conservative ideology is built on the premise of communal affection, of morality and love. But in the 1950's the only legacy which remains of Southern Conservatism is racial hatred.

Russell Kirk: The Illusion of a Burkean Revival

IDEOLOGY AND OBSCURITY. The new spokesman for reactionary Conservatism is Russell Kirk. As with most of the earlier reactionaries, Kirk has childhood roots in the soil and still prefers agricultural society; like them, he wants to see "aristocracy" restored from among the older middle classes rather than from the new industrial classes or institutions. But he has gone back to Babbitt and More for inspiration, largely ignoring distributism and agrarianism as temporary aberrations. The emphasis in his writings, as in those of the earlier reactionaries, is on criticism of the very foundations of modern society. But like all American Conservatives he manages to make his premises sufficiently obscure to discourage their use in evaluating his conclusions.

Kirk is representative of the reactionaries' shift to religion and American tradition as the means of Conservative salvation. He lists six primary postulates of Conservatism: (1) the divine foundation of society; (2) affection for tradition; (3) recognition of the need for "orders" and leadership; (4) the linking of freedom and property: (5) faith in prescription and the primacy of emotion over reason; (6) slow, cautious change.[4] The most important assumption for him is the thesis that the divine intent of God rules men and societies, and he insists this is not obscurantist. Now it is not necessarily objectionable to begin an ideology with a "self-evident" value, provided that the value is clearly definable and consistent with the conclusions which one draws from it. If the assumption of divine rule is to serve as the real postulate of Conservatism, it must provide the actual basis on which Conservatism makes its judgments. But the obvious difficulty with divine intent is that every conceivable ideology can claim and has claimed to be on the side of God. The real problem is that one cannot jump directly from a belief in God to a statement of human values without first making the all-important assumptions about the nature of man which are the real beginnings of meaningful ideology. The existence of God as an abstract affirmation tells us nothing about values unless it is followed by such assumptions.

The difficulties which Kirk has in getting started, once he has declared his theism, illustrate the problem quite clearly. Speaking for both Burke and himself, he insists that the divine will is "commonly . . . inscrutable" and inaccessible to reason. The only thing clear about this assertion is its meaninglessness. If God's will is inscrutable then one man or group has as much or as little claim to understand it as any other. If Kirk means to deduce from this that inaction or slow, cautious change is the only safe course, then the argument is a *non sequitur,* since there is no reason to conclude that God's purpose in history does not work through action and rapid change as well as passivity, unless a completely new set of assumptions is subsequently introduced. On the other hand, if Kirk does not mean to reason directly from divine rule over society and history, then why does he make this seem like his first premise? Naturally Kirk cannot remain stuck forever with the idea of inscrutability, so he begins to cut himself loose. He asks himself the inevitable question of how men may know God's will, and answers, "Through the prejudices and traditions which . . . have [been] implanted in the mind of the species." [5] To the extent that this is supposed to represent Burke's position, it is, as we have seen, untrue, because Burke was never able to maintain simple traditionalism throughout his writings. But this is no more meaningful a premise than divine inscrutability, since he provides no clear criterion for good or bad traditions or prejudices. Yet without a further criterion, the attempt to found an ideology on traditionalism becomes an acceptance of everything that ever has been or will be implanted in human society, including Communism or atheism. One need only note that Stalinists have become the traditionalists of contemporary Russia to understand the absurdity. The acceptance of change which is made slowly and cautiously is equally compatible with any ideology in history, since caution is always relative to circumstance, and since no ideology has ever advocated changing everything in society every day of the week, like used underwear. On the other hand, to insist that "slow" change must always be so slow as to be imperceptible is to obliterate human history, since its periods of "imperceptible" change have always been built on preceding periods of upheaval and transition like our own.

Lest one think that traditionalism might be more convincingly presented as the real beginning of Conservative values, it may be well to pause here to consider two other treatments of the subject. The first is one commonly used by Conservatives. It is the assertion that true tradition refers not to entrenched values in a particular country but to the Hellenic-Judaeo-Roman-Christian tradition. The difficulties in this position must be the despair of all serious Conservatives. What do we include in this tradition? Why not Greek Sophism and Roman Epicureanism? Why not ancient traditions of blood-

shed and oppression? Why not the Christian heresies? Why
not Roman authoritarianism and imperialism? The answer is,
of course, that this is only a circuitous way of accepting a very
specific tradition, usually that of the Late Middle Ages, sometimes that of a slightly later period, almost never more recent
than the French Revolution. But when the central question
remains: why the medieval tradition? Certainly not on the
grounds that any elements of an earlier tradition which survive are good and those which disappear are bad, for then we
must also accept the changes of modern culture. Certainly
not on grounds of mere antiquity, for then pure Hellenism or
Judaism would be superior to medieval Christianity. Of
course, the whole problem could be made to rest on religious
faith, but whose religious faith? Conservatives can be found
among very diverse religions. And even if the field were nar-
rowed to religions which are properly Conservative (those
which predate the seventeenth century, let us say), why the
elaborate additional rationalizations? If the whole matter
rests simply on faith, then make the assertion and let it go at
that. But if rational discussion is still essential, then we must
have a criterion of tradition which can be discussed.

The other treatment of traditionalism is by Richard M.
Weaver, another of the reactionary new Conservatives. Weaver
ostensibly begins his exposition of Conservatism with tradition,
and justifies it on the ground that it is primary because intuitive, and because myth-making man is more elemental than rational man. From this elemental intuition of values man is im-
pelled to "clarification, arrangement, and hierarchy," [6] he says.
But notice how the argument has proceeded. He begins with
intuitive values which could be the beginning of any ideology.
He continues with the "classification" and "arrangement" of
the intuitive values of a society. Then comes the injection
of "hierarchy," a concept which Weaver interprets with true
Conservative assumptions to mean a harmonious hierarchy in
which each accepts his position. But there is no necessary connection between intuitive societal values and Conservative

hierarchy. The real connecting link between the two is implied in the brief discussion which precedes the assumption of intuitive tradition. In that discussion, Weaver assigns conscious reflection an inferior role in value-making, because its "worldliness" must "eventually bring disharmony and conflict," while the "metaphysical dream" of tradition makes it possible "to think of men living together harmoniously over an extent of time." [7] But though the concept of communal harmony is thus clearly the primary one and remains implicit in all Weaver's subsequent discussion, he makes it seem that tradition or "instinct" is the real postulate, just as Kirk does. Both men sometimes neglect to make clear that the Conservative "instinct" is affection directed towards the community, and they never make clear that this affection is measured by the absence of conflict and tension. Both often make it seem as though any tradition can be Conservative, and both periodically resort to the convenient but misleading thesis that all hierarchy or "orders" and "leadership" are necessarily Conservative. The reason for the obscurities is simple—clarity on the positive primacy of harmony and the negative primacy of minimal conflicts and tensions would also clarify the contradictions in reactionary New Conservatism. It would make untenable the insistence on trying to preserve a disappearing tradition which is not based on Conservative harmony, with an ideology which can only create new conflicts. We shall see this more clearly by the time we have concluded with Kirk.

Further examination of Kirk's formulations reveals one vagary after another. He goes on to enumerate the conclusions which presumably follow from a belief in God: "that individual station in life is assigned by a 'divine tactic'; that original sin and aspiration toward the good both are part of God's design; that the reformer first should endeavor to discern the lineaments of a Providential order, and then endeavor to conform political arrangements to the dictates of a natural justice." [8] He then pointedly denies this position to be obscurantist. But what else can it be called? Why is a change in one's station in life any less God's design than one's station at birth? If Kirk is including both, then what is he excluding? He cannot be excluding resentment against the distribution of prestige, since he does not accept the present distribution, which usually by-passes the "moral" men. There is nothing in the formulation to prohibit an ethic of open competition for wealth. It is not even necessarily a contradiction of radical equalitarianism, since the abolition of station altogether, once attained, may seem just as much a "divine tactic" as its existence in the past. That men aspire to the good and that politics should be just are truisms which Kirk should have little trouble getting accepted by an assemblage of every philosopher who ever lived.

In a later book, *The Intelligent Woman's Guide to Conservatism,* Kirk is somewhat more cautious in his use of theism as the basis of Conservatism. He admits the obvious—that not all religious people are Conservative—and grants that not all Conservatives are religious, since he knows perfectly well that Henry Adams and George Santayana, for example, were bluntly agnostic. What then is left? Simply that Conservatism should have a religious foundation.[9] But this, depending on one's definition of religion, could be true of almost any position. Still, he insists on drawing specific conclusions from this ethereal religiosity. Democracy is weak, he says, because popular judgment commits many blunders, but divine justice is the real source of political truth, though it may be only imperfectly perceived.[10] If it can be only imperfectly perceived, why should it lead to any fewer blunders than democracy?

Elsewhere, Kirk opens his exposition of Conservatism with the "principle" that man is not perfectible either morally or in terms of true happiness.[11] If this means that societies have a tendency to degenerate, then it is real Conservatism, provided that morality and happiness are first defined in terms of communal harmony. If it means that man cannot do without restraints but that the restraints should be moral and social rather than authoritarian, it is also real Conservatism. But Kirk uses it, without further clarification, as an argument for accepting a presumption against change because imperfection in society is unavoidable. But since he adds that one age may be better than another, and that some change is necessary, it is an empty "principle." The knowledge that there will be imperfection in the world for an indefinite period in the future is compatible with all the theories Kirk means to exclude, whether Liberalism, positivism, or Marxism. Surely imperfection is no argument against change or in favor of "caution," and more important, it is not a criterion which tells anyone when change is good or bad. Interestingly enough he adds that a perfect Utopia would be boring anyway, because it is the struggle to bring order out of disorder that makes life interesting.[12] Here is a paradox indeed. It is bad enough that historical conditions force Conservatives to the contradiction of having to struggle to achieve harmony. But for a man who is spending his life trying to find out how men and societies may avoid conflict to say that struggle is the spice of life suggests a serious blurring of his own assumptions.

There are a number of other empty formulations in Kirk's books, such as the definition of justice as "the right to one's own,"[13] but this line of criticism is already becoming tedious. The crucial counterpart of these observations, however, is that whenever Kirk is faced with a tangible problem, his Conservative assumptions become sufficiently clear to presume in his favor that when he says "Never disturb that which is at rest,"[14] he means "Never disturb that which is harmonious." When he considers "the problem of wants," he emphasizes the value of a simple life and the insatiability of material desires.[15] In economic analysis he uses the Platonic concept of justice as the proper performance of one's assigned societal functions, because cooperation and not conflict is essential.[16] The key societal virtue is honor,[17] and honor is the basis of aristocracy.[18] The "natural aristocrats" and the "moralizers" should lead society,[19] and the goal of political order is "the harmonious arrangement of classes and functions" so that all give "willing consent to law." [20]

The point is obvious without carrying the examples any further. Kirk knows what Conservatism is. Why then all the smokescreen about God, traditionalism, imperfection, and all the rest? Why weren't these concepts integrated in the first place with the fundamental postulates of communal harmony and the minimizing of conflict? We suggest that it is because this Conservative harmony does not exist in twentieth-century America and that if reactionaries like Kirk admitted it, they would be forced to the conclusion that when traditionalism no longer sustains a harmonious society, the Conservative may as well abandon it. But though obviously aware that it is communal harmony which appeals to them in their favorite traditions and that this harmony no longer exists, the reactionary New Conservatives insist on maintaining the traditions anyway. When Kirk includes freedom and private property among the postulates of Conservatism without pointing out that these are the Liberal elements of liberal Conservatism, he is merely providing the basis for the convenient rationalization that because America's traditions are based on freedom and private property, American traditions are therefore Conservative.

When it suits his purpose, Kirk makes this argument the basis of his historical treatment of American Conservatism. He considers John Adams to be the native model for Conservatism. He insists that the American Revolution was a Conservative restoration of colonial prerogatives and that the other early leaders, for example, Jefferson and Hamilton, were at least "partly" Conservative. He refutes the thesis of men like Hartz and Hofstadter that the American tradition is Liberal by arguing from an arbitrary definition. Liberal individualism, he says, cannot be traditional, because tradition is by definition anti-atomistic. It is not necessary to dwell on the weakness of this argument. We need only turn to the content of what Kirk considers to be the American tradition. These include natural rights, self-government, the balance of power concept in the Constitution, private property, religion, and the family.[21] None of these contradicts pure Liberalism, and they are compatible with Conservatism only if subordinate to the Conservative moral and social ethic. But Kirk never really maintains that there is a Conservative social system in America, and he never really frees himself from the dilemma of defending a Liberal tradition.

Even if we assume that the original American tradition was in some sense Conservative, Kirk knows that this tradition has "degenerated" steadily. He accepts Tocqueville's description of nineteenth-century American democracy as ignorant, impetuous, coarse, undignified, incoherent, superficial, and conformist. He is as unhappy as any Burkean about universal suffrage. He admits that American character has always been resistant to tradition because of its individualism, covetousness, and contempt for restraint. He traces the decline of American Conservatism from John Adams to its virtual disappearance by the end of the nineteenth century, and agrees that it has been weak and vague in the twentieth century. Yet he counters Babbitt's fear that the battle has been lost with the argument that American respect for traditional morality can yet save the day. But he adds that it is at any rate easier to criticize Burkean solutions than to suggest alternatives.[22]

Kirk's surface optimism about the Conservative nature of American tradition forces him to try to reconcile Northern and Southern Conservatism in order to present a single tradition. He does this by raising Calhoun to a rank almost equal with John Adams and by preferring Southern "particularism" to the later nationalism of the house of Adams. Most important is his defense of the Southern position on slavery. He admits that slavery was a bad moral basis for Conservatism, but insists that the problem was insoluble because the slaves were a potentially discontented class who could upset Southern tradition and solidarity. This, of course, is a correct analysis of the Southern Conservative contradiction, but it is hardly a comfortable place to rest. From there a Conservative could just as easily reject Southern society as accept slavery, and this is just what the Adams family did. Somewhat later therefore, Kirk finds a way out in the common argument that the problem of slavery would eventually have solved itself because of the economic and moral forces which were making it impossible. This implies that imperialist expansion of the slave-plantation system would not have been a legitimate way out of impending decline. But there is no reason why a Southern Conservative could not have rationalized expansion, even through Latin America (and many of them did). If social cohesion was so important that slavery was not too high a moral price to pay for it, then imperialism too would have been justifiable. Kirk elsewhere accepts just such an argument, for he says that Disraeli's imperialism was consistent with his Conservatism because without the advantages of empire he could not have saved a prescriptive British society.[23] At no time does Kirk seem to notice the inconsistency between readiness to accept Conservative imperialism and his assumption that the Southern slave system would have disappeared "naturally" if left to itself. At any rate, in spite of his difficulties in making Southern Conservatism compatible with his moralism, in spite of his characterization of later Southern politics as corrupt and hypocritical, in spite of his criticism of "distributism" as based on individualistic fallacies, he welcomes Southern agrarians like Davidson and Tate to the fold of American Conservative tradition. Having discussed the Conservative weaknesses and cleavages of the past he now looks forward to a "recrudescence." Not only does he find American tradition to be intact, but he takes hope from the current revival of the churches, the increased veneration for the past, and the new "search for roots."

While Kirk is forced to discuss some of the nineteenth-century Mugwumps because there were no other Conservatives during that period, he glosses rapidly over the "adjusted"

Conservatives of the twentieth century. He mentions men like Henry Cabot Lodge and Theodore Roosevelt, but refers to them as leaders who diverted the aspirations of their class rather than as representative of the prevailing tendencies of that class. Of men like A. Lawrence Lowell he says nothing.

SOCIAL AND ECONOMIC IDEOLOGY. Kirk is well aware of the primacy of morality and social relations in Conservatism. He is also aware of the weaknesses of twentieth-century American society from the point of view of Conservative values. Love or affection, he says, is the basis of community, and it is heightened by common attachment to local neighborhoods, emulation of moral leaders, and deep traditional roots. But industrialization has been destroying tradition, mobility has been destroying local attachment, and democracy has been destroying the natural need to emulate superior men. The consequent loss of the sense of community and common affection has spread boredom throughout society, and this pervasive boredom has led to a restless obsession with trifles, a proclivity to violence, and sexual immorality.[24] The family as the central institution of love and affection has also been weakened as industrial society has taken over many of its functions and as cheap transportation and amusements have deprived it of its roots and its cohesion.[25] The result has been a marked tendency for the birth rate to fall. As the central moral purpose provided by traditional religion has been fragmented, men have become manipulable material for totalitarianism. The Liberal "inner-directed" man did not realize how much his values depended on traditional morality. It is only now when tradition is being seriously weakened that the value-less "other-directed" man is emerging, ready to accept any norms that may be offered to him. Instead of using his leisure for contemplation, self-improvement, and proper emulation, the other-directed "mass-man" uses it for self-indulgence and allows himself to be manipulated by the mass culture. Instead of seeking the psychic harmony which is founded on mastered passions, he is torn by endless tensions.[26] He is consumed with an avarice for material goods which is beyond possible satisfaction, and he is constantly exposed to sexual stimuli and erotic tensions which can never be gratified.[27] In such a society maladjustment may be the only honorable course. But since the acceptance of inner moral restraints is the only alternative to the imposition of external restraints,[28] the disappearance of morality only paves the way for an authoritarian state. The contemporary identification of freedom and moral anarchy is false. In Christian tradition, freedom is the result only of submission to God, and in Stoic and Indian thought freedom is the absence of desire.[29]

Most men, Kirk says, want only to live quietly, regularly, and securely, and they can be virtuous only through routine. It is the superior few who deserve rewards. The qualifications for honor should be contribution to the conservation of society, giving each "his own," fulfilling contracts, expressing "high-minded spirit," and realizing "noble order and balance" in personal character.[30] Honor in turn should be the basis of aristocracy. But the social and economic conditions for the existence of gentlemen are becoming precarious. Even in the rural areas of America, Kirk admits, there are few such men to be found,[31] and the land has been the traditional sustainer of aristocrats and gentlemen. Yet without such men there is no moral leadership for the rest of the people to honor through emulation; without emulation there is no community; without community there is no reservoir of love for the family to draw on; without the family there is no carrier of traditional morality; and without traditional morality there is moral chaos.

Kirk's admission that contemporary Conservatism has difficulty expressing itself coherently [32] is one which is deserving of our most unreserved concurrence. But having drawn together Kirk's scattered comments on the American social system, we can easily discern the absurd incompatibility between the profound contemporary Conservative crisis (of which Kirk is fully aware) and the "whistling-in-the-dark" nature of his solutions. On the all-important questions of social and moral relations Kirk can bring himself to present a "program for Conservatives" only because he does not make Conservative values and the American reality clear at the same time but keeps them carefully separated, like express trains which would collide if they crossed the same track at the same time.

His solution to the problem of morality and harmonious social and moral relations is simple: preserve and strengthen the family, the pluralism of "groups," and religion. Now it is bad enough that vague talk of strengthening the family is a nebulous response to the powerful influences being exerted by mass communications, public schools, government, and corporations. But to talk as though "the" family is necessarily a Conservative institution is to befuddle the entire problem. The family can be a vehicle for any kind of values, and Kirk knows from David Riesman (whom he admires as a social analyst) that it is increasingly an institution in which the children, rather than the parents, set the values because the values are continually changing. Furthermore, the older type of family in America teaches self-reliance and success, rather than self-denial or emulation of honorable gentlemen. To make things worse, Kirk does not expect moral leadership from businessmen, laborers, or white-collar workers, but from lawyers, doctors, clergymen, and teachers.[33] It takes a strong dose of the Conservative imagination which Kirk is always extolling to think that these people exercise the determining moral influence on society today, that they receive most of the deference, or that it is Conservatism they are teaching.

The desire to preserve American group pluralism may be genuinely traditional, but it is difficult to see what it has to do with Conservatism, and it is positively misleading to equate it, as New Conservatives do, with Burke's acceptance of diversity in imperial relations, religion, or class structure. The mere fact that Burke wanted to let India and Ireland follow their own traditions in imperial relations has no bearing on what he wanted as the basis for a single Conservative community. When he advocated toleration for religious minorities, it was always limited by the acceptance of a single established Church, and he refused toleration for "excessively" Liberal religions such as Unitarianism.   To say that aristocracy rests on a concept of diverse but harmonious classes is to say nothing about diverse conflicting groups.   Nothing in Burke's ideology is relevant to American pluralism.   Furthermore, Kirk admits that immigration weakened American traditions by bringing conflicting traditions into the country.   He admits the tensions caused in American society by racial differences.   He rejects labor unions as oligarchic.[34]   He dislikes big business corporations.   His pluralism, therefore, seems to include only professional and religious rather than economic, racial, or nationality groups.   But he says nothing of the conflicts which are stimulated in American society even by professional and religious diversity.   American pluralist ideologies are predicated on conflict and compromise, but this has nothing to do with Conservatism.   To laud pluralism and diversity as Conservative is as blundering a confusion as to equate American tradition with Conservatism.

Everything rests finally on religion, and we begin to see why Kirk began his whole exposition of Conservatism with religion. This is the final solution to all the social problems—"boredom," "morality," "the family," "community."   And this is Kirk at his most obscurantist.   He denounces Liberal Protestantism, and by implication, Liberal (that is, Reform) Judaism.   He refers to himself as an "archaic Puritan," and hopefully predicts that Catholicism may be the majority religion in America in two or three generations.   He accepts Job's unquestioning resignation as the model of religious conduct.[35]   He therefore accepts only orthodox forms of religion.   Yet he carefully avoids relating this aspect of his position to his optimism about the "return to religion," preferring to use the word "religion" in the same abstractly vague sense as it is used in the current slogans. In this way he avoids the obvious embarrassing problems.   The assumption of a real return to orthodoxy of any kind in America, let alone to the morality of a Job, is at least questionable.

The widespread admission by clergymen that the "return to religion" has little real moral or theological content; the club-joining motivation behind much of the "return"; the manipulative packaging and marketing of religion; the tendency of American Catholics to divide along all the usual lines which divide Americans, rather than to embrace Conservatism; the frequent failure to find real solace in religion today—these are problems of which Kirk usually seems blessedly unaware. "Adjusted" Conservatives like Peter Viereck are far more realistic than reactionaries like Kirk on the subject of religious revival, as they are on many other subjects. To the extent that Kirk's restoration of a socially cohesive community depends on orthodox religious revival, let alone on the mere preservation of existing religious affiliations, it rests on a flimsy foundation indeed.

A Conservatism which cannot rely on a cohesive social system is in an extremely vulnerable position. It cannot, as Burke did, unreflectingly accept a Liberal economic system, for it has no Conservative moral framework to superimpose on the economy. Yet this is exactly what Kirk does. He talks vaguely about the need for frugality and simplicity in living standards, about "just" prices and wages, about giving workers a sense of status and pride in workmanship even at the cost of efficiency, and about the effect of machinery on the nervous system. But he is obviously uncomfortable about the whole subject. He is most at home in the Liberal economy of John Locke, where private property and the "natural right" to the fruits of one's labor set the standards of value. He is critical of the distributists for their ideological confusions, especially their tendency to overemphasize individual freedom. But the distributist program of the economist Röpke is the only one for which shows any enthusiasm. This program includes the agricultural "way of life," decentralization of industry, marketing cooperatives, smaller factories, and a system of "domestic economy" in which workers supplement their incomes with vegetable gardening and similar activities. Kirk wants especially to preserve the shopkeeper and the small farmer, and provides a striking example of the manipulability of natural law theory by insisting that we observe the "law" that population should be diffused in proportion to the soil.   He is hostile to social welfare programs because they prevent a sense of moral achievement by the donor and a sense of gratitude on the part of the receiver; and he disapproves of progressive income taxes and inheritance taxes because they weaken the institution of private property and incentives to talent.[36]

Nothing further need be added to the earlier discussion about the shabbiness of a Conservative structure which rests on an American lower middle-class base.   Kirk himself seems well aware of the difficulty when he admits that though culture and morality should be supported by a wealthy, leisured aristocracy, he can find no such class here.   He talks of Platonic class harmony, but has no proposals for settling economic conflicts of interest in industrial society.   He talks of returning to a society of simpler economic demands, but never considers the impact such a retrenchment would have on the contemporary American economy nor any way in which it might be done. He talks of "just" prices and wages, but unlike Hayek, on whom he frequently calls for support of his "free enterprise" views, he neglects to point out the extent to which medieval ideas of "just" economic relations depended on long usage and economic stability, even stagnation.   He remains caught between a social system which is not Conservative and an economic system which is not Lockean, still repeating Burkean liberal Conservative formulas as the catechism for salvation.

Kirk thus represents contemporary Conservatism in its most contradictory position.   On the one hand, he is well aware of the fantastically wide disparity between the Conservative social ideal and contemporary America.   From this point he could quite consistently go on to a kind of total alienation from society and seek refuge in religion.   On the other hand, he also knows that Conservative features have all but disappeared from the economy, and he should know that the classical system of capitalist private property is not the only or even the most congenial system for Conservatism. He does say, for example, that where older societies still have some system of communal property, it should be preserved and allowed to change only slowly and only if "necessary." [37] He could therefore also come to the conclusion that the Conservative task now is to study the problem of introducing harmony into an industrial society within the framework of the modern corporation. This would send him in the direction of Conservative corporatism. Either of these two directions—alienation or corporatism— could lead to relevant conclusions about twentieth-century society. But Kirk refuses both, and insists instead on identifying Conservatism with traditionalism. The result is to combine an almost total critique of society with "standpattism" and moral exhortation. In view of his admission that lamentation has become a congenital Conservative weakness, one seeks in his writings for some real solution, but in vain. When all the excess verbiage is cleared away, nothing really remains except the old platitude that great moral leaders who are determined to lead society back to justice can always succeed.

IDEOLOGY AND POLITICS. Given the contradictions in his social and economic ideologies, the fruitlessness of his intellectual and political analyses follows as a matter of course. Naturally, his criticism of the American intellectual system is sweeping. Contemporary education, he charges, is purposeless factualism and pragmatist indoctrination; mass culture is degenerate mediocrity; mass communications stimulate political passions and destroy tradition;[38] universal education produces uniformity and dullness;[39] progressive education is inimical to traditional moral disciplines and conducive to "other-directedness." His solution to this degeneracy is to create a new "intellectual aristocracy" (an old American Conservative solution) by teaching college students to be Conservative gentlemen.[40] But aside from the weakness of the colleges' influence when compared with all the other sources of information and persuasion in society, Kirk himself admits that they cannot make up for the moral deficiencies of the contemporary family. He also admits that the colleges are teaching less and less about Virtue and Truth (in his sense, of course) and more about the technical training needed to succeed in society.   Furthermore, he cites studies which indicate that very few college graduates do any serious reading after graduation, and that this practice is continuing.[41]   Yet he insists that most professors are "true" scholars, presumably the kind who could train Conservative gentlemen, and that with good leadership the natural Conservatism of "the people" would be restored,[42] "the people" apparently meaning the old lower middle class (the workers may become Conservative "later").

The centrality of the colleges in Kirk's ideology led him to write a short separate work under the title of *Academic Freedom*.   In spite of his sometime optimism about professors, it must be obvious to him that there are as many cleavages on college faculties as there are in American society at large.   Undaunted, he accepts intellectual conflict as necessary "to avoid ennui," but quickly adds that such conflict should be part of a quest for "justice."   Characteristically, he does not define "justice" here, but he cites the Platonic Academy and the medieval university as models of the kind of academic freedom which is possible when scholars are consecrated to Truth and teleology instead of aimless groping.   True academic freedom, he says, must be based on loyalty to the "consensus of opinion of the ages" as well as to the basic values of the present age and to a transcendent moral order.   Since Communists violate all these loyalties they may be excluded from teaching, subject to "prudent" exceptions.   He also clearly denounces (but tolerates) McCarthyite "Liberals" like William Buckley, "doctrinaire Liberals" like Henry Steele Commager, and even liberal neo-Thomists like Robert M. Hutchins.   But Kirk is most worried about "pragmatists," whom he considers to be the really dangerous authoritarians.   Magnanimously, he does not recommend their exclusion because, unlike Communists, "we can reason with them." [43]

But his real reason for tolerating such opposition becomes clear only at the end of the book. It is not because conflict is good for the soul. Rather it is because expulsion of the "Sophists" would only endanger the "Philosophers." He recalls that until recently it was Conservatives who had to bear the brunt of academic pressures, and he implies that it could all too easily happen again. We can only guess at what Kirk's attitude would be towards academic freedom if a Conservative "aristocracy" did exist. He admits, however, that the necessary consensus for teaching a single philosophy does not exist. Against the threat of the new "Age of Manipulation," the only realistic course is to defend the Liberal "Age of Discussion." [44] We cannot return to the "Age of Faith." Therefore, the way for Conservative intellectuals to gain control of the colleges and to build a new "aristocracy" is to persuade their colleagues of the Truth. Yet Kirk insists elsewhere that Conservative values are only effective if one is steeped in them, and that they cannot be instilled by logic.[45] Before Conservatives can create a new society of "gentlemen," they must make the teaching of tradition and Conservatism dominant in the colleges. In order to do this, they must persuade the professors by rational argument that tradition is superior to reason, which they consider a Liberal aberration. Kirk is thus back to the dilemma of the Platonic technique. How can Conservative harmony, which depends on "unconscious" acceptance, be taught by reason? American Conservatives have been talking about creating an intellectual aristocracy since the beginning of the century. Kirk says they needed a masterful Conservative thinker in order to succeed. Obviously, they must still await the master. But if they should ever find him, he will, like Plato's philosopher-king, find himself immobilized by the cleavage in his nature. Forced by the disappearance of Conservative traditions to reason about "Truth," the Conservative "philosopher" will flounder like a fish out of water while the "king" "does in Rome as the Romans."

Kirk's political ideology consists of a simple pretense that the American Constitution is Conservative and that it must be preserved in its pristine eighteenth-century form. Checks and balances he considers to be pure Burkeanism. Since the "orders" are at present out of balance, he favors the proposed Bricker Amendment [46] to curb the powers of the President in relation to Congress and of the national government in relation to the states. His traditionalism leads him also to accept constitutional civil liberties, but he is strongly in favor of "prudent" moral censorship, and, in spite of his emphasis on judicial review for safeguarding tradition, he is unhappy about those recent Supreme Court decisions which have weakened censorship. He is extremely hostile towards bureaucracy, which he considers to be an instrument of authoritarianism. The only branch of government on which he does not focus his criticism is Congress, in spite of the fact that the sensitivity of Congress to private interest groups hardly makes it a paragon of Conservative virtue. His repetition of Burke's dictum that the Conservative must often shift his defense in "balanced government" is only another quotation out of context, and he hardly even mentions the problem of pressure groups. Kirk's policy recommendations are indistinguishable from those of the NAM or the Chamber of Commerce. He wants less taxes, approves of the Taft-Hartley Act, objects to social security as a form of hidden taxation, and rejects the school-lunch program as "creeping socialism." He has nothing to say of political parties except to quote Burke and call for more "principles," obviously assuming that Burke's discussion is relevant to American politics. He expects political support from farmers, rural townspeople, lawyers, clergymen, professors, and families of "old wealth." Naturally he is unhappy about universal suffrage, a system which is kept within bounds only by the divine law that the "number of fools in opposite factions usually is in balance." [47] Finally, he is adamant about identifying Conservatism and political decentralization. He wants to maximize the authority of state and local government as well as private voluntary associations. Yet such a program is Conservative only if harmony is in reality characteristic of all the relationships involved. Kirk never bothers to consider whether or not this is true, and the obvious problems of segregation would alone be enough to make it highly doubtful.

Kirk is perfectly well aware that there is a difference between liberal Conservatism and conservative Liberalism.[48] It is therefore all the more striking that his thundering denunciations of modern society should be climaxed in a squeaky defense of a conservative Liberal tradition no longer relevant to contemporary problems. He knows how unlikely it is that a Conservative aristocracy will evolve from the colleges, and the space rockets must have dashed any flicker of hope he may have had about stopping the emphasis on technology. Even while he insists that the purpose of science is to learn fear of God and not the conquest of nature, he knows how little chance there is that this will become the prevailing attitude in the colleges. He knows that the industrial age demands more authoritative societal discipline than ever before and that the Conservative problem is somehow to reconcile this historical reality with its values, but he has no answer for the problem. Far from really expecting a return to simple material standards, he knows that economic forces have not only been able to satisfy "Avarice" but are now "encouraging Gluttony." At one point he even puts his finger squarely on the root of his social dilemma, when he admits that the struggle for both "harmonious personality" (in the Platonic sense) and a "just society which will recognize the best" of such personalities is "most desperate today." [49] Small wonder that he repeats again and again that Conservatism cannot be expected to produce a definite program because it is not "abstract" like other ideologies, or that we must not expect perfection but should learn "honorable resignation," or that it is the struggle and not the goal that makes life "interesting." When all his contradictions have canceled themselves out, Kirk is really left with only moral exhortation and religious orthodoxy.

In the preface to his recently published book of pessimistic

essays he seems to understand the hopelessness of his position.
The preface opens with Santayana's proclamation that the
"voice of dispossessed and forlorn orthodoxy prophesying evil
cannot be silenced," and closes with St. Augustine's prayer for
"the night" that he "might be invisible in God." In one of
the essays he confesses his pessimism about the possibility of a
real Conservative revival and his fear that what looked like
Conservatism will turn out to be only another passing fad.[50]
But the following year his pessimism seemed to have disappeared, perhaps because *The Intelligent Women's Guide to
Conservatism* was much less a "guide" to Conservatism than a
traditionalist tract, replete with religious vagaries, and hence
somewhat more compatible with the "American tradition."
Since then he has turned to editing a new Conservative periodical called *Modern Age* and writing introductions to a paper-
backed series of classics in political theory. As long as he can
continue to ignore historical reality and self-contradictions, the
potential productivity of the Conservative intellectual is pro-
digious.

Other Prophets in Babylon

The same ambivalence between total pessimism and almost
pathetic attempts at forced optimism about the possibilities of
"regeneration" can be seen in the writings of all the reactionary Conservatives. In 1948 Richard M. Weaver wrote a book
which was in some ways more precise in defining Conservatism
than Kirk's exposition because he based his philosophy directly
on Platonic rather than Burkean theory.[51] This enabled him
to make the interesting point that the advance of materialism
and the abandonment of the Conservative life of simplicity
really began when the Middle Ages surrendered Platonism in
in favor of the easier ethic of Aristotle. In spite of this remote
origin and the long subsequent process of degeneration which
he traces up to contemporary society, Weaver is still hopeful
about "restoring lost ideals." But his program condemns itself to futility without the need for any outside criticism, for

the process of regeneration is to be launched by teaching poetry and precise dialectical definition in the schools. His awareness of the absurdity of this "counterattack" on at least seven centuries of history becomes apparent at the end of the book. Here he admits it may now be too late for a Conservative restoration and that little is being done to this end.[52]

In 1953 Weaver wrote another book which omitted much of the pessimistic analysis of his earlier work. His concern was to show the importance of linking rhetoric to proper definition of principles and to commonly accepted traditions. Earlier American rhetoric, he argues, was based on such common traditions, and statesmen like Lincoln were clear in their basic principles. If we taught the difference between rhetorical persuasion and definitions of first principles, he says, it would provide the needed tonic for representative government,[53] which now puts too much emphasis on manipulative rhetoric.

But while this concentration on tradition and Platonic dialectic may have helped him achieve some reconciliation to "American tradition," it produced some curious conclusions. The most striking was the conclusion that Burke was not really a Conservative, because he usually argued from empirical circumstances while Lincoln's arguments from definition were more truly Conservative. Weaver also points out, correctly, that Burke's frequent arguments from mere traditionalism were without meaning as long as he did not abstract the essence of the traditions he was defending.[54] These observations prompted Kirk to retort that Burke often did argue from "principles" and that Burke's Conservatism is by now a well-established historical fact. Actually, both positions are half-right. Burke's empiricism was not really "natural" to Conservatism. It was the result of the generally Liberal framework of British thought and was one of the Liberal elements in Burke's Conservatism. To the extent that Kirk insists on identifying this "concreteness" with Conservatism, he is elevating a passing historical circumstance to the level of universal ideology when he should be shedding the adaptation to historical conditions in order to arrive at the ideological core of Conservatism. But on the other hand, as we have seen, the Platonic assumptions in Burke's thought are undeniable, while even Weaver's rationalizations fail to uncover any such assumptions in Lincoln's position. It may be true that Platonic epistemology is most easily related to Conservatism, but it is sheer confusion to make total adherence to that epistemology the sole criteria for identifying historical forms of Conservatism. The real purpose is to provide Weaver with some specious grounds for mitigating his pessimism. Incidentally, the analysis also reveals ideological cleavages even within the ranks of reactionary Conservatism.

Several other New Conservatives are equally ambivalent in their failure to follow Conservative standards of criticism through to corresponding conclusions. Alan Valentine denounces the present "age of conformity" primarily by Conservative criteria, but ends with vague hopes that American democracy may yet decide to raise its masses to the level of aristocracy.[55] Anthony Harrigan, a Catholic Conservative, was clear in his assertion that the leadership of the Eisenhower administration has not really been Conservative in spite of popular terminology, but hoped in 1954 that the true Conservatives might be able to capture the imagination of the Republican leadership. In 1957 he reviewed the "degeneracy" of contemporary America and the corruption wrought by mechanization and urbanization.[56] But he shifted three times in one short article: first he hoped for little more than being able to "hold the line" against further degeneration; then he talked of evolving a sense of community through voluntary groups; and finally he sighed that it may be too late for any salvation and that we may have to await utter despair and chaos. One month later he denounced the tendencies to "other-directedness" in the modern corporations, but ended with the hopeful observation that many corporations were now learning to take the interests of the public and the local community into consideration.[57]

Frederick L. Wilhelmsen, another Catholic Conservative, has been perhaps the most nearly consistent in his frank acceptance of pessimistic conclusions, and reveals the ease with which the reactionary moves to a kind of Late Stoa, admitting his sense of alienation without claiming to have any solution. He is clear about the medieval basis of Conservatism and cautious in his use of Greek tradition, which he admits to be perhaps more compatible with Liberalism.[58] He also admits the absurdity of Catholic Conservative attempts to prove that American institutions are products of medieval tradition. He frankly accepts the alienation of the Conservative professor and realizes that "the world no longer wants him." [59] But he tries to make it seem as though this is also Kirk's position. It is, he says, wrong to attack Kirk as one who is trying to conjure up an American Tory tradition which never existed. Kirk might have lapsed into disillusion as Santayana did or he might have launched a doomed quixotic movement like distributism. But, Wilhelmsen claims, the path he has chosen is that of a social critic, exposing the failures of modern society.[60] This tendency of Conservatives to reinterpret the positions of other Conservatives is itself an interesting commentary on their confusions and on their frequent attempts to introduce an illusory unity to the hopelessly fragmented Conservative ranks. But to take the reverse side of this coin, Wilhelmsen is well aware (as many of the non-Catholic Conservatives are not) that the American Catholic Church is not necessarily the progenitor of New Conservatives, least of all the Kirk and Wilhelmsen varieties of Conservatism.[61]

In spite of Wilhelmsen's attempt to make Kirk seem like an "alienated" Conservative, the predominant characteristic of reactionary Conservatism is its refusal to follow the logic of its own ideology. It continues to talk as though it were launching programs for the regeneration of the world when it is really launching "doomed quixotic movements." Russell Kirk might indeed be happier if he confined himself to the role of critic.

He certainly would be more consistent. He might indeed find salvation with St. Augustine in "the night," where he "might be invisible in God." He certainly would find repose there. But in the meantime he does not confine himself to criticism, and he does not find repose. He is too busy writing "programs" and "guides" to Conservatism for "intelligent women."

VI

The New Conservatism:

Burke Readjusted

Alongside the "recrudescence" of reactionary Conservatism in the period since World War II, there has been a "revival" of "adjusted" Conservatism. The adjusted group accepts the crucial changes of the twentieth century and refrains from programs designed to restore lost traditions or alienated classes. But there are important internal variations in the degree and the direction of its "adjustment." In many respects John Hallowell resembles Russell Kirk, but he differs in accepting the ideology of democracy as the most desirable framework for moral development, unlike Kirk, who accepts it in a grudging resignation to the unavoidable. The "new" Herbert Agar of the 1950's has gone much further than Hallowell, because he accepts the American system of pressure groups and party compromise, as well as a strong presidency, on the ground that they result from an irreversible historical trend. In the process of analysis, his terms of justification become difficult to distinguish from those which a Liberal might use to justify the same institutions. Peter Viereck is emphatic in pointing out that American traditions are Liberal but still insists that it is the function of Conservatives to preserve those traditions. Even more, he accepts the reforms of the New Deal not only as inevitable but as positively desirable when evaluated by Conservative standards. Clinton Rossiter goes further than any of the group. Like Hallowell he accepts democracy enthusiastically (subject, of course, to some Conservative interpretation).

Like Agar he justifies both the American party system and the American presidency. Like Viereck he accepts much of the New Deal. But he goes beyond the others in frankly accepting the entire business class as the necessary base of American Conservatism, and he is willing to listen to any proposals for the future, including the corporatist society envisioned by men such as Peter Drucker. The degree of adjustment to industrialization also increases as one passes from Hallowell at one end to Rossiter at the other. In adjusting to American Liberalism and democracy, these men represent the typical tendency of their type of Conservatism to follow the lead of other ideologies. We shall see that their adjustment extends also to changes in the direction of authoritarianism.

John Hallowell: The Adjustment to Democracy

John Hallowell combines two incompatible theses in his analysis. On the one hand, his moral code rests on an orthodox interpretation of Christianity. On this basis he interprets modern history as a process of continual decline from the high point of the Middle Ages. This interpretation rests on the Platonic theory, which, as we shall see, views history as a process of degeneration from an initial period of moral harmony. If this position were continued to its logical conclusion, Hallowell could either be an "alienated" Conservative who surrenders all hope of improvement or a reactionary Conservative like Russell Kirk, who thinks that the lost past can still be restored. But when he comes to analyzing contemporary American democracy, Hallowell suddenly shifts his theoretical base from Plato to Aristotle. By identifying the American Constitution with Aristotle's "polity," he manages to justify the American system while insisting on a Conservative, moralistic interpretation of democracy.

Hallowell's ideology, like that of most contemporary Conservatives, ostensibly begins with Christianity. The essence of this religion he considers to be the concept that "the reorientation of one's will and thoughts from self to God is the only requirement for entrance into the Kingdom of God." Happiness and peace are by-products of the love of God; they cannot be attained by direct pursuit. But since man's nature is corrupted by original sin he cannot reach this goal by himself or through the historical process. Perfection will come only at the end of history and by the grace of God.[1]

To take this conception literally is to reject contemporary society, because it is obviously not based on the surrender of "selfish" will. Yet, though Hallowell often speaks the language of alienated orthodoxy, he is unable to rest content with this position alone. Although a Conservative Christian withdrawal from society might bring spiritual consolation to the individual, it could not have any historical effect on society unless there were a great number of other Christians who were also prepared for spiritual withdrawal, and then it would hasten the dissolution of society. This actually happened during the decline of the Roman Empire. But in the twentieth century few Christians accept such orthodoxy literally, without qualifications; and Hallowell has no desire to promote the dissolution of modern society. Under contemporary conditions, a man who insists that no human group is really good because all men are sinners, and that men should strive constantly for religious regeneration through surrender to God is, for all practical purposes, acquiescing in society as it is, at the same time that he is alienated from it; because he is likely to have little company, though revivalism is currently popular.

To avoid the difficulties of this position Hallowell, like any realistic ideologist, insists that it is possible to formulate a practicable conception of societal justice and that human institutions can approximate this justice. His criticism that Reinhold Niebuhr offers no standard of justice by which one could judge the comparative merits of societies is really a criticism of Niebuhr's tendency to a literal interpretation of original sin. On the other hand, he also rejects Catholicism on the grounds that no human institution can claim *total* identity with righteousness. The Catholic Church, he says, has seemed too often to follow an opportunistic policy in which it placed its existence as an institution above its adherence to the Gospel. It has taken a clear stand on Communism, but failed to be equally clear on Fascism and has too frequently adjusted itself to the *status quo*. At the same time, he continues, it has tried to dictate too closely the pattern for a Christian society. The hero of the story is the Anglican Church, since it confines itself more to Christian criticism than to specific societal proposals but yet offers some standard of "justice." [2]

Though there is a relation between Conservatism and the orthodox Christian idea of the surrender of the self to God, it is impossible to reason directly from Christianity to societal ideology because the connecting assumptions have changed throughout Christian history. The mitigation of demands on the individual and the institutionalization of Christian authority in the Catholic Church made possible the justification of a modified Conservatism during the Middle Ages. The Calvinist combination of Christianity and a self-appointed "elect" produced a kind of authoritarianism, and the later inclusion of economic activity in the concept of "serving God" helped to justify Liberal capitalism. Even radical theorists have been able to call on Christianity for support, by choosing an equalitarian concept of the "brotherhood of man" as the meaning of dedication to God. Hallowell, of course, accepts the more Conservative patristic Christianity, but he still has to add further qualification in order to make this the basis of a Conservative theory of society.

In Anglicanism, Hallowell finds two positive standards for the good society. The first is that the individual should be given "the widest possible extension of personal responsibility," for this is the meaning of freedom. But since no further standard is given of what is "possible," the standard is valueless, except to indicate a somewhat Liberal predilection. The second standard is that a man must serve his immediate community according to the community's values, but subject to the values of the wider community and of Christianity.[3] The obvious traditionalism here is potentially Conservative, but Hallowell makes little attempt to integrate the Christian surrender of self, freedom, and tradition into a coherent ideology.

As with all contemporary Conservatives, one must search in less emphasized and more remote corners of Hallowell's work to find his real assumptions. Clinton Rossiter has referred to Hallowell as an Aristotelian. This is at best a half-truth, because Hallowell's sympathies lie primarily with Plato. He cannot devote much space to Plato since he is dealing with modern thought, but Plato is one of the few theorists for whom Hallowell has virtually no criticisms (Burke is another). Indeed, he goes out of his way to defend Plato (in the notes at the end of his book), not only against modern critics but even against criticisms of Aristotle. He treats sympathetically Plato's concept of harmony as the true nature of man and society.[4] But the really important indication of his Platonism lies in his entire treatment of the history of Western society which is based on the Platonic idea of historical change as regressive.

The high point of political and moral history for Hallowell lies in the Middle Ages. The process of change since then has been a process of steady degeneration. The earliest important symptom of this degeneration was the rise of Liberalism. Although Liberalism at first retained many of the older elements of the Western heritage, its distinguishing feature was the emphasis on the autonomous individual. God was increasingly retained only as a logically necessary premise, and scientific empiricism was substituted for theology. This concept of autonomous reason was a departure from the medieval tradition in which faith sustained reason. The organic nature of the human community was ignored, in favor of the individual. Liberalism, however, did not degenerate completely as long as it retained the idea of conscience. But when conscience was destroyed by scientific positivism, Liberalism degenerated further into mere license or into pure coerciveness and tyranny. In an earlier work, Hallowell quotes a description of Liberalism as the attempt to restore a lost harmony without relying on revelation. But, it is asked, was there any shore to which Liberalism could return once it cut loose from churchly tradition and infallible revelation? [5] He accepts the thesis of the Conservative Ortega y Gasset that the abandonment of religious salvation for the "plenitude of science" has led to the modern totalitarian state. Totalitarianism is thus near the nadir of the process of degeneration which began with individualism. Like Burke, Hallowell really accepts freedom only on condition that it remain subordinate to Conservatism.

Lest there be any doubt that Hallowell is primarily a Platonist, one has only to read a recent book in which he specifically identifies his whole analysis of modern thought with the Platonic argument that when original traditions are destroyed man degenerates into license and tyranny. He identifies the Middle Ages with the concept of harmony and he sees that subsequent history has been a process of degeneration from this early harmony. He accepts the Platonic concept of true love as attraction to harmonious perfection, and he insists that in a true democracy all must aspire to the Platonic life of virtue.[6]

Hallowell's critiques of contemporary society are similar to those of other Conservatives. The Western world, he says, faces a crisis which is the result of moral and cultural breakdown. Industrialization has dehumanized man to a mere cog in the machine. "If his appetite for goods lags, it must be stimulated artificially; he must be stimulated if for no other reason than envy of others who buy . . . he must buy if the producers are to go on producing." In such a society the laborer has no sense of dignity. Culture becomes abstract and dehumanized. Civilization is in danger of perishing. The only way out of the conflicts to which man is prone is through the Cross. The only redemption for modern society lies in Christianity and a return to the spirit of the Middle Ages.[7]

If Hallowell went no further than this, his position would be virtually identical with that of Russell Kirk, and subject to the criticisms which have been directed against Kirk. But when he comes to the subject of American democracy Hallowell seems to be completely incapable of following the logic of his own assumptions. Now, indeed, Aristotle becomes his standard-bearer. The American constitutional system becomes the incarnation of Aristotle's "polity." Democracy is justified because it institutionalizes consent and lets the individual determine his own political destiny. The spiritual equality of man requires opportunities for the individual to develop his moral potentialities. Furthermore, as Aristotle said, the reasoned judgment of the many is best. It is because of the need for individual consent and moral responsibility, as well as the greater reliability of the many, that government should rest on deliberation, on free elections, and on personal civil liberties. The primary difficulty with all this is that it contradicts his seven hundred pages of historical analysis. His historical treatment of modern thought rests on an assumption of continual moral decline, for which Liberalism and positivism bear the primary responsibility. But if democracy is a morally superior system, then modern history has been progressive and Liberalism has been one of the essential instruments of this progress. Even if we assume that Hallowell's extolling of democracy is confined to the original American Constitution, it must be pointed out that, unlike Kirk, he makes no attempt to deny that the Constitution was based on Liberal and not on Conservative premises.[8] This central contradiction in Hallowell's writings is connected to two further problems.

The first is his repeated obscuring of the differences between Plato and Aristotle. Hallowell is aware that these two men disagreed in many important respects, but he prefers to stress what he considers to be their similarities. He repeatedly passes from quoting one to quoting the other, as though they had both said the same thing in different ways, and at least once indicates that he considers the Platonic and the Aristotelian concepts of justice to be identical.[9] Actually, though Aristotle defines justice as "giving each his due" and maintaining "the Golden Mean," his only tangible test of justice is the achievement of political integration and stability. If Plato's "solutions" lie in unconscious social cohesion, Aristotle's lie in conscious political authority. If Plato thinks men will surrender their desires for the satisfaction of inner peace and communal affection, Aristotle insists that only coercion can make most men good. While Plato advocates harmony through renunciation of desires, Aristotle advocates the maximum satisfaction of individual desires consistent with the need for political integration. While Plato seeks to eliminate tensions, Aristotle treats them as inevitable and wants only to prevent them from disrupting society. If coercion is for Plato an admission of failure, Aristotle repeatedly insists that it is fundamentally legitimate as long as it is used "properly." Aristotle's concern for political integration and authority above all else in society was mitigated by his acceptance of Platonic values as subordinate qualifications. But this does not make the two positions compatible, let alone interchangeable. Plato's position was profoundly Conservative. Aristotle's was really authoritarian, though usually a conservative form of authoritarianism. When Aristotle looked at history, he saw political change as paramount and ultimately as the cause of social change. For Plato the reverse was true. For Aristotle, therefore, history is a process of enlargement of satisfactions and integration rather than the deterioration of harmony, even if he cannot see this process extending beyond the Greek city-state. Hallowell's obscuring of these differences enables him to make the contradictory shift from a Platonic analysis of continual moral decay since the Middle Ages to an Aristotelian vindication of American democracy as a high point of historical development.

The second problem in Hallowell's analysis is that his apparent justification of modern democracy is so qualified by Conservative criteria that one may question whether he really accepts democracy at all. He sees democracy as a system in which all may aspire to a life of Platonic virtue. He takes the trouble to point out that democracy is compatible with aristocracy if the "best" (and this means the morally best) are elected by the people. Effective democracy, he says, depends

on the Christian submission to God, and the statesman, like
the doctor, must restrain the evil and release the naturally good
tendencies of the citizen [10] (We might note here that this medical analogy, which was a favorite of Plato, was rejected by Aristotle as irrelevant to the problems of politics). His theory of
political parties is based entirely on that of Burke. The striking thing about these ideas is that if American democracy depended on their fulfillment for its justification, we would have
to conclude that it is a complete failure. No one can seriously
maintain that the American citizen aspires to Platonic virtue
or submission of self to God, and we have already seen the
irrelevance of Burkean ideology to American party politics.

But Hallowell does not really attempt to apply these criteria
to American democracy. When he comes to actual evaluation,
he lowers his sights considerably, transforming Plato, Burke,
and orthodox Christianity into a modern form of democratic
Aristotelianism which could easily pass for a conservative
American Liberalism. This requires further obscuring of
Aristotle, however. When Hallowell cites Aristotelian concepts
of consent and political equality, he does not make clear that
these applied only to people equally capable of maintaining
stable political power, and that Aristotle's concepts were therefore based on assumptions very different from those of individual freedom in American democracy.

Hallowell's vindication of democracy is largely on Aristotelian grounds of political integration, though he also moves
to Conservative and Liberal grounds with utter disregard for
problems of consistency. He emphasizes that democracy depends on common values, that this requires minority willingness to accept the decisions of the majority, and that this in turn
implies that disagreements should be only on means and not on
ends. Having thus accepted a concept of common values
broad enough so that it can include common Liberal values,
Hallowell is able to reinterpret Burke's theory of political
parties so that he can apply it to American parties. He accepts
American parties because they do not disagree on fundamen-

tals and because they integrate diverse interests reasonably well. He criticizes them only to the extent that they do not effectively control pressure groups such as tariff and farm organizations. Government must be limited by "natural law," and the function of the representative is to use mature moral judgment, as Burke says, rather than simply to reflect the views and desires of his constituents.[11] Hallowell's major concerns are to reject any contemporary form of Liberalism which emphasizes only adjustment of private interests while ignoring transcendent morality and to reject forms of pragmatism which he fears will encourage pure authoritarianism. He thus concludes with an affirmation of twentieth-century American democracy, though he does not come to this position from Liberal premises and though in his own historical analysis even eighteenth-century Liberalism was a degenerate precursor of all that he detests in the modern age. The result is the anomalous combination of moral crisis, a dehumanizing economy, and a deteriorated culture with an acceptable (indeed justifiable) political system. His problem is similar to Kirk's in this respect, but his inconsistency is worse than Kirk's because he attempts a moral justification rather than mere acceptance of democracy.

Herbert Agar: The Adjustment to American Politics

The degree of "adjustment" in Hallowell's Conservatism is slight, but with Agar's writings in the 1950's we come to an unmistakably marked change in the tone of Conservative ideology. One can still find Conservative criticisms and agrarian nostalgia in Agar's recent works. He still attributes the moral and political fragmentation of the world to the Industrial Revolution. The purpose of science, he says, is to "catalogue the world" so that we may hand it back to God the way we got it and not to war with nature. Work has dignity, especially agricultural work,[12] but industrialization has been spiritually frustrating, cruel, and shortsighted. America, he warns, has done everything but compose her soul. She has never known a time of rest, of calm self-possession. But there is now a new element in Agar's tone, resignation. "The flight from the land is a road of no return whose lure none can resist," he sighs. And beyond resignation is the admission of the efficiency of large-scale business,[13] an admission which the distributists flatly refused to make in the 1930's.

Agar still speaks also of the moral "natural law" engraved in conscience. The prohibition against murder, treachery, perjury, and the like are moral constants in any society at any time, he exclaims. But he is extremely cautious about basing actual political decisions on natural law. All political spokesmen, he remarks, find that government decisions coincide with natural law when they agree with them and that they do not when they disagree. Furthermore, one cannot solve all the complex problems of history with the Ten Commandments. His political natural law therefore becomes distilled to just two elements. The first is that conscience itself must never be coerced, since it is the repository of natural law, however varied its expressions. The second is that the Western conscience does not permit the absorption of the family, the enterprise, the church, and the state into a single comprehensive unit.[14] Agar admits that the whole idea of natural law has been progressively weakened since its separation from the established Church of the Middle Ages, and he is obviously trying to save two last pieces of it. But aside from the fact that virtually any Liberal could accept these two "rules," it is difficult to see who in America would reject them.

His example of a violation of conscience by the state which would justify resistance is the passage of a law requiring Catholics to practice divorce.[15] Since the Catholic attitude towards divorce is a purely "internal" matter which does not affect any other group in society, no government would be justified in failing to respect it, he says. But one is hard pressed to imagine circumstances in which anyone would care to advocate such a law, or to see what Agar has saved by affirming this prohibition. Not even the experiments in the USSR during the 1920's can be cited as examples of violating moral conscience in Agar's sense, since merely facilitating divorce does not directly cause it unless one's moral code also changes. Certainly this norm would be of no use in the problem of school desegregation. If one cites the "Southern conscience" as an entrenched value against proposed interracial contact in the schools, there is just as much reason to cite opposite Negro values. Actually, desegregation would not be a legitimate example of a purely internal matter of conscience, since it affects more than one group. The "natural law" against the consolidation of all institutions of society is, of course, Agar's argument against totalitarianism. But this is not relevant for non-Western countries, which do not have any traditional "conscience" against such consolidation. More important, it is of little value for the United States, where the Conservatives fear a coercive totalitarian state much less than the indirect consolidation of societal institutions by mass manipulation. As for the private moral injunctions against murder or treachery, these will not be very widely disputed as long as there are no clear standards by which to judge a society's interpretations of them. Ideologies dispute about the grounds which justify taking human life, not about the existence of unjustifiable killing. On the one hand, no society has ever completely abdicated the right to be final judge of the conditions which justify homicide. On the other, no rational ideology has ever commanded man saying, "Thou shalt murder."

The confusions in Agar's moral standards are contemporaneous with his adjustment to other changes besides industrialization. He rejects the tradition of the French Revolution because it was equalitarian and "lower class," but accepts that of the American Revolution because it was Liberal and middle class. He even speaks of the American Revolution in terms of "uncontrollable forces," a strange stand for a Conservative who used to talk of the omnipotence of moral determination. Shifting from his earlier criticisms of the American constitutional system, he now justifies its near deification as essential to unity in an otherwise fragmented country. He rejects excessive faith in the efficacy of purely "spiritual" reform. It was force which finally determined who was right in the Civil War, for though the use of force against evil is self-defeating in that it merely creates another wrong, man cannot avoid resisting evil, and by force if necessary. Especially revealing is his praise of Theodore Roosevelt for having enabled the transition to twentieth-century America to occur "without anyone realizing it." Although Roosevelt did not, like Henry Adams, see the potential evils of this new world, he made it possible for the change to occur peacefully and with a sense of continuity from the older world.[16] Here is the distinguishing trait of the "adjusted" Conservative. He is not happy about the great changes which have been occurring in the world, but great changes, as Burke said, may have been prepared by God as part of his divine plan. Rather than quixotically break a lance against this onslaught of history, it may be the better part of both prudence and piety to accept it, and by accepting it to save at least something of value. As the sage said, "If you can't lick 'em, join 'em."

Agar now sees American history in terms of oscillating relations between freedom and authority. He is ready to admit that American federalism is "illogical" but defends it on the pragmatic ground that "it works." The one time it failed, the problem had to be decided by violence—the Civil War. During unagitated periods the Federal government abides by the limitations on federalism, but in time of crisis it must act like a unitary government, returning to the more "normal" system after the crisis has passed. Yet the over-all drift has been towards centralization, and while Americans have followed Jefferson in their hearts, they have followed Hamilton in their deeds, for centralization seems inevitable. Within the Federal government, the historical trend has also favored the emergence of a strong presidency, subject to the same limitations and fluctations as federalism. The President has necessarily become the focus of popular democracy because of the inefficiency and irresponsibility of Congress, its inability to discipline itself, and the confusions resulting from its fragmenting representative base. Nor is the Constitution a real barrier against the further strengthening of the presidency, because the Constitution is what the Supreme Court makes it, and the Supreme Court is ultimately what the President makes it. It is true that we have been fortunate in the Presidents who have led us in crises, and that we got superior leaders such as Lincoln and Theodore Roosevelt only through political accidents, but no system can guarantee political genius at the right time. The separation of powers with its differing bases of representation in Congress and the presidency is essential in a country as large and diversified as this one. It combines the demand for satisfaction of interests with the need to act decisively in crises, and works successfully where a parliamentary system would long ago have destroyed the country. But it is our political parties on which the whole system rests, for when all other governmental resistance to the growing power of Franklin Roosevelt had disintegrated, the party system still preserved "balanced government." [17]

The party system is then the cornerstone of the American union. It mitigates the selfish demands of regions and groups through compromises which offer something to everyone. It softens majority rule, diminishes the separation of powers, and strengthens the presidency while resisting excessive centralization. The parties, however, seek patronage and bargains, not principles. They give favors to each noisy group and ignore issues that rouse deep passions. On important issues, each party takes both sides. Since each interest which is strong enough to make trouble must be satisfied, easy obstruction lies in the way of new policies. The system thus facilitates inaction through its chaotic nature and action through its pragmatic flexibility. It allows the President to lead on the one hand and special interests to obstruct on the other. Each party appeals to the Constitution, but the party in power tends to interpret it loosely while the party out of power insists on stricter interpretation. Since the majority learns to yield even when it could insist on having its way,[18] what we really have is a rough approximation to Calhoun's "concurrent majority" without the stalemate that his actual plan would have caused in crises. As for party followers, we have both the loyal vote which makes for stability and the independent vote which makes for honesty and change. It is true that we pay the price of corruption, of vulgarity, of ignoring grave issues, and of confusing the national interest for the sum of private interests. But the one time when the parties did adhere to principles, the result was the Civil War. As for the shortcomings of the party system, they are part of the "price of union," and a small price it is compared to the alternatives of disunion or an authoritarian party system and unchecked majority rule.[19]

The foregoing elements of Agar's analysis of American parties have not been cited because they contain anything unique or even characteristically Conservative. On the contrary, the analysis probably represents the prevailing approach to the subject among political scientists today, and it is based on typically Liberal values, combined with a sprinkling of authoritarian arguments. By confusing this interpretation with Calhoun's "concurrent majority" (a mistake he refused to make in the 1930's), Agar can make it seem as though his shift is consistent. What he is really doing, however, is to expose unwittingly the confusion on which the acceptance of the party system by men like Kirk and Hallowell rests. When they laud the party system because it is based on common ends, they fail utterly to point out that the common ends can include the thesis that every group should have some of its demands satisfied. If this qualifies as a Conservative value, then Kirk and Hallowell had better tear up their books and begin all over again. Of prime importance also is Agar's implicit refutation of the Conservative criticism of American parties. Kirk and Hallowell reluctantly accept the catering to private demands because the parties serve "common ends," but insist that the party system move closer to Burke's ideal by stressing "principles," the "national interest," morality, and decorum. Agar shows that the absence of even these isolated Burkean ideals is part of the necessary price for unity which the parties preserve with their common Liberal ends.   Closer attention to the "national interest" or to "principles" might produce a more exclusively authoritarian or a more democratic party system, but it is hardly likely to result in Conservatism.   As for Agar's new argument, it amounts to saying that the Conservative in America must become Liberal whenever possible and adjust to authority whenever necessary, if he is to avoid the even worse fate of pure authoritarianism or radical democracy.   By the same arguments a Conservative could also justify both authoritarianism and radical democracy if the alternative is "anarchy." The ideological obscurity of Agar's position raises an obvious question: if Conservatism must adjust to prevailing historical forces, then why not adjust without Conservatism?

Peter Viereck: The Adjustment to the New Deal

Agar has always favored much of the New Deal, but his early support was based on reactionary agrarian grounds, and his present support is based on historical inevitability.   Viereck's adjustment to the New Deal has, however, been on more self-consciously Conservative grounds.

Several features of Viereck's Conservatism are strikingly "different."   After the obscurantist religiosity of the men we have already considered, it is rather startling to hear Viereck say that he does not really know whether the Christian ethic is divine, though he does feel that it is innate and universal in man.   He even says that if there were no such innate basis for morality, it would still be socially necessary.[20]   Equally unusual is his discussion of tradition.   He readily admits that the elements of the Western heritage "sometimes" conflict, and goes on to say that the constant need for resynthesis "goads us to greatness."   The only constant he can find in that heritage is the belief in "the uniqueness of the individual soul," and he does not balk at agreeing that this is compatible with any ideology (except totalitarianism).[21]

His basic Conservative postulates are those we have already

encountered numerous times: public service, decorum, an inner check, *noblesse oblige;* the moral restraints of tradition; the inner grace to be able to face calamity; the need to experience ethical restraints for long periods of history in order to make them effective; the primacy of morality over economics, because economic ambitions are disruptive while ethical aspirations are cohesive; a tendency to "concreteness"; and the burden on those who propose innovations.[22] But, Viereck says, there is no such thing as pure Conservatism. The tendency of Conservatism is to range from admixture with Liberalism at one pole to influence from authoritarianism at the other. He leaves no doubt that his sympathies lie at the Liberal end. His hero, of course, is Edmund Burke, because Burke understood the possibilities of self-discipline and hence of freedom. The continental Conservative for whom he has most respect is Metternich, a "Burkean" who understood that nineteenth-century Europe needed repose above all and that only an "inner balance" could resist the "pull towards extremes." All American Conservatives, he affirms, are Burkeans, since they agree that liberty must be protected by tradition.[23]

To understand Viereck's position fully, however, it is necessary to mention those Conservative values which he omits as well as those he includes. Of the societal elements which we have outlined as the basis of Conservatism, Viereck emphasizes only the concepts of tradition, moral restraint, and the primacy of social cohesion. He is not very much concerned with a harmony of economic functions, or with minimizing material desires, and he has some praise for the material achievements of industrialization. Aristocracy, he says, is functionless in modern society; it is only the "aristocratic spirit" which is "precious." Since aristocracy is vulnerable when it performs no service, the Conservative must now prefer democracy as the "repository of folk traditions," and seek, in the United States, to make all men into aristocrats.[24] Here only "natural aristocracy" can succeed.

Viereck prefers to identify himself more with the reformist

rather than the traditionalist side of Burke, and Winston Churchill is his current model. He criticizes Burke for choosing between contradictory traditions sometimes on the basis of natural rights and sometimes simply because of their age. In fact, Viereck goes so far in perferring the reformist spirit of "Tory democracy" that he strongly recommends cooperation with democratic socialists in Europe, and, if necessary, the adoption of segments of their program. But his adjustment to Liberal democracy is not simply a consequence of the need for a common front against totalitarianism, nor does it even refer to the fact that transitional periods of history are "always uncomfortable for Conservatism." [25] He is prepared to admit that both the Conservative and Liberal "impulses" are equally basic to human thinking and that the debate between them is therefore endless. He thinks that Conservatism is not an ideology but a "way of thinking." He even says that Conservatism is best when it "serves a Liberal party." [26]

It is not surprising, therefore, that he pointedly opposes Kirk's Conservatism, and insists that if the Liberal tradition is rejected in America there will be nothing left to conserve. The true American tradition, he says, consists of "revolution-preventing reforms." [27] Now we must assume that when Viereck says that the Conservative and Liberal "impulses" are equally "basic" he does not really mean that they are equally valid, but simply that we will always have advocates of both "ways of thinking" in society. If he really granted them equal validity his position would be impossibly contradictory, since there would never in a given situation be a better argument for tradition and inner restraint than for change and freedom. Nevertheless, it is clear that he is prepared to grant a much larger measure of validity to Liberalism than Kirk or Hallowell. Unlike Kirk (who only pays lip service to the idea), Viereck is seriously prepared to accept change on its own terms without first having to reinterpret it. And unlike Agar, he tries to justify this adjustment to change in Conservative terms. He does not explain it as a simple bowing to the inevitable. His argument is that by yielding to important changes, even to demands for greater equality, the Conservative preserves harmony by preventing serious conflict from breaking out. In this sense, he says, violent revolutions occur by default,[28] when no one in power is prepared to play the Conservative role properly. In a way, the same reasoning is implicit in Agar's argument, but when Agar talks of "the price of union" his arguments are usually Liberal and when he accepts historical change he does not justify it on the specifically Conservative ground that resistance would mean less harmony and more conflict.

The "adjusted" Conservatives' criticisms of American society are less sweeping than Kirk's, but of this group Viereck's criticism are the most trenchant, though his solutions are mild. His social analysis is especially incisive because he does not allow himself the illusions from which Kirk suffers. He not only criticizes the contemporary emphasis on "group adjustment," but says bluntly that even the current "anti-materialism" is being sold like a cellophane-wrapped commodity and that the "return to religion" is largely a parlor fad. He dismisses talk of a restoration of Christian unity as absurd and regressive. It is, he emphasizes, a mistake to consider Catholics to be "naturally" Conservative, since in America they are much more likely to be middle class in outlook, and he will not accept Puritan morality as being identical with Conservatism. Instead he frequently abandons the ponderous self-righteousness of the reactionary Conservatives for the "gracious idleness" of the aristocrat. What modern man craves are the "courtly images of custom, ceremony, and stately calm." The "cash nexus" can lead only to frustration and loneliness, and the businessman's ethic of "tax-deductible donations and . . . celery juice" to ease his conscience and his ulcers is inferior to the aristocratic indulgence in "courtesans, horses, and champagne." [29]

But Viereck's talk of making everyone in a democracy into aristocrats does not really mean that he wants social equality. On the contrary, he still retains the Conservative affection for status inequality, and wants only to give all the opportunity to reach the moral level of the aristocrat. The "best" should still be the moral leaders of society and they should guide it to a communal unity. But this unity must be based on pluralism and it cannot be consciously "organized." Furthermore, there is no reason for status inequality to carry special privileges in a democracy, and certainly no reason for a class system in the United States. Instead the Conservative ethic should filter throughout the entire society, with the saloon and the burleque house, for example, serving as the lower-class counterparts to the corresponding aristocratic institutions. His final solution to the problem is to build on the traditional American capacity for voluntary cooperation in solving problems, and to spread the Conservative ethic through "friendly persuasion and a sense of humor" on the level of private relations.[30]

In a way, Viereck's adjustment to the contemporary relaxation of moral taboos under the guise of diffusing the old aristocratic ethic is an interesting attempt to cope with the problem of social and moral tensions. But the attempt does not really come to grips with the problems. Kirk's observation about the tensions created by constant sexual stimuli that cannot possibly be gratified is more relevant here than Viereck's apparent sophistication. A burlesque house is after all not really analogous to the "institution" of courtesans. If tensions measure the difference between desires and satisfactions, then we must conclude that no degree of moral relaxation acceptable to Viereck could possible ease this problem. The same is true of stimulated desires for material goods, which Viereck hardly bothers to consider at all. Nor does Viereck have any real answer to the problem of "over-adjustedness" which he himself poses. It is of no help to have him tell us that the aristocrat was able to avoid such excess because he was secure in his hereditary position and could therefore afford accentricity, since aristocracy is no longer relevant to the terms of Viereck's analysis. Nor can he be seriously optimistic about the prospects of "friendly persuasion" by Conservatives, especially since he argues cogently that all new insights now tend to become adulterated in the process of faddish adoption by the "Over-adjusted Man." (He mentions the popularity of Reinhold Niebuhr as an example of this fashionable dilution.) [31] The weakness inherent in mere adjustment is nowhere clearer than in the fact that Viereck's own adjustment brings him no closer to his goal of widespread "inner graciousness" than does Kirk's adamant reaction. And we must remember that a society which does not have a Conservative moral and social base has little on which to build a Conservative political system.

Viereck's economic adjustability is also far-reaching. It is true, he says, that industrialization causes havoc in society, but this has really been less true in the United States than anywhere else. The same American superiority can be seen in our brand of capitalism, and our economic system is now beginning to change markedly in the direction of greater responsibility. Intellectuals should therefore stop "baiting" businessmen and understand that moral inadequacies would remain in any economic system now.[32] Besides, industrialization and capitalism have also brought great benefits to mankind. As for unions, they are Conservative institutions since they give the workers a sense of belonging, and, because of unions, workers are probably the most Conservative class in society. Self-restraint and the "brotherhood of suffering" can solve many of the problems of industrialism. For those problems which require political and economic measures, as the problem of depression does, we should not hesitate to use the kind of techniques developed by the New Deal.[33] Aside from the usual generalities about the moral responsibilities of business, Viereck's characteristic position is that American industry is now efficient enough to be able to afford some nepotism. This imitation of lost aristocratic times is now desirable because nepotism is based on personal loyalties and softens the Calvinist-capitalist ethic.[34]

Having adjusted to modern economics, Viereck fails even to consider, much less to solve, the problems of greatest importance for a Conservative. The major fallacy in his approach is

the unspecified assumption that the Conservative task of preventing conflict applies only to conflicts of revolutionary proportions. It is on this basis, for example, that he concludes
that the New Deal was Conservative. But the fact that such
conflicts are absent from the American economy does not mean
that there are no problems of sufficiently grave importance to
raise serious difficulties for Conservatism. One can hardly
assume a very high degree of harmony between management
and labor, or industry and agriculture, or big business and
small business, or even within any one of these. The fallacy in
Viereck's argument is obscured by the fact that he compares
the degree of harmony which follows major changes with the
conflicts that would have occurred if no settlement had been
made. But this is not really different from Agar's position in
spite of Viereck's more self-conscious Conservatism. It actually
eliminates any standard of evaluation except the strength of
historical forces (a position which is inherent also in blind
traditionalism and in the idea of a mysterious divine plan of
history). On this basis, a Conservative would have been obligated to support Russian communism, German fascism, and
the American New Deal with equal fervor in 1935.

Actually, the Conservative should compare the harmony in
new settlements with that of previous historical settlements,
particularly the periods of maximum harmony. The extent of
either social or economic conflict in the America of 1950 should
be compared to 1900 rather than to 1931, and that of 1900
should be compared to 1800. It is probably true that, with
only Conservative harmony as the standard, the thirteenth
century in Western Europe represents a higher point than any
since then. To avoid passing a verdict of decline on modern
society, adjusted Conservatives compare contemporary periods
of settlement with periods of conflict or with potential conflict.
Of course, a Conservative can accept recent historical changes
with the argument that reaction would cause conflicts even
greater than those which already exist, but he must also admit

that the changes tend to carry society ever further away from the Conservative ideal.

Viereck not only fails to consider problems of economic conflict but, what is worse, he fails to cope even with the problems of status conflict which he himself raises. Though he makes an interesting case for the thesis that status resentment was the prime mover in lower middle-class movements from Populism to McCarthyism, he offers no way out of this conflict. He cannot take the position that these conflicts need only be restrained by counterforces, for this would be a Liberal argument. He cannot ask us to wait until the organizational forces set in motion by industry establish a new integration, because this would involve accepting the very kind of "group adjustment" which he rejects. Worst of all, he cannot rely on the settled status system which is effected by an established aristocracy, because he rejects the idea of aristocracy. All he can do is analyze the problem; he can offer no escape from it except through "friendly persuasion and a sense of humor," or the American tradition of "voluntary cooperation."

Viereck's cultural analysis is not significantly different from that of Kirk or other Conservatives. He speaks of culture rather than politics as the center of Conservative influence in America, and insists that in the long run the influence of intellectuals as the "conscience" of society is decisive. If he is willing to grant to art the occasional function of shocking a society out of its complacency, he feels nevertheless that we have had enough of such agitation now and that what we need is "calm, ennobling art." [35]

It is not surprising to find that Viereck's political ideology consists largely of the thesis that Liberal democracy cannot dispense with Conservatism. Since the "will to power" is the cause of tyranny, the best preventives are adherence to tradition on the one hand and institutions for channeling change on the other. Without traditional rules both freedom and the democratic parliamentary system are endangered. Like most contemporary Conservatives he frequently refers to the feudal and aristocratic roots of the Western tradition of freedom. As for democracy, besides its provisions for change, its great advantage lies in the capacity to combine stability with a check on abuses of power. The best kind of democracy is constitutional monarchy because a king provides balance and cement for the system, but in the United States the Constitution and the Supreme Court are adequate substitutes for a monarch.[36]

Two comments should be made about this analysis. The first is that if Conservatism must depend on the simple existence of rules in order to justify its importance to democracy, then it has fallen to a pitifully low estate. Since the rules may be used for any purpose, from the pursuit of self-interest to the changing of the rules themselves, it is difficult to understand why proving the need for such rules is any more a justification of Conservatism than proving the inescapability of habit in individual life, including, let us say, the habit of destructiveness. Certainly the argument for rules is not one which would encounter any opposition from American Liberals. Since Viereck's argument about the need for rules is coupled with an insistence on democratic machinery for changing these rules, it might be used against an American Communist revolution, but would be worthless against the Communist revolution in China where there was no political democracy. Secondly, Conservative claims about the aristocratic roots of freedom are equally pointless. The weakness of Liberalism in the Russian tradition indicates that aristocracy is not in itself a carrier of freedom. More important, Conservatives can hardly claim that aristocrats sought to maximize freedom in feudal society just because they wanted to protect their own privileges. If one takes the position that resistance to central authority, no matter what its motivation, is to be lauded as a source of individual freedom, then one would have to bestow similar praise on savages and revolutionaries. To justify aristocratic privilege because it led to middle-class freedom in spite of continual aristocratic opposition is to parody both Conservative and Liberal arguments about freedom.

The Liberal might be willing to acknowledge a kind of abstract historical gratitude to the medieval aristocrat for letting history "move behind his back," but this cannot possibly be of any real consolation to the Conservative.

Like all American Conservatives, Viereck praises the Liberal concept of mutual opposition as though it were the same thing as Conservative harmony. He is even prepared to use current Liberal terminology like "countervailing power" to describe the relation of nineteenth-century European monarchs and aristocrats to the middle class. Since he maintains that no one class can qualify as the carrier of Conservatism, and that the poor are more Conservative than other American classes,[37] he does not lament the defeat of the "squirearchical" Federalists.[38] American political parties since then may always have been Lockean in ideology, as Louis Hartz says, but at least they have always been Conservative in practice, Viereck is happy to report. This seems to be such great compensation to him that he claims to be glad that America has no real Conservative Party, and he admits that the parties differ primarily in degrees of overt emphasis on liberty and equality.[39]

The really important political contest now, he says, is between the moderates and the extremists of both parties.[40] The extremists include the Midwestern "isolationist" wing of the Republican Party and the Southern racist wing of the Democratic Party. As between the moderates, he would be equally happy with either party (though he is disappointed with Eisenhower's leadership). Franklin Roosevelt, Adlai Stevenson, Averell Harriman, Christian Herter, Irving Ives, and Clifford Case are all examples of "natural aristocrats" for him. Viereck naturally stresses the need for reverence and honor of political leaders, but "all other things being equal" (which apparently means "given two equally bad candidates"), the best course is to vote for the least efficient and most corrupt candidate as a defense against a mechanized and over-efficient society. The function of American elections is to decide which "elite subgroup" will dominate, but the frequent criticisms of wealth and status help keep men like Harriman and Stevenson responsible by forcing them to maintain self-imposed standards. Indeed the American political system may be described as "a benevolent squirearchy tempered by character-assassination." [41]

Viereck, like all American Conservatives, prefers political decentralization, pluralism, and localism if possible, and like all adjusted Conservatives he feels the need for strong presidential leadership. Not only does he champion civil liberties, but he holds that civil liberties are endangered by mass democratic groups and protected by the "natural aristocrats." It is, he says, the Southern masses who are lynchers and the old Populist classes who were McCarthyites. But such "natural aristocrats" as Chief Justice Warren and Senator Watkins were leaders in the fights for desegregation and against McCarthyism. Viereck is, at the same time, astute enough to recognize that even civil liberties can be used today as instruments of political manipulation. Recalling Senator McCarthy's careful avoidance of racial or religious bigotry and the "inter-faith" implications of the symbols of Rabbi Schultz, Father Coughlin, and the Reverend Mr. Gerald L. K. Smith, he quips that if *1984* ever comes to America, it will be through a "team of buddies" from all faiths, displaying model "cooperation" in their zeal to burn books "without restrictions of race, color or creed." [42]

There is little which need be said about Viereck's analysis of politics beyond what has been said previously. Even if American political conflict were confined to that between "moderates" and "extremists," this should be small consolation to the Conservative; and the assumption that the "moderates" are led by "natural aristocrats" is gratuitous. Nor does Viereck have anything to say about conflicts within the ranks of the moderates, and the enforcement of political responsibility by "character assassination" should afford him little occasion for exuberance. His conclusion that American parties are Conservative assumes Rossiter's distinction between our Liberal ideology and our Conservative practice. We shall examine this thesis shortly.

But Viereck's analysis of civil liberties merits some further criticism. In part it is simply based on wishful thinking, particularly when he confines Southern racism to the lower classes. It may be true that *most* racists have come from the lower or lower middle classes. But William J. Cash, in his classic, *The Mind of the South,* found that the Southern plantocracy also was frequently engaged in violent racism during the late nineteenth and early twentieth centuries. Nor could Viereck ever prove that aristocrats have generally been civil libertarians or opponents of group prejudice without rewriting the history of the European aristocracy in modern times. Even in the United States, it is just as easy to cite the anti-Semitism of a Henry Adams and the antipathy to immigrants of a Conservative civil libertarian like A. Lawrence Lowell as it is to point out similar prejudices among the Populists.

Viereck's approval of the desegration decision is particularly interesting because it illustrates the continuing dilemmas of American Conservatism. If one evaluates the problem of race relations as the Southern Conservatives or Russell Kirk do, then the prevention of conflict is the prime standard by which to judge desegregation. By this standard the Supreme Court decision in 1954 would have to be considered a serious blunder, if not consciously anti-Conservative. If one approaches the problem morally, as the Court did and as Viereck apparently does, then the evaluation would have to be an opposite one. But there is no more reason for a Conservative to take the one approach than the other. Furthermore, unless Viereck is prepared to abandon the Conservative position that equality is a purely internal condition of moral responsibility, he must conclude that the reasoning of the Court about racial equality was Liberal and not based on the Conservatism of any "natural aristocrat." His entire use of this latter term is, in fact, so vague as to be totally useless. As Agar pointed out about the manipulative use of the term "natural law," Viereck is prepared to call anyone whose policies he approves an "aristocrat." And, to return to Viereck's major fallacy, even if he takes the position that the Court decision is necessary to settle racial tensions which already exist, he would be hard pressed to show that any conceivable settlement after 1954 can match the racial quiescence which existed in the South in 1854.

Clinton Rossiter: The Adjustment to Industrialism

It would be tedious at this point to repeat, even in summary form, Rossiter's enumeration of the elements of Conservatism. He reiterates all the values of American Conservatives, including the characteristic confusion of "balance" and stability with Conservative harmony and the convenient assumption that Conservative ideology is no older than Burke and that it has therefore always embraced the ideal of liberty. But Rossiter distinguishes Conservatism (with a capital C), which is based on the conscious reflections derived from Burke, from conservatism (with a lower-case c), which consists of unreflective or interest-motivated fondness for established habit and tradition on the one hand and an adjustable American brand of Conservatism on the other. As it turns out, these categories correspond roughly to reactionary and adjusted Conservatism as distinguished in this book,* and his preference is clearly for the second group. He rejects that Conservatism which is "suspicious, gloomy, passive, and elitist" in favor of one which is "more daring, hopeful, individualistic, and democratic," one which seeks not to block change but to divert it into "channels of progress," one which never forgets that it is dealing with an America which is "experimenting in atomic power plants and automatic factories." [43]

Rossiter objects, however, to the misleading American tendency to equate laissez-faire Liberalism with Conservatism. He points to the exclusive use of economic achievement in evaluating social status and to the instability which its advocates caused by opposing reform as indices of the anti-Conservatism

---

* In this book, conservatism, with a lower-case c, is used only to describe the technique of defending existing traditions and institutions, no matter what their nature. It is also used as an adjective which describes modifications of other ideologies, as in "conservative Liberalism."

of laissez-faire. The latter, he emphasizes, was almost the contradiction of Conservatism in preferring the individual over the community, conflict over harmony, acquisition over enjoyment, self-interest over "fraternal sympathy," and competition over cooperation. Yet, like most adjusted Conservatives, Rossiter is quite prepared to admit, indeed to insist, that it is Liberalism which the Conservative must seek to preserve, since the American tradition is Liberal. In fact, he is happy that America had no feudal past, for historically this meant that liberty here was always a fact and that it had only to be preserved. But if America has been Liberal in its ideology, Rossiter hastens to add that it has been Conservative in its institutions and its practices. American affection has, after all, been bestowed on tradition, "the community," self-restraint, religion, and natural law as well as on the values of Liberalism. Such organic communities as the family, the neighborhood, and voluntary associations have been at least as important here as individualism. Only in economics and technology have we been really unconcerned with tradition. Even our more radical Liberals, from Jefferson to the Populists, never challenged the institution of private property itself, and though there have been many changes in American history they were always carried out through established institutions.[44]

Like most contemporary Conservatives, Rossiter now sees more favorable conditions in America for Conservatism. These conditions include less social mobility, a maturing economy, increasing conformity, the "return to religion," group consciousness, greater economic security, the diffusion of property, growing traditionalism, and the external pressures of Communism.[45]

But what makes Rossiter's Conservatism different from that of the others we have considered is that he is prepared to have future Conservative leadership come from the business class as well as the professions, and he even wants to appeal to the white-collar class. "An American aristocracy, if it is to be truly functional, must draw far more heavily on the business class than does the aristocracy of . . . almost any other country." This is, he says, not incompatible with the concept of a "democratic elite," because we may need separate elites for economics and politics, as well as culture. But his fondest hope is that America's business leaders will become transformed into an aristocracy by developing a tradition of public service in government. He is even willing to consider seriously Peter Drucker's proposals for a corporatist Conservatism (though this is, as we shall see, a distinctly separate "type" of Conservatism). When property becomes a form of power, he asserts, it can justifiably be regulated in the public interest,[46] though the various groups in society, including economic groups, should be encouraged to regulate themselves as much as possible, so as to preserve the equilibrium of "contervailing powers." Rossiter is explicitly calling for Conservatism to adjust itself to industrialism and industrial classes, a position which cannot clearly be found in the writings of any of the other Conservatives we have discussed. It is not a grudging adjustment as in Agar, nor one that may be inferred as in Viereck. It is clear and it is optimistic, as though he expects a great Conservative future in the industrial society. Nor is there any nostalgia for the past. Rossiter's eye is on the future.

Along with this acceptance of industrial society, we find considerable adjustment to the strong role which has fallen to government in our time. He wants government to be the "major equilibrating force" in the balance of social groups, to promote moral responsibility in corporations and unions, to perform humanitarian welfare services, to increase equality of opportunity, and to "make private enterprise work." The Conservative should understand, he says, that government is not the only danger to freedom, and that compulsion can take social and economic forms also.[47] Therefore, "paradoxically, our last defense against dangerous abuses of social and economic power is political power." Naturally, Rossiter does not want this role of government carried too far. He prefers to see social welfare handled as much as possible by private enterprise in the form of pension plans, health insurance, and corporation welfare programs. But the final responsibility for unsolved problems will apparently rest with the government. Though he favors political decentralization, he wants some type of decentralization more practical than the "surrender of legitimate functions by the national government." [48]

Rossiter agrees with Agar that the American party system is the "price of union," so he is willing to let it alone. In fact, he exhorts Conservatives to emphasize its virtues and explain away its follies.[49] Of course, they can work for more responsible methods and "better" candidates through either party, though his own preference is for the Republicans and for luring the South away from the Democrats.

On civil liberties, Rossiter takes the common Conservative position that freedom is something to be defended, not something to be sought.[50] But he is highly critical of America's failure to "extend justice to the Negro," and he strongly supports the Supreme Court decision on desegregation.

In an early book, Rossiter argued in favor of quasi-dictatorial power for the President during emergencies as long as this power was used to defend the existing order. The crises which would justify such power included war, rebellion, and depression (and why should we not now add inflation?). For ideological justification of this position, he agreed with Lincoln's argument that the purpose of law is to protect the state rather than vice versa, and though Rossiter recognized that this thesis could also be used to justify authoritarianism, he insisted that at least in emergencies it becomes obviously true. Furthermore, though he cites Rome as the original model of constitutional dictatorship, he concludes that in Rome it became an instrument of authoritarianism when Roman wars were no longer of limited duration.[51] (The parallelism, in this respect, to the current situation is interesting).

In a more recent work, he discusses the general increase in the power of the President and the new roles he is expected to play. The changes, he emphasizes, did not occur because of institutional alteration but because of the emergence of new customs, the foundation of which is the fact that the people now expect the President to perform the new functions. The President is now the Manager of prosperity, the Protector *and Expander* of civil liberties, and Protector of peace (which includes acting in droughts, floods, violent strikes, and strikes which interrupt production in wartime or emergencies).[52] Furthermore, Rossiter says, we shall be turning to the President even more in the future, as the economy grows more interdependent, as emergencies increase, and as Congress grows more unwieldly. Since the President, though the partisan political leader of some, is the moral leader of all, since only he can lead Congress, since power can ennoble as well as corrupt, and since the President brings "unity and harmony to a system of diversity and antagonism," these changes are, for Rossiter, apparently not only acceptable but desirable. Of course, he would not want to see the President get too much power, and he is glad that the American system has so many effective checks on him. Although the courts do not provide an effective barrier against the growth of presidential power,[53] Congress the parties, and the administrative services, among others, are real checks on his power. On the other hand, Rossiter wants to increase presidential control of administrative services, and to discourage "excessive" Congressional obstruction. He also stresses the need to have Presidents skilled in political manipulation,[54] though one might suppose that such skill can only reduce political responsibility in a party system which has neither class anchors nor clear ideological standards.

In the writings of Kirk we have already encountered the convenient assumptions that "the family" or religion-in-itself or voluntary groups are inevitably Conservative by nature. But Kirk is obviously uncomfortable about this rationalizing fiction, and he often perceives the real nature of the Conservative social problem. Rossiter's use of the Conservative social concepts is so undiscriminating and vague, however, that he hardly seems aware of Conservative social problems at all.

When he says that the increase in religion, group consciousness, and conformity are promoting Conservatism, he offers no reason why they may not be simply facilitating manipulation. He merely assumes that the changes in American social relations make it unnecessary to worry much about this realm.

Rossiter's economic analysis is equally unrelated to Conservatism. Why should a Conservative be joyous about "diffused property" which includes everything from the family farm in Iowa to stock ownership in General Motors? How can he accept modern industrial society without even bothering to consider whether or not it is compatible with Conservative values? Rossiter throws Peter Drucker's corporatism into his program as one of several alternatives from which a pragmatic choice can be made. But we shall see that Drucker's is a fundamentally different type of Conservatism which requires sweeping changes in the nature of modern industrial relations. Yet unless such changes can be made, the contradictions between Conservative values and industrial society remain insoluble.

When Rossiter insists that only business leaders can provide the class base for an American aristocracy, he never bothers to ascertain whether they can be a *Conservative* aristocracy, though he is aware that some would challenge his view. The fact that second and third generation men of wealth like Nelson Rockefeller and Averell Harriman may devote themselves to "public service" or philanthropy rather than to increasing their fortunes does not mean that their leadership is Conservative. There is not the slightest shred of evidence that these men radiate Conservative moral values throughout the community. On the contrary, they seem to reflect much of the prevailing ethic through their skills in "public relations." Their prestige may emanate from their great wealth or their political acumen, but not from any superior moral code. They have no Conservative program to offer. On the contrary, they are found on opposite sides of the political fence, though at no time in opposition to the prevailing currents of American society. There is not the slightest reason to assume that American millionaires of inherited wealth who turn to political careers are any more Conservative than nineteenth-century British Liberal manufacturers who sat in Parliament or than the equestrian class which held political power in the Roman Empire.

The pressure of foreign affairs, which Rossiter sees as promoting Conservatism, is at least as conducive to authoritarianism. Nor is there any way of distinguishing his position on the role of government from the actual drift of American society towards increasing government authority. He does not discuss the difficulties of supporting both a wide degree of power or responsibility for private groups and final power or responsibility for government. There is nothing, for example, about the problem of inflation, a problem which John Kenneth Galbraith, the originator of the term "countervailing power," admits would upset the whole balance. More important, Rossiter is already attuned ideologically to considerable further extension of the power of government. The implications in the position that government authority may be necessary to control other forms of power and compulsion are virtually unlimited in the direction of authoritarianism. If private corporate and union power aggravate inflation, then what are the justifiable limits on the scope of government action in inflation? If inflation is now becoming a permanent problem, what are the time limits on government action? If the power of a church over the intellectual activities of its members is strong enough to be a form of compulsion, what are the limits on the responsibility of government to restrain that power? If consent to the exercise of such private power legitimizes it, is it legitimate if such consent is motivated by religious fear, and how can this be determined? Naturally, Rossiter would not sanction any of the implications in these questions, but they are available for future use if they should become "necessary." Since Conservatives are not persons to hold that history can be planned and directed by men, the question of what is "necessary" depends on "the way the wind is blowing."

Rossiter's Conservative position on civil liberties is completely incompatible with his attitude towards desegregation and the presidency, and it is untenable as an explanation of the growth of civil liberties in general. How can the right of Negro children to attend desegregated schools in the South be considered as defending an existing liberty? Indeed, if freedom is only something to be defended, why should Negroes have been given citizenship or civil rights or the right to vote in the first place? Russell Kirk is at least consistent in wondering whether the Negro should even have been freed from slavery after the Civil War. Besides, Rossiter accepts as legitimate the new role of the President in expanding as well as defending civil liberties. The fundamental illusion of the Conservatives, however, is to suppose that traditional rights have no beginning, that they "just growed." But the defense of established rights in the mid-twentieth century already includes defense of the whole range of freedom won by Liberals in modern history. There is no reason why a British Conservative should have supported freedom of the press in the eighteenth century, since it was not yet established. By 1950 it was a tradition. If, as Conservatives sometimes infer, freedom of the press could be derived historically from the limited freedom of discussion in the medieval university, then the right of revolution could be derived from trial by combat, or from the freedom of prehistoric man from political authority altogether.

All this is, of course, nonsense, but so is the idea that the history of modern freedom has been simply the defense of existing rights. Furthermore, on the basis of Rossiter's position about the multiple nature of compulsion, one could easily justify the use of government power to restrict discrimination through social pressures, for example, by enforcing desegregation in Southern hotels and restaurants. And, in fact, though he is not too happy about using government power to enforce civil rights, he is prepared to accept anything, from passive acquiescence towards advances in Negro rights to the advocacy of "strong, compulsive action by the federal government," as legitimate Conservative positions. When a man accepts all the civil rights categories that Liberals have been able to think of, and is prepared not only for Liberal interpretations of them as conditions change but also for the use of political power to enforce them, then it becomes quite difficult to understand what distinguishes his position as a Conservative. The only clue Rossiter gives us is that a Conservative must be "a gradualist lest he be a liberal or radical." [55] But aside from the fact that "gradualism" is a tactical and not a valuative concept and could quite validly be adopted by any political group under the sun, how gradual is "gradualism?" By what norm can one decide if the use of troops in Arkansas, three years after the Supreme Court decision, was "gradual?" The fact is that Rossiter's "adjustment," here as elsewhere, carries Conservatism so far that it is, so to speak, open on one end, and there is little limit to the potential distance it can travel in the future.

Rossiter's analysis of the American presidency is the most realistic of any we have considered (though Agar and Viereck might well agree with virtually all of it), but its realism does not make it Conservative. The Liberal elements of his discussion have been omitted as factors which may be assumed. But almost all of the arguments which have been cited are significant because they are concessions to authoritarianism, and the concessions are so broad as to leave the way open for adjustments to considerable further enlargement of executive powers. Most of this is obvious, but it should be pointed out specifically that no type of unity which can be imposed upon a "system of . . . antagonism" could possibly qualify as an example of Conservative harmony. Rossiter takes the trouble to point out that there is a difference between authority and authoritarianism. But this is a half-truth, well designed to cover his own contradictions. When a Conservative accepts increasing measures of centralized political authority as a modification of his Conservative values, this does not make him an authoritarian. But it does mean that he is adopting an increasingly authoritarian kind of Conservatism, and that he should at least attempt to resolve the resultant tensions in his values. Rossiter does not even seem to recognize the problem.

Worse yet, although there is much of both Liberal "checks and balances" and executive authority in his latest book, there is virtually nothing which can even remotely be construed as explicitly Conservative. He is not really following Conservative values when he says that we should avoid tampering promiscuously with established institutions such as the electoral college or the presidential system as a whole Tinkering, he emphasizes, does not really solve the difficult problems and is only likely to create new and greater difficulties for each one it seems to solve. The electoral college balances the overrepresentation of rural areas in our legislatures by overrepresenting the cities, so it is progressive in spite of its apparent inequities. Anyway, he says, the college system has at no time altered anything fundamental in the course of American history. Nor will tinkering reforms change anything essential in the presidential system, and drastic changes do not seem necessary. Since America does not have the conditions which could make a parliamentary system work, we must pay the price of political unaccountability for "safety." [56] Since there is no real choice between "our safeguards and British harmonies," Rossiter tells us, we may as well "relax and enjoy the inevitable." [57] But this analysis is not really Conservative at all. The rejection of "tinkering" does not imply the acceptance of Conservatism, and the preference for "our safeguards" over political responsibility need not be construed as anything but the American form of Liberalism. The thesis that feasible choice lies only between letting a system be or making drastic changes in it when it becomes historically necessary is one which a Marxist might have little difficulty accepting. The only thing Rossiter clearly rejects here is "tinkering," a very special and highly transitory form of Liberalism.

Rossiter's analysis of the presidency is not Conservative even when he says that changes will come through alterations in custom and prescription.[58] When we recall that Rossiter includes as a customary change the popular "expectation" of strong presidential leadership and that this sanctions all the changes in presidential roles which have occurred since Franklin Roosevelt, we are moved to wonder whether custom now means anything more than the prevailing drift. The traditionalism which in Conservative ideology has always meant the accumulation of centuries now means the accumulation of a single generation. But how can we know while the changes are occurring which will become "custom" in the next generation and which will not? Roosevelt's attempt to pack the Supreme Court failed, but it did help force the "adjustment" of the Court to the New Deal. Does this justify the attempt? On the basis of Rossiter's standards, what position should the Conservative have taken at the time the issue was raised? If, as he has explicitly admitted, the changes of one generation become the Conservative traditions of the next, what limits can there be on the attempted changes? When we consider his analysis as a whole, he makes out an excellent case for the thesis that we should be prepared for continual adjustment to increases in presidential power. If we should reach a point where a further quantitative increase is equivalent to a fundamental qualitative change (to authoritarianism, let us say), then we might remember Rossiter's warning that law is made to protect the state, especially in time of crisis (and what period of drastic change is not a time of crisis?). But what became of Conservatism?

The fact is that there is no way of telling whether Rossiter is really a Conservative who has adjusted to Liberal values or a defensive Liberal who thinks he can strengthen his case by arguing from Conservative premises. Yet, the difference between liberal Conservatism and conservative Liberalism is not one of mere hair-splitting, whether we consider their "classical" or their contemporary American formulations. Burke's liberal Conservatism held that a fairly wide measure of freedom to satisfy individual desires could be granted without upsetting the essential Conservative harmony of British society, and that it *should* be granted as long as it did not distrub that harmony.

On the other hand, conservative Liberalism, in John Locke for example, maintained that many of the existing traditions could be continued as long as they did not seem excessively repressive of the need for freedom. The mere fact that these two positions could coalesce at a given period of history, let us say sometime in the eighteenth century, must not obscure the fact that a century or so later the adherents of each theory were at diametrically opposite poles. Those who tried to adhere consistently to Conservatism (Coleridge and Scott, for example) found it necessary to call for a halt in the widening realm of individual freedom, which was in fact upsetting the older harmony of the society. Those who followed in the Liberal stream found it necessary to call for the increasing rejection of traditions, because these were in fact becoming burdens on individual freedom.

The defensive conservative Liberalism of contemporary America seeks to protect existing individual rights and Liberal institutions rather than to extend freedom. Those liberal Conservatives who are now willing to adjust can accept these values and institutions, provided that they also admit that such institutions are lesser evils rather than positive goods. But Rossiter's position is a kind of "no-man's land" between the two ideologies because it virtually obliterates all distinction between them.* A Conservatism that is prepared to be enthusiastic about Liberal institutions simply because they are established, and to "adopt" other classes because it has none of its own, is not even an ideology—it is a totally blind and passive inertia, and its reasoning is mere rationalization. When, to make things worse, Liberals are converted into Conservatives by fiat, simply because they do not want to destroy their own

* If Rossiter is really a defensive Liberal who is relying on Conservative arguments, then he is open to the charge of having deprived Liberalism of any real defense. If, as he has claimed, the "conservative" should try to prove that "whatever is, is right," (*Conservatism in America*, p. 271) then he has no argument against *any* changes, once they occur. (See Chapter VIII.) But if he does not intend to identify himself with Conservatism, then why does he begin with Burkean Conservatism and insist on drawing periodic inspiration from it, in spite of his intention to reject Burke?

institutions and traditions (of which private property is the
most preeminent), then we must conclude that the Conservatives feel so desperately "the need to belong" that they are willing to desert to the enemy if only they can convince themselves
that it is the foe who has really surrendered in his heart.
Speaking magisterially for "the Conservative," Rossiter produces the following:

> He wants it clearly understood that some of his ideas are private
> property. If the Liberal wants to share them, he will first have to
> abandon Liberalism. Certainly the Liberal cannot challenge the
> Conservative's peculiar claim to the preference for liberty over
> equality, emphasis on constitutionalism rather than democracy, fear
> of majority rule . . . and devotion to the rights of property.[59]

A long list of converts to "Conservatism," from Voltaire to Jefferson and Gladstone, has thus been made by a stroke of the
pen. And although Rossiter does not identify himself with
"capital-C Conservatism," he nowhere repudiates this particular confusion, which is endemic to his whole book.

   Rossiter's bewildering identification of Conservatism with a
defense of any established tradition is explicit in his admission
that the progressive attacks of one generation often become the
Conservative defenses of the next.[60] Not unexpectedly, John
Crowe Ransom (who has become "adjusted" in recent years)
uses this conclusion as an argument against Russell Kirk.[61] But
which is the better Conservatism: one which refuses to abandon its standards even if this means being isolated from reality,
or one which adjusts to reality at the expense of its standards?
The only tenable answer is that neither is "better" and that the
very terms of the choice indicate the insoluble nature of the
American Conservative dilemma. But each side runs from
the problem and seeks refuge in illusion, Kirk by reinterpreting reality and the "adjusted" group by reinterpreting Conservatism. If Kirk insists that the American tradition is Conservative, Rossiter admits that it is Liberal but insists that defending it is Conservatism, even if it is changing with each

generation. If Kirk can find solace in the delusion that an intellectual aristocracy can rise on a lower middle-class base, Rossiter calls for political leadership by multimillionaires who have real power already, and then jubilantly concludes that this is Conservatism.

But Rossiter's analysis is important because it reveals most clearly that a truly adjusted Conservative in America must adjust to authoritarianism as well as to Liberalism. This is not surprising since much of contemporary American Liberalism has made the same adjustment, and a historically relevant Conservatism must not appear to be less "realistic" than Liberalism. Hallowell's partial adoption of Aristotle; Agar's acceptance of force as an indication of historical "inevitability" and his acceptance of transition to a world he dislikes as long as the transition occurs "without anyone realizing it"; Viereck's justification of any changes which prevent revolutions; and Rossiter's acceptance of the changes of each generation as "custom"—all these are compatible with Rossiter's conclusion that a forward-looking Conservatism must be prepared to support further increases in the authority of government in general and of the President in particular, based, among other things, on the capacity for political manipulation and support by "big business." The "adjusted" Conservatives have accepted Liberal democracy, but like a new Middle Stoa, they are also prepared for a more authoritarian future.

Realistic about American society, Rossiter is also realistic about the "adjusted" Conservative. "The new conservative's mood," he confides, "will not be a harmonious unity of habits and humors; his mind will display its share of inconsistencies, contradictions, and tensions." [62] This statement merits our unreserved concurrence, since almost everything we have examined in his position illustrates it. But if any lingering doubt remains on this score, we may note three particularly disquieting statements:

(1) [The] conservative message [is] that the equation of human liberty balances emancipation with order, confidence with caution,

experiment with experience, adventure with steady habits, self-expression with self-discipline, idealism with realism.[63]

(2) In the field of education, the new conservatism can steer a steady course down the middle—between Deweyites and anti-Deweyites, vocationalists and generalists, all-out democrats and unrealistic elitists, traditionalists and progressives, sectarians and secularists, advocates of "moral education" and advocates of studied indifference. . . .[64] [Russell Kirk finds this passage particularly unnerving.]

(3) There will be room in the camp of the new conservatism for wide differences of economic view. Both . . . the critic of bigness in business and . . . the apologist for it will be made welcome. So too will . . . the critic of factory sociology and many of the men he condemns so forcefully. The only tests for admission should be earnest devotion to "private enterprise regulated fairly in the public interest" and willingness to face new facts about the economy and set new social goals for it.[65] ["Factory sociology" here refers especially to Peter Drucker's corporatism.]

It is clear that there can be no objection to Rossiter's conclusion on the contradictions of the "New Conservatism." But one must object most strenuously to his rationalization that classical Conservative ideology reacts with indifference "to charges of inconsistency" because of its concern with the practical.[66] From Burke's proud defense of consistency as his "highest virtue," Conservatism has now come to this. And what are we to make of a Conservatism which is prepared to admit that perhaps Conservatives should always be in the minority?[67] Here is an ideology which has adjusted itself so far that it is questionable whether it has any objective content left.

Yet if Rossiter's is the most extreme and explicit form of Conservative adjustment, is there any place where this adjustment can logically be stopped once it has started? Rossiter, like all contemporary Conservatives, rejects the new American ethic which David Riesman has described. But it would now be illuminating to recall for a moment what Riesman's "other-directed" men are really like. What is common to them, he says, is that

their contemporaries are the source of direction for [them]. . . .
The goals toward which the other-directed person strives shift with

[guidance from contemporaries]; it is only the process of . . . paying close attention to the signals from others that remains unaltered throughout life.[68]

The primary need of the "other-directed" man is therefore to develop a kind of psychic radar system capable of receiving the signals, Riesman says. If this is inapplicable as a description of the "adjusted" Conservatives, it is only because their radar operates with a time lag of a few years. But little is really lost since they all insist on the vital importance of the "Liberals" in our "Conservative" American society, and presumably the "Liberal" radar is up-to-date. From Hallowell to Rossiter the New Conservatism is a study in the process of "group adjustment," and with each gradation in adjustment another piece of Conservative ideology is reinterpreted into its opposite. Apparently unable to escape the Conservative conscience completely, they convince themselves that society itself is at last becoming Conservative. But Rossiter simultaneously insists that Conservatism must adjust both to America and to the mid-twentieth century. If the "other-directed," "over-adjusted," "organization" man is the symbol of up-to-date-America, then he has succeeded in the adaptation. After a long and arduous journey away from the history of his country and century, the American Conservative can at last come to rest. He "belongs!"

VII

The New Conservatism:

Corporatist Utopia

The schizophrenia of American Burkean Conservatism lies in its total inability to integrate its values with reality. The reactionary Conservatives, obscure though their presentation of Burke may be, remain reasonably faithful to the values of their tradition. But they have been completely incapable of developing a feasible program for the realization of their values. This is not a temporary phenomenon or a result of the fact that the "master" Conservative thinker has not yet appeared on the scene, as Kirk hopefully suggests. It is a necessary result of the historical dilemma in which these Conservatives find themselves.

It is clear that the relatively harmonious conditions of the Middle Ages have been over for a long time. But in spite of all the mental gyrations of the contemporary Conservatives, it is also clear that the historical conditions to which a Burkean ideology could feasibly belong are also confined to the past, and probably never existed in America. The Burkean position made sense only as long as there seemed to be some ground for thinking that Conservative social values were still stronger in the existing society than Liberal economic values. Since it is obvious that no Conservative can claim this to be true of contemporary America, the entire Burkean thesis has become untenable. Even the fragmentation within reactionary Conservatism bears witness to its ineffectiveness. It is not simply that no two of them say the same thing. The telling defect is that the difference between them have been fundamental and irreconcilable. The mutual opposition of harmony and morality, which pinpointed the difference between Southern agrarians and "Northern" reactionaries, was an unbridgeable contradiction. Even with the passing of the agrarians from the scene, the continued emphasis of the Kirk group on morality rather than harmony indicates that they can no longer find harmony in the real world. The inability to formulate a program which is both intelligible and relevant to their ideological values makes it clear that the historical "day" of the Burkeans is over. When the connection between values and reality is severed, then the only activity left for the adherents of the values is criticism. The path is open for a Conservatism of alienation which will frankly abandon practical hope of improvement.

If the inability to put values into practice shows that the values have no relevance for a particular period of history, the mere capacity to be "practical" or "realistic" does not in itself prove one's ideological predilections to be correct. The potential dichotomy between values and reality works both ways. Although the "adjusted" Conservatives begin with Burkean values, they end with non-Burkean conclusions. But a willingness to adjust to the changes of reality at the cost of abandoning values still indicates that the values are now unrealizable. No amount of bravado about facing up to contradictions can hide the impossible position of the adjusted Conservatives. The often-heard argument about the inescapability of contradictions in "real life" is an easy rationalization for a bewildered ideology, and may have propaganda appeal for a "practical-minded" society. But as a serious intellectual position it borders on inanity. If it means that one can never find the realization of a single value in society without admixture of contrary values, then the argument is a pointless truism, recognized by every ideology in history. If it means that, although the value which one affirms to be of prime importance over all others exists as an obscure segment of reality, one can still act as though it were in fact paramount, then the argument is nothing but another obscurantist smoke screen. We always come back to the same conclusion—the adjusted Conservatives have separated "theory" and "practice" just as decisively as the reactionary Conservatives, though in reverse. There is nothing necessarily wrong with the adjustedness itself, as long as they admit that their values recede with each adjustment and do not pretend that they speak as Conservatives when they advocate adjusting.

In a sense, the confusions of adjusted Conservatism began with Burke's own erroneous assumptions that a Conservative could consistently adjust to changing historical reality. The dichotomy between reactionary and adjusted Conservatism reflects the original contradictions in the "source" of modern Conservatism. But the very fact that the Burkean descendants have now split into a reactionary ideology and a "practical" one, prepared to adjust even to authoritarian changes, is clear proof of the historical irrelevance of Burkean Conservatism. The fact also that there is no more compelling reason to adopt one position than the other and that their respective adherents can have made their choice only because of personal interest or temperament is all the more proof of the irrelevance. Once the relation between value and reality is decisively broken it does not really matter which one is falsified to maintain the illusion of integration. If it gives them a feeling of being intellectually active, they can go on debating this question indefinitely.

In the meantime, however, final intellectual proof of the need to speak of Burkean ideology in the past tense is provided by the appearance on the American scene of fundamentally different historical "types" of Conservatism. Although both Peter Drucker and Reinhold Niebuhr retain varying amounts of Liberalism in their respective positions, they represent Conservative responses to history whose very nature necessarily implies the passing of the Burkean context. Drucker's approach to contemporary society is a return not to Burke's principles but to Plato's; and Niebuhr's theoretical model is St. Augustine. The frequent indiscriminate inclusion of these men in the catch-all category of "New Conservatives" only makes it clear that the contemporary Burkeans do not even understand themselves, let alone their relation to the world around them. Unlike the Burkeans, these men are concerned with sweeping changes in the nature of contemporary society. But the changes which they advocate are designed to promote Conservative values, not mere adjustment to current drift.

The Reappearance of the Platonic Problem

It should not be supposed that the American exponents of Platonic Conservatism always identify themselves as Platonists or even that their theoretical premises are in fact purely Platonic. On the contrary, we shall see that there are crucial differences between their ideology and Plato's, forced on them by the altered historical context of twentieth century America. In spite of these differences, however, their problems, their aims, their solutions, and their dilemmas are at bottom the same as Plato's, and the changes which history has forced on them has only made their task infinitely more difficult than that of Plato.

The basic historical fact which Plato faced was that the age-old traditions on which Conservatism depended were no longer effective, and that his world was irretrievably different from that of the past. Since the ancient traditions no longer dominated society, since therefore there could be no identity of tradition and harmony, it was necessary to arrive at the concept of harmony through a process of abstraction and to think in purely rational terms of the prerequisites for a harmonious world. The distinctive features of these contemporary "Platonists" is that they also no longer find it possible to pretend that actual traditions contain the realization of Conservative goals. There is no hedging in their admission, indeed their insistence, that the world has changed so decisively that Conservatism must return to its first principles and think its problems through in totally new forms. We shall see that in this process of reevaluation the unsolved dilemma of Plato recurs in modern form; that they escape from the contradictions of conflicting traditions and "gradual" adjustment to Liberalism or authoritarianism only to be forced in the end to rely completely on repressive authority; and that the modern form of their position only compounds their difficulties.

But our first concern is to emphasize that the nature of this historical "type" of Conservatism is fundamentally at variance with the other contemporary types which we have considered. The transition even from the adjusted group is not a quantitative one of degree of adjustedness but a qualitative one in which the entire context and outlook have been transformed. Although the other New Conservatives are cautious in their evaluation of a man like Peter Drucker, it is only the fact that they avoid a real analysis of the nature of his position which enables them to pretend that the differences between them are merely minor differences in the interpretation of contemporary facts. As usual their tendency to use amorphous categories of thought only perpetuates the illusion that there is a single "Conservatism" in contemporary America, and beclouds the fact that once Conservatism has made the transition to Drucker's assumptions there can be no return to Burke.

In Drucker's earliest work, he attributed the cause of fascism to the collapse of Liberal democracy. Freedom and equality, which presumably had been Europe's ideals since the rise of Christianity, could be developed no further within existing societal forms. Fascism was the result of the failure of Liberalism, of the negativity of its theory, of its inability to build new societal forms to replace those of the medieval system it had destroyed, and of its concept of "Economic Man" as the essence of human aspirations. Liberal capitalism had promised not mere profit alone, Drucker says, but the expectation that the profit system would lead to ever-widening freedom and equality.[1] Contrary to its promise, the profit system had produced an industrial society which required stratification and social discipline. As long as capitalism seemed to maximize individual freedom and equality of opportunity, its Liberal property system made sense to the society. But as property has become only a means to privilege and as social mobility from the lower classes fell off, the system has come to seem like an irrational fiction. That the conditions of the lower classes have improved is unimportant compared with the loss of faith in the capacity of Liberal capitalist-democracy to fulfill its promises. Fascism actually occurred only in those Western countries where the roots of Liberal democracy were shallow, where Liberalism had only been secondary to the force of nationalism, but the crisis which its advent exposed was one which every Western country faced, even though the inertia of long-established forms might prolong the façade of Liberalism after its content had disappeared.

"Christian" (that is, Conservative) critics of Liberalism and capitalism had long understood the nature of the developing crisis, Drucker says. He traces this line of criticism from the French counterrevolutionary de Maistre to the German corporatist von Ketteler, both nineteenth-century ideologists. But the churches, he emphasizes, really had no feasible solution for the problems. They tried only to restore feudalism, to apply old forms to new problems, and to combine a potentially radical program with the continued support of reactionary churchgoers. They wanted to make the churches a new force without surrendering their position in the old order, not understanding that religion becomes a constructive force only after its forms have been destroyed. The failure of the churches to provide real alternatives for Europe, he continues, makes it clear that the fascist crisis was not due merely to the "godless spirit" of the age but to fundamental problems for which no real solution had been worked out. Nor were secular Conservatives of the early twentieth century, such as Gilbert Keith Chesterton in England or Henry Adams in America, able to produce any realistic solutions; and while the revival of religious orthodoxy may give some sense of peace to the individual, it cannot recreate society or make community life sensible even for its supporters.[2]

In his next book, Drucker carried this analysis further. A fundamental historical change occurred in the shift from the capitalist "mercantile society" to the new "industrial society," he says. But while the reality was now industrial, the institutional forms were still mercantile, in spite of the fact that mercantile society had stopped "functioning" by 1918. A "functioning" society means for Drucker one which gives the individual a meaningful and rational status based on his societal function. Society must also be based on commonly accepted values, but though Drucker leaves no doubt that orthodox Christianity is for him the correct value, he emphasizes that a society can function on the basis of any values provided they make sense to the individual. Furthermore, since values can be realized only through the society, the problems of function and of social status remain his primary interest. He is also concerned that societal power be "legitimate," by which he means that it be justifiable on the basis of the specific beliefs of the society and exercised in the interest of the ruled, because illegitimate power must always depend on pure force and repression. Without a sense of social status the society will become repressive because its members will become "masses," and masses can only express themselves through tyrants.[3]

The capitalist mercantile system functioned as long as it could make wealth and property the basis of prestige and status and could integrate men through the market system. It was legitimate as long as social and economic power centered in the market and as long as political power corresponded to this reality. But the market system is no longer the center of power, wealth can no longer be accepted as the basis of status, and mercantile capitalism can no longer integrate men. The corporation has replaced the manor and the market as the basic socio-economic institution. The corporation is the first really autonomous institution to arise in the modern state, Drucker emphasizes, because it arose from the free contract, and not from the granting of exclusive government privileges as the early monopolistic corporations of the modern state did. But the corporation no longer depends on private property, because its stockholders are interested only in dividends rather than in their corporate rights, and the corporation no longer needs the individual stockholder as a source of capital.[4] Yet the law does not recognize that it is control of the corporation rather than ownership which now determines power. Thus, while the corporation has become the modern reality, the societal forms and beliefs are still those of the mercantile age. The result is that corporate power is neither functional, responsible, nor legitimate.

For these problems the romantic European Conservatives of the nineteenth century offered no solution, for they could only look backward to the mirage of the Middle Ages. But Burke was not a mere traditionalist, since he "ruthlessly discarded" traditions when he saw that they did not work. He understood that because man is imperfect he cannot foresee the future and must therefore accept the present reality. This is true also, Drucker finds, of American "Conservatism" because it was the American Revolution and the "Conservative" Founding Fathers that translated Burke's ideas into reality. Neither Burke nor the American Fathers tried to restore the past, because they knew that the reality of the present had changed, and, Drucker affirms, the true Conservative always agrees with the true revolutionary on the facts. What he seeks is to integrate a new society on the basis of the old principles.[5]

We can agree with Drucker that Burke was not simply a traditionalist and that tradition is not necessarily identical with Conservatism. But it is not true to say that Burke would have been prepared to abandon tradition altogether and accept revolutionary change or that the American Revolution and Constitution translated his ideas into reality, and we shall return to both these subjects in a later chapter.* Our interest here, however, is in the nature of Drucker's position. The acceptance of

* See Chapter IX.

"revolutionary" facts, the rejection of old forms, and the abstraction of Conservative principles from concrete traditions of the past—these are the essential elements of the Platonic setting, in spite of the fact that Drucker thinks he is following Burke. With the transition to Drucker we have passed irrevocably into the twentieth century and to a different Conservatism.

Platonic Conservatism had already made its appearance in twentieth-century America in the ideology of George Santayana. Unlike Drucker, Santayana knew that he was a Platonist and began with articulately Platonic premises. His concern was not with tradition as such but with reason, and the aim which he assigned to reason was to harmonize man's natural impulses. The goal of man for him was to use reason to achieve the blissful state of equilibrium which animals achieve instinctively, to find peace, even nirvana, the Buddhist state of bliss in which all desire ceases. Santayana also saw that the kind of harmony he wanted was virtually absent from the modern world. But what distinguished him (and other contemporary Platonists) from his original Platonic model was that he accepted not only harmony but also the freedom "which liberates human imagination" as his key values. In this sense, although harmony remains the ultimate criterion of value, the impact of Liberalism on Conservatism has been a permanent one. The attempt to combine these two values, however, produced an apparently insoluble tension in Santayana's thought. In his more optimistic early works, the final ideal for society was a democratic "timocracy" based not only on Conservative "merit" but on the substitution of free and equal opportunity for hereditary rule. Such a system would have to be based on a new kind of societal organization, rooted in unions and new "guilds." [6] But his final conclusion even here was that such a society would have to curb freedom, and since this would arouse the opposition of those incapable of appreciating moral perfection, it was not likely to succeed. By the time he wrote his last major analysis of society, however, he no longer held any hope at all for the realization of his ideals. The human tragedy, he said in this last work, is that man can perceive the need for harmony, but can never really achieve it. He presented his ideal as simply a "preference for harmony in strength, no matter how short-lived," [7] but expected to find this ideal primarily in artistic beauty rather than societal relations, and saw in philosophy only a means of consolation.

Santayana and Drucker were both born in Europe, but they differed from their "corporatist" European counterparts in placing much greater emphasis on the value of freedom. European corporatism, at least in the nineteenth century, also sought to restore societal harmony through the framework of the modern corporation, but it had little to say about freedom, and both the classes and forms of corporatist organization were still largely medieval. European corporatists therefore expected much more harmony in society than did Santayana. Drucker even rejects the form of corporatism which can be found in the papal encyclicals, on the grounds that it is applicable only to pre-industrial countries such as Portugal.

What distinguishes Drucker in particular from Santayana as well as European corporatists is his insistence that any feasible societal organization must now make provisions for permanent economic expansion. Because he accepts economic expansion as an essential value of the modern world, he is not very harsh in his historical evaluation of Liberal capitalism as long as it continued to function. He agrees that it performed the invaluable service of making wealth potentially plentiful. He even claims that it made men less mercenary by making wealth more easily available. [8] Now that man has learned the secret of production, the task, as Drucker sees it, is to build a new "functioning society" without abandoning productivity and expansion. Unlike the earlier European corporatists who wanted to freeze societal functions, to preserve disappearing classes such as the peasantry, and to ignore the question of increasing productivity, Drucker insists that a fluid socio-economic structure is still vital and that no group should be immunized against technological change, though the impact should be cushioned.

Unlike Santayana, he sees nothing necessarily repulsive about industrialization itself. Drucker's is a highly realistic, modernized, and Americanized brand of corporatism.

We should, at this point, dwell for a moment on the meaning of the term "corporatism" as it has been used here. It is especially important to distinguish "corporatism" from the "corporate state." What is common to them both is acceptance of the corporation as the basic social unit. But the fascist corporate state seeks to impose political power on this social unit, while corporatism seeks to make political power dependent on it for legitimation. The elevation of social relations to the ascendant position in society has been a basic characteristic of Conservatism since Plato. Drucker does not, like the European corporatists, want to organize all socio-economic productive units into national political "corporations" or to base governmental authority on them, but he does want the social community of the corporation to be the dominant element of society, and we shall see that his position does really demand a change of political forms.

Peter Drucker: Industrial Platonist

Drucker considers freedom to be a permanent element of Conservatism. Its origin, he says, is in the Christian concept of man as a creature who knows there is right and wrong but who is imperfect and must therefore be free to choose the right in concrete problems. The principle of political freedom assumes that we cannot know what kind of government will be good, because good government depends on intangible factors such as the moral character of society and the genius of individual statesmen. But freedom is not just the negative idea of the absence of restraint; it also connotes the positive participation of the citizen. Burke developed the idea of mixed government, as well as consent and property, as limitations on government power; [9] but he also understood the need for positive participation and for a functioning society as a primary need, distinct from freedom. The American Revolution translated Burke's ideas into reality, both here and in England, where the king was forced to abandon pretensions to arbitrary power. It was also successful in solving an old Conservative problem: the separation of "political government" and "social rule." St. Augustine was the first to achieve this in what later became the medieval separation of church and state—the doctrine of the Two Swords. Sir Edward Coke later achieved a similar separation of government power and the traditional common law. But until the eighteenth century the separation had always led in practice to the supremacy of one sphere over the other. The American Revolution for the first time brought the two spheres into actual balance by making the market system into the "socially constitutive sphere" and by balancing private property against majority consent.[10]

Drucker's identification of Burke's mixed government and the American system of checks and balances is only one of a number of misinterpretations of Burke, but these are of little concern to us now. Several points, however, are of some importance. In the first place, while the concept of "positive freedom" contrasts appealingly with "negative freedom," it has no clear content and is apt to have no relation to individualism or Liberal values. "Negative freedom," that is, freedom from restraints, is a clearly individualistic idea which affirms an ethical "right" to oppose society. The aim of "positive freedom," on the other hand, is to minimize the conflicts between the individual and society. The question of how this is to be done is one way of stating the fundamental issue of political theory. The concept of communal harmony was Plato's answer to this question and is, of course, that of Conservatism in general. When Drucker says we need local self-governing groups to maximize individual participation and hence positive freedom, he means, as we shall see, that the crucial categories of social integration will be status, function, harmony, and a fundamental delineation of authority which will in reality leave only a limited sphere in which individual choice will matter. Since it turns out that "positive freedom" means

Conservatism, it is clear that such terms must always be read cautiously.

Secondly, Drucker's discussions obscure his concern for maintaining the supremacy of "social rule." His apparent acceptance of economic relations as the basis of social power is really limited to a period of history which he regards as closed, and is due to his accepting the achievements of that period as the starting point of contemporary society. Except for this bygone era of Liberal capitalism, Drucker rejects the concept of "Economic Man." Furthermore, though he says that political and social power should be separated and praises the American Revolution for "balancing" the two, he does not fail to add later that they must both serve the same societal end. He goes on to say that we do not know yet what this end will be, but that it will certainly not be economic.[11] However, his subsequent analyses make it clear that his preference is for "Social Man" as the common value. Thus through a highly circuitous process of reasoning, Drucker finally arrives at the point from which he really started: the need for the supremacy of social power.

Thirdly, the appeal of the American Revolution for him and the rejection of the question of "good government" as an irrelevant "Platonic" problem only becloud the real nature of his position. At several other points Drucker takes the trouble to criticize Plato, often as a "totalitarian" and once as a "rationalist liberal." We have seen the irrelevance of totalitarianism as descriptive of Platonic theory, and it is obviously absurd to refer to him as a "rationalist liberal." But this is due to Drucker's linking of rationalism, abstract Liberalism, and totalitarianism as inherently interrelated categories. There is a recurrent Conservative error here which Drucker should be the last to make, and which in fact he nullifies by the use he makes of the American Revolution. Rationalism—the use of abstract reason to propose alterations in society—is the natural approach of any critical ideology to a period of profound change, when the institutionalization of one's values can no longer depend on existing relationships. Plato, Hobbes, Marx, and the French eighteenth-century Liberals were all rationalists in this sense because each faced a revolutionary situation in terms of his own values, though the values were different in each case. We shall see that it is impossible to distinguish between French, British, and American Liberalism in terms of their values and that attempts to do so in terms of Burkean theory are self-contradictory. The essential historical difference between them is that British Liberalism developed very early and with relatively less upheaval of institutions and traditions; that American Liberalism had only to fight outside domination and did not have to fight its past at all; that French Liberalism was abstract because France was not a Liberal society and that it was ultimately violent because of the strength of the forces which opposed it. There is hence no necessary relation between rationalism and Liberalism. Liberalism is distinguished by its values, while rationalism is a response to particular historical problems.

Nevertheless, rationalism is not a comfortable mode of expression for Conservatism, because it implies the severance of traditions from values, a separation which in turn implies the Platonic dilemma. Conservatism almost always insists that the building of an effective tradition requires protracted periods of time and that attempts to shorten the time are self-defeating because they require the use of coercive power. Drucker's dilemma is that he necessarily takes both sides of this question. He knows that traditions need time to develop, but he insists that there is little time in which to solve the contemporary problems, and that there are few desirable traditions left. His disavowal of Platonism and his attraction to the American Revolution are expressions of this dilemma. According to Drucker, Platonism is bad because it is rationalist and rationalism implies upheaval and coercion. But the real achievement of the American Revolution was that it developed a "new society and new values without social revolution, decades of civil war, or totalitarian tyranny." The Platonic "question of good government" is irrelevant, but the question of "positive freedom" is crucial. We must use present institutions as much as possible but there will still be plenty to build and cut.[12] No matter how Drucker tries to straddle this problem we always come back to the same conclusion: except for the inclusion of "negative freedom" and economic expansion, Drucker's position and problems are essentially Platonic.

However, Drucker's analysis of the problems of contemporary society is realistic from the Conservative point of view, even if incomplete. Political power has become increasingly dominant, he points out, as the social sphere has failed to solve the problems of status and function. The real world revolution has not been in machinery, but in the organization of people for production in factories. Hence the shattering impact on traditional relations. The emotional significance of the family may have increased in recent times, but only because the divorce of the family from the process of work has made it functionally irrelevant and weak.[13] The essential social and economic unit of our time is the corporation, which sets the pace for contemporary society, even though it does not yet pervade all fields. There is no way of returning to the earlier society, because the big enterprise cannot be allowed to collapse without inviting disaster. It is the enterprise as a permanent institution which has become the supreme reality, far overshadowing the importance of any of its components.[14]

The corporation has achieved a kind of integration of its members, but in its hierarchy those furthest from the top have the most difficulty in making sense or purpose out of its operation. There is no real harmony among the industrial classes; labor, white-collar, management, and investors. Each has its own way of looking at the corporation, its income, and its process of work. The investor is interested only in dividends and expects them to be paid in proportion to current profits. The worker is more interested in secure and predictable wage income and needs it most in bad years when profits are low. Therefore, attempts to integrate workers by profit-sharing plans which distribute dividends to the individual worker are pointless, because the worker's attitude towards dividends would still conflict with his attitude as stockholder. Management wants high salaries, regardless of profit or tax rates, because in our society high salaries are symbols of status and authority. The worker thinks only in terms of his immediate job and the people working alongside him. The supervisors of the industrial white-collar or "middle" class think in terms of specific departments or functions. Only top management thinks in terms of the over-all performance of the enterprise, including its general economic aspects.[15] The investor is not really concerned with the enterprise as an institution at all. Each group mingles socially only with its own kind, and this tends to prevent movement within the enterprise from one class to a higher one. The prerequisite for joining management is experience in viewing the enterprise as a whole, but none of the other levels can acquire such experience either socially or on the job. The tendency is therefore to bring candidates for management in from the outside, from the brighter college graduates, and to groom them for management from the beginning.[16] Each group thus gets the feeling that opportunity is disappearing, although objectively there is more than ever. Since status in the enterprise tends to determine the total social status of its members, the impact of this feeling is intense.

The worker, Drucker continues, tends to be unhappy in his work because most jobs are overspecialized and increase fatigue by gearing movements to those of the slowest man in the line.[17] Furthermore, he says, there tends to be little relationship between a man's work and his personality needs, because personality needs cannot really be measured by objective tests. Only within the union does the worker acquire a sense of purpose and status as well as opportunities for advancement. But the union for these reasons becomes an opposition power which rejects the corporation and its purpose (or lack of purpose). In addition to this, the union is essential for the worker in his fight for security, but here too the problem is primarily a social one, because the most serious effect of unemployment lies in its destruction of all sense of status and societal identification. For the new "middle" class also the work process is unsatisfying. The worker can at least identify his contribution in the finished product, but for administrative personnel this is much more difficult because their contribution is intangible. Furthermore, the workers can at least have some meaningful social contact with each other on the job, but the supervisors and administrators often work outside their own group and with rank-and-file laborers, by whom they are regarded with hostility. The easiest psychic compensation for them is to become "bullies," but this only aggravates the hostility and the sense of isolation.[18] The purely economic problems, those of the division of the income "pie" among the various classes, Drucker regards as of least significance.

It is in this context of social alienation, Drucker insists, that the problem of the growing politicization of society be understood. As the individual loses his identification with society on the one hand while the industrial need for social discipline and cohesion increases on the other, the only way out is through the intensified use of political power. In this sense, Drucker admits that the process of politicization is itself an admission of Conservative failure, and the advent of socialism in Europe and other parts of the world is one of the measures of this failure.[19] But in the United States, with its "conservative" revolutionary tradition, the process can still be stopped, and if the solution can be achieved here it will have world-wide repercussions. Many of the preconditions for solution already exist, Drucker finds. We need only channel them in the right direction.

The basic concept which Drucker applies to all these problems is that of Conservative harmony. He defines harmony as the condition in which the interests of different societal groups coincide. The essential societal categories are status and function, because these are terms of belonging and harmony, and because they resolve the conflict between the claims of the individual and those of the group. Without acknowledging the

Platonic source of these ideas, he takes the trouble to reject what he thinks is Plato's assumption that *total* harmony can actually be achieved.[20] All his postwar books are concerned with the application of these concepts to the contemporary corporation.

According to Drucker's postwar analysis the distinguishing characteristic of industrial society is that it subordinates the social function of its key societal unit (the corporation) to the economic function. This is different from both the medieval system, which reversed the relationship, and the capitalist market system, which separated the two functions. The reason for this shift is that for the first time economic change occurs by increased productivity, that is, expansion from within the economic system itself. Because of this supremacy of the economic function, the managerial wielders of socio-political power cannot always rule in the interests of the "ruled" classes, but must be responsible first for the economic survival of the enterprise. Aside from the question of status, this concern for economic survival over the workers' interests is the under-lying power motivation for the emergence of unions.[21] Further-more, the economic survival of the individual enterprise must be subordinate to the economic expansion of the society.

If these dichotomies were unbridgeable, there would be no solution to conflict, except through political power, but each in fact rests on a foundation of potential harmony. The con-temporary profit system ensures that the individual enterprise will be judged on the basis of its compatibility with society's need for economic efficiency. It does not matter that profit no longer has the same significance it had in classical capitalism, that is, as an individual motivation. Its importance now is that is provides an objective yardstick by which to judge the performance of the enterprise, and that it channels the drives for power and prestige into constructive paths. It provides the standard in an expanding society which tradition provides in a static society. But the criterion of profitability does not mean that the enterprise must necessarily have an income surplus;

it simply means that it must not have continual loss, because loss would indicate failure to measure up to the current economic standard.[22] The price system makes possible the measurement and integration of individual desires. It does not matter that neither the profit system nor the price system operates perfectly, because no economic system ever has. As for the divergence of economic interests within the enterprise and the conflicts over division of authority, these can be minimized if the common social interests can be maximized, because while the primary interest of the enterprise as a whole is economic, that of its members is social.[23]

It is with this problem of harmony within the enterprise that Drucker is primarily concerned. The major proposals that he makes are the following:

1. Training, employment, work speed, and rhythm should be varied, as much as possible, for each individual.[24]

2. Workers and supervisors should be taught the importance of their contributions to the finished product and the importance of the product in the life of society. By learning to look at the enterprise as a whole, they will understand the function of management, and this will give managers what they really want—the status of a "genuine aristocracy." [25]

3. Worker and white-collar "plant communities" should be formed and entrusted with social decisions (about recreation, cafeterias, etc.) and control of guaranteed annual wage funds, the latter subject to managerial veto. Personnel problems should be decided by the "communities" and management jointly, subject to negotiation. The elected leaders of the communities will thus acquire experience in exercising authority, and this will make them candidates for promotion to the managerial ranks.[26]

4. The worker really wants status and predictable wages for himself and the men who work alongside him. High wages are only secondary. If a guaranteed annual wage were coupled with government unemployment compensation, full income

could be guaranteed for half of the labor force and a two-thirds income for another quarter of it. This would be enough to give the entire labor force a feeling of security. It is essential, however, to have an escape clause for periods of falling profit in the individual enterprise or the whole economy. On the other hand, managerial income should also be geared to profit by fixing salaries at multiples of wage categories and having additional bonuses depend on over-all profit. Drucker also hints that dividends to stockholders may have to be confined to a kind of "service fee," since the providers of capital no longer perform the same kind of economic functions they once did.[27]

5. Wage negotiations on the industry-wide level should be tied to a flexible, objective standard such as the cost of living, profits, or productivity.[28]

6. Government cannot prevent depression because its sensitivity to pressure groups hinders it from controlling the booms before depressions. Effective minimizing of depression requires counter-cyclical planning of capital expenditures by the individual enterprises, encouraged by tax exemptions.[29]

7. Corporations must have an objective standard for managerial promotion. But they cannot use the standard of adaptation to established traditions as the older types of community did, because the essential qualification for corporation management is the ability to initiate change so as to increase productivity. The best way to test this ability is by applying the principle of "federalism" to industry. "Federalism" means that the operating units should be given actual autonomy through control over a definite finished product and a specific regional market. By applying cost-accounting "measurements" to the autonomous plant, objective criteria could be provided to judge the success of its management, and the more capable plant managers would move into the ranks of top national management. Top management would have the authority to replace the personnel of the autonomous units or to eliminate the units altogether, but once it grants authority, it should

not otherwise be able to infringe on the exercise of that authority. This program has been used effectively in General Motors, but if it is to become significant in the nation as a whole, it must be instituted quickly. Writing in 1950, Drucker pointed out that the average age of top managers was now sixty. These managers would have to replaced in the succeeding five to ten years. If the changes which he advocated were not made within that period, the new generation of managers would only entrench the existing system of succession from "the outside." [30]

8. Strikes cannot be banned without destroying unionism and inviting totalitarianism. But the increasing interdependence in our economy is making strikes intolerable. If the unions had the security of the union shop and if management's authority and functions were recognized and appreciated, the strike might become only a symbol of union cohesion which is never invoked. In the meantime, there should be agreement in advance, enforceable through law, to arbitrate all contract disputes (in the courts, if necessary). In strikes which endanger society, the government should take temporary control of the enterprise, but during this period only a minimal profit rate and the old wage rate should be operative, in order to encourage rapid settlement. The internal authority of unions should be made subject to legal controls, and union power should not be used to restrict advances in productivity or to freeze social status. Drucker hopes that the plant communities and the use of objective standards in wage negotiations will lead to union decentralization and that this will in turn reverse the tendency towards oligarchic control. On the other hand, managerial authority should be made subject to an independent board of "management auditors" which will preserve the distribution of "federal" powers and enforce the use of objective criteria in promotion policy. Legal title of ownership should be vested in the Board of Directors, which might consist of representatives of investors, managment, the plant community,

and the management auditors, instead of belonging directly and exclusively to the investors.[31]

9. In his most recent book, Drucker forsees continuous inflationary pressures during the next twenty years. These pressures can be relieved only by the potential increases in productivity offered by automation. But automation requires a complete redesigning of the enterprise and a high degree of stability and predictability in sales, costs, and labor force. More than ever, the basic requirement is for the "harmonious integration" of the whole economic process, for a "pattern behind the flux," for the organic industrial philosophy which Henry Adams understood to be essential. The fact that only institutional investors can provide the needed extra capital underscores the impersonalization of investment in modern society.[32]

10. We cannot abolish the new administrative agencies and functions of government, but government power must be controlled, because military technology has made any modern "right" of revolution into a mere abstraction. The development of responsible social authority within the corporation will make it possible to entrust the administration of the new welfare functions to autonomous self-governing bodies, and this would reverse the trend towards centralization "for the first time since feudalism." Effective plant community government would revitalize local government (and the family's sense of status), which has declined primarily because its vital functions have been taken over by the corporation.[33]

Drucker also discusses a number of political issues which will arise in the next twenty years and which will presumably have to be solved within the framework of the contemporary system of parties, pressure groups, and government. In the most critical problems—foreign relations and inflation (which "breeds class hatred")—he doubts, however, that adequate solutions can be found through the party system and the "normal political battle." The solution of the inflation problem, he suggests, may have to await the drawing up of "fundamental state papers" like those of Hamilton. He does not say how these state papers would then be put into effect, though one gathers it would be by circumventing the "normal political battle." He feels that parties do not yet offer the necessary policy leadership, because each is still fighting battles of the past. The first party to outgrow the past may gain leadership for the next twenty years, he says hopefully.[34]

The question arises, however, as to whether his position does not demand a change in the entire political system. In an early work, he considered the American party system to have no contemporary European counterpart, but to be similar to the estates of the Late Middle Ages, because it was regional and anti-authoritarian. He also felt that the historical roots of American voluntary associations extended back to medieval England because of their quasi-governmental functions.[35] But on the other hand, he frequently pointed to the inadequacy of Liberal democratic government as a framework for harmonious solutions because of its susceptibility to private pressures. Most American Conservatives talk of private associations within our society of conflicting interests as though they were the same as associations in a Conservative society. Robert A. Nisbet, for example, argues from Conservative premises for the need to strengthen societal groups in order to increase harmony, but he belies his assumptions when he concludes with a call for "group laissez-faire," in which the final burden of harmonizing group relations would lie with democratic government. Drucker understands this confusion, but he hedges on the subject. He knows that industrial harmony requires an alteration of political relations and that it cannot be achieved through bargaining, because bargains are only temporary solutions which do not change the conflicts themselves. He knows, on the one hand, that he cannot accept the Liberal thesis that the national interest is the sum of private interests and, on the other hand, that an acceptable "ruling class" is not feasible. But he does not draw the necessary political conclusions from his analysis, because he is afraid to disturb the political *status quo*. He concludes simply that the pressure group system must be made to work properly! [36]

The Utopian Nature of "Pure" Conservatism in Twentieth-Century America

Yet, to attempt to harmonize group relations through American democracy, insofar as that democracy rests on pressure groups, is to travel in a continual, self-defeating circle. Assuming that Drucker's (or anybody's) proposals for Conservative harmony are feasible, the only way they can be put into practice is to have someone work them out and propose them to the groups concerned, and then to have the groups accept them. Once they are accepted, assuming again that they are feasible, there is no further need for "group laissez-faire" in the sense of open and unhampered competition for power, because objective norms will be available for the settlement of all conflicts which have been foreseen. If Drucker's proposals for the corporation were successful, there would be few political functions left for union or business pressure groups in their present forms. They would indeed become "medieval" associations with settled functions and powers. If finished proposals for harmonious group relations must first be worked out and then accepted in order to minimize conflicts, the same thing must be done with future conflicts and problems once the start has been made. This is apparently what Drucker has in mind when he talks of "fundamental state papers." But the question then is: if all this can be done successfully, what is the use of political parties and pressure groups or indeed of majority rule? None is conducive to the evolution of new frameworks for harmonious Conservative group relations, because they are all predicated on political conflict. The whole nature of parties and hence of government would have to change in order to secure the correspondence between the political and social sphere that Drucker seeks. Political leadership would in large measure have to be immunized from popular pressures, and the discussions by various groups would occur only after the proposals of the political leaders had been made, perhaps through some kind of institutionalized functional representation. Drucker's entire position thus seems to demand a new form of political organization along the lines of earlier European corporatism, though without its assumption of frozen relationships.

Nevertheless, it should be clear by now that Drucker is a far more realistic Conservative than any we have considered. If a Conservative society is possible at all today, it must be along the lines he proposes, even if the details of his "program" must still be worked out. This is not a subject on which Conservatives can pick and choose what appeals to them empirically, as Rossiter seems to think. If the fundamental problems are as Drucker describes them, then the Conservative must see himself in a new world environment, and he can only reject Drucker's proposals if he offers something more likely to create societal harmony. Furthermore, as Drucker indicates, if Conservative solutions are to be put into practice, they must be started in the near future; because each time a generation commits itself to following a given line of development, it becomes more difficult for it or the next generation to reverse it. But the future appeal of Drucker's position for Conservatives lies in the fact that several "parts" of it seem already on the way to becoming reality, or at least to becoming popular. The idea that industrial relations should emphasize conceptions like status, belongingness, and harmony was advocated for years by Elton Mayo and others; and it is now part of the ideology of the "organization man." Corporatism thus offers a way to combine continued "adjustment" with the hope for a real Conservative society in the new world. Nevertheless, such "piecemeal" adjustment is in itself an admission of Conservative failure, and Drucker's acceptance of it only obscures the central contradiction in his whole position.

Drucker justifies a pragmatic, piecemeal approach to the problems he has outlined, on the ground that this approach accounted in large measure for the early success of the American experiments. Moreover, he insists that if the basic institution of the corporation is properly organized today, society would be able to tolerate "dissenting institutions." [37] But although the appeal to American experience seems realistic on the surface, it actually beclouds the important issue of whether Drucker can in fact avoid the "totalistic" (not totalitarian) implications of the Platonic position. The piecemeal approach to societal problems in American history was, at least until the twentieth century, usually based on Liberal values in a Liberal period of history. Such an approach is feasible when one is swimming with the historical tide, so to speak. To adopt it when there is no clear relationship between the prevailing trends and the values one wants to see institutionalized, however, is to drift, not to be "practical." Since the over-all historical movements of the twentieth century are not in the direction of Conservatism, as Drucker himself admits, a piecemeal approach is, for the Conservative, equivalent to surrender.

At the end of Drucker's major work, he admits that his proposals will not overcome the "profound spiritual crisis of Western man," though he adds that they can at least help us fight our "man-made demons," [38] whatever this means. Elsewhere he makes the unqualified statement that ethical beliefs exist before organized action or institutions.[39] At the same time, it is clear that the kind of moral attitude needed to support a harmonious society or institution could not possibly evolve within a single generation, the maximum time limit within which Drucker says the key changes must be made.[40] Yet without the proper moral attitude, it is impossible to see how his proposals could conceivably work. The solution to each of the problems he raises cannot depend on bargaining or the use of coercive power, both of which he rightly rejects as contradictory to his goals. It depends on voluntary acceptance by all groups concerned. But such acceptance in turn assumes a change of moral attitude in the direction of his own Conservative values. His whole program therefore depends on a moral change which he has no way of achieving, because his piecemeal approach (in contrast to Plato's) completely ignores the whole problem of education and mass communications in American society.

A consideration of mass communications would have forced Drucker to widen his whole perspective. What good does it do, for example, to try to teach workers that their social status and functions are of prime importance, when advertising tries to teach them that their level of economic consumption determines their status, and that income is, after all, of prime importance? We have seen that Drucker's socio-economic program requires an altered political framework, but how could this be obtained when both the educational and communications systems teach a different conception of American democracy? Can legal recognition of the divorce of ownership from control in large industrial corporations possibly be obtained when powerful business groups and public relations firms insist on telling stockholders that American Telephone and Telegraph or General Motors or Ford is "your company" and go out of their way to surround the annual stockholders' meeting with an aura of "positive participation?" The dominant conceptions of American culture continue to be anti-Conservative. In the new ideology of the "organization man," a sense of status and belonging is something which must be "sold" to people whose more natural inclination is to feel a sense of economic and political conflict with others. Under these circumstances, the piecemeal promotion of particular Conservative ideas in industrial relations may help achieve some kind of unity; but it will not be a Conservative unity. Conservatism requires an unchallanged sense of cohesion, not an artificial integration which depends on a constant barrage of propaganda. Conservative symbols may be useful in an age which is prepared to use any ideas which will work, and the manipulation of these symbols may be good public relations. But it is not good Conservatism.

Nor is American pluralism of much use to Conservatives who

are relying on "the group" to be the vehicle for a restored sense of status and for a renascence of moral and social identification with the community at large. Without a traditional moral code and a secure status system, emphasis on the social motivations of diverse groups is today as likely to be divisive as cohesive. The racist and anti-immigrant prejudices of fundamentalist rural groups are directed precisely at proving the status of Negroes and urban immigrants to be "alien" to America. Much of the behavior of Midwestern "isolationists," especially those of Germanic origin, has been explained in terms of a defensive, almost compulsive, need to prove an "Americanism" superior to that of those who have dominated American foreign policy in the past. Similar status motivations have been found in the hostile behavior of some Catholic groups in recent years, and the list could be extended almost indefinitely to other religious, racial, and nationality groups.

Nisbet's assumption that the individual can restore a lost sense of status and belonging through "group laissez-faire" is therefore self-defeating. It is one of the ironies of the contemporary Conservative illusion that the status motivation has been disruptive in America. To the extent that groups are concerned specifically with status and belonging, open competition among them can only serve to increase doubts about who really does "belong," and no one who identifies strongly with one of the groups can identify confidently with the society as a whole. This is not in itself a serious problem for Liberal "group pluralism," which requires only enough cohesion to prevent conflicts from disrupting the society, rather than a maximum identification of the individual with society as a whole. Pluralism has been successful in America largely because group competition has been confined to "bread-and-butter" economic issues and temporary access to political power, and because individual identification with society does not really depend on mediation by the group.

No one can really claim that American groups, like those of the Middle Ages, accept the same everyday values from religion or tradition, and no Conservative tries to do so. If there is a long-term tendency among the contemporary groups for socio-moral conflicts to disappear, it can only be due to a kind of group "other-directedness." Until the new morality has more definite content, however, a piecemeal approach by Conservatives to the problems of "group society" can only play into the hands of Liberals or provide new material for manipulation under the guise of "belongingness" and "togetherness." The mere use of Conservative slogans today is no sign of an approaching Conservative reality. A society that always wants to be 'together" is obviously one that does not feel "together"; and without a cohesive social base, a pragmatic Conservatism will continue to "play the other fellow's game." The Platonist is ultimately forced to the Platonic solution. His approach must be totalistic and the answers adopted all at once. Ideological, moral, and political changes must accompany the social and economic. Have we thus come back to the need for exiling everyone over the age of ten? If not, there is no feasible alternative solution offered by Drucker.

If Drucker has not been able to escape the need for a Platonic solution, he has been able still less to escape the Platonic dilemma. He says that his major book on the "new society" is really concerned with "political action." Yet a program of political action is conspicuously absent from all his books. All he does is to reiterate the need for voluntary acceptance of his proposals, with the accompanying threat that government control is the only alternative in each case. But what if managers refuse to accept salary limits as the condition for bonus arrangements? In reality no one seriously thinks they would accept. When Drucker considers the possibility that labor may refuse to submit voluntarily to his proposals, he insists that the proposals would only be felt as restrictive if the unions were blind in their opposition to legitimate power limitations.[41] Is this different from Plato's talk of his "corrupt generation?" When Drucker writes about teaching workers to feel pride in their status by understanding their functions in the total product, he asks himself whether anyone can feel pride because he has participated in the production of a can opener. But he immediately answers that the true "managerial attitude" results from a process of abstraction beyond the product to the view that the enterprise itself is the essential focus of identification.[42] Furthermore, the enterprise is only a step in the process of identification with the society as a whole, which requires further abstraction. How such a complex process of identification can occur spontaneously within a short period of time and without a strong relevant tradition is one of the key difficulties of the Platonic position. Drucker's answer (which needs no comment, except for the italics) is that

We must actively induce, coax, *even force* the member of society, whether rank-and-file worker, middle management, or top executive, to see the society he lives in.[43]

His only practical hope for labor is that the new generation of union leaders will be "more flexible" and that the rank-and-file members are "certain" to support a "functioning plant community." [44] Even if this were true, the "community" and other benefits must be offered to them first. But what if the new generation of corporation executives are not "flexible" enough to make the offer? If the new executives continue to come from "the outside," their outlook will not be different from that of the old executives. They can, for example, be expected to favor the "one-man control" which Drucker says is predominant today rather than "federalism." But by Drucker's own assumptions this would perpetuate the feeling that there is a lack of opportunity for advancement within the enterprise, accentuate feelings of hostility, and make unlikely the acceptance by anyone else of his proposals. Actually, the program is an interdependent unit even within its own scope, and the failure of any one item would cause total failure. This does not mean that historical change must always be total and sudden. But proposed changes that are contrary to those which prevail during a period of transition must be total and sudden, which is another way of saying that they cannot succeed without repressive authority.

Drucker's own early generalizations imply an admission that the scope and intensity of political authority must now be increased. He says that the collapse of "Spiritual Man" in the thirteenth century and of "Intellectual Man" in the sixteenth century were periods of transition and "totalitarianism" (he really means "authoritarianism"). The present is the period of the collapse of "Economic Man." Why does this collapse not also demand increased authority, since the implication is that when the old values are irrelevant the creation of new ones presupposes a transitional period of coercion? On the other hand, he criticizes Liberals who insist on the primacy of majority rule, because the only safeguard they offer for civil liberties is self-restraint; and this, he insists, is inadequate both theoretically and practically.[45] But is the self-restraint, including the economic self-restraint, required as the precondition for his proposals exempt from this criticism?

Drucker sees World War II as the cause of the new industrial developments which are making his program feasible; and his assumption that the worker can be given meaningful status by understanding the importance of his function in the production process is based on wartime experience with educating the worker to understand his responsibility in the production of military equipment.[46] Yet what is wartime harmony but the abandonment of internal conflict only because of concentration on external conflict? Drucker and other Conservatives are quick to point out that totalitarian unity depends on foreign conflict. Why should Drucker not conclude that the development of Conservative harmony, status, and function also depends either on the application of prior internal coercion or on the threat of war? Indeed, in view of Burke's admission that medieval harmony was preceded by prolonged periods of force, and in view of the long centuries that elapsed between Plato's proposals for harmony and their approximate realization, the question arises whether prolonged repression is not always the precondition of Conservative harmony. Drucker's own analysis points in this direction, but he does not draw the obvious inference that the use of coercive authority may be the inescapable condition for the adoption of his proposals.

We are thus back to the Platonic dilemma. A Conservative cannot advocate the use of repressive authority without abandoning hope of achieving harmony. But in a period when harmony does not prevail, the conditions necessary for its achievement turn out in practice to require coercion. This is true not only of the socio-economic changes which Drucker proposes and of the political changes which are implicit in his proposals, but also of his conceptions of representation and federalism. In discussing the plant community, where presumably the "citizen" is to have an opportunity for "positive freedom" and participation, his stated assumption is that the attitudes of the leaders will be reflected in the membership.[47] This assumption is implicit in other discussions, the expected acceptance of "fundamental state papers," for example, where the role of the citizenry would be passive. The assumption that the attitudes of leaders and followers are basically identical and that leaders may therefore be "presumed" to represent the rank and file underlies the Conservative idea of "virtual representation." But this conception is, at best, applicable to a Conservative society only. Where there are divergent interests in the community and no common tradition, as in modern society, "virtual representation" can in practice be nothing but a mask for authoritarianism. To extend Drucker's assumption to the whole of contemporary American politics would be to maximize repression. Yet, though he never suggests that it should be instituted, "virtual representation" is the only consistent basis for a Conservative political system.

His concept of "federalism" is also misleading. In the first place it is a complete misnomer for a system in which the central authority can abolish the constituent units or remove their officials. But this is only the usual cloak of Liberal terminology with which the contemporary American Conservative feels compelled to hide the real nature of Conservatism, even from himself. In reality Drucker correctly describes under the guise of "federalism," a truly Conservative system of decentralization, in which autonomy can be given to the local unit because there is no difference in the values, functions, or operations of central and local units, and because harmony is ensured by the subordination of both central and local units to a common standard, in this case the dubiously Conservative standard of profitability in the production of specified commodities. Yet, again, the application of this kind of "federalism" to the United States as a whole would make it clear that the use of Conservative ideas today can only end in a reality of authoritarian centralization.

If Drucker's dilemma is the same as Plato's, there is another, more ironical element of similarity. The proposals for altering by law the nature of property ownership, for universalizing the union shop, for ensuring technological advance and expansion, for considering profit to be the avoidance of loss rather than the accumulation of surplus—these and others are most likely to be resisted by the older middle classes who are being displaced by the advance of the corporation. Certainly Russell Kirk would refuse to accept them, and so would the hangers-on of Southern agrarianism. The status resentments analyzed by Viereck are directed precisely against the thesis that the corporation is necessarily the new center of social status. Worst of all, not even Rossiter's business "aristocracy" is likely to be enthusiastic about this program. Any of these proposals could cause bitter political disputes which would nullify the harmony of Drucker's "new society," even if it were tried. The final irony is thus that Conservatism becomes its own worst enemy. Both the adherence to traditions and obsolete harmonies of yesterday and the adjustment to conflicts of the present make the achievement of new harmonies remote. We are back to Plato's problem with his aristocratic relatives, whose very existence made the *Republic* utopian. Drucker's Conservative "relatives," too, help keep his "new society" in the ideological stratosphere.

The Future of the New Conservatism

It should by now be apparent that the New Conservatism, far from being a single entity, is a microcosmic reflection of all the major types of Conservatism in history. The corporatists are "pure" Conservatives, though of the Utopian-Platonic rather than the medieval variety. The reactionaries are liberal Conservatives like Burke. The "adjusted" group has reformulated Burke to fit the growth of authoritarianism; and in this respect they resemble the Middle Stoics. An occasional Conservative, Frederick Wilhelmsen, for example, has confessed himself to be "alienated," with no feasible solution for society's "degeneration." To complete the list, "radical Conservatism" has also reappeared, in the neo-Augustinian doctrines of Reinhold Niebuhr.

Unfortunately, we cannot enter here into an analysis of Niebuhr's ideology. The complexity of his thought makes a brief treatment impossible. Furthermore, Niebuhr has in fact gone so far toward severing the orthodox moral conceptions of love and self-surrender from his analyses of society that he hardly seems Conservative at all, especially if one reads his books as isolated units. In any event, there is such a great gulf between him and the New Conservatives that it would be of dubious merit to treat them in the same work. There are, however, several general observations about radical Conservatism in general which are necessary to round out our coverage of contemporary Conservative ideology.

In the first place, orthodox Augustinian Christianity is, in the twentieth century, no longer "radical" at all. Its original radical elements were relative to what preceded it and relative to a period when the offer of forgiveness of sins had a real impact on the psychic problems of the time. There was a striking difference, for example, between the pessimistic resignation of the Late Stoa and the intense activism of early Christianity, although the premises of the two groups were, in many ways, similar. Furthermore, although patristic doctrine accepted slavery at first, its formulations could easily be used to reject slavery later. In the twentieth century, however, the idea of the equality of souls before God is not even remotely radical, and in comparison with other ideologies, it is now orthodoxy which seems pessimistic.

Secondly, therefore, when contemporary Conservatives turn to Augustinian Christianity, it is only because they find in it some personal consolation, not because they can feasibly expect orthodoxy to have any significance for society as a whole. In the twentieth century, Augustinianism, in itself, is a form of "alienated," not of radical, Conservatism. It is now a sort of Late Stoicism. This underscores the importance of viewing the changing forms of ideologies as historical rather than as logical "types." An ideological "type" never has exactly the same form or the same significance more than once in history. When we say that all the forms of Conservatism can be found in contemporary America, it should be understood that the forms are in no case completely similar to early counterparts. In particular, all the contemporary "types" accept Christian and Liberal values. The differences among them lie beyond these historical changes to which they have all alike adjusted.

Thirdly, when we speak of Niebuhr as a radical Conservative, we refer not simply to his Augustinianism but to the fact that he has combined orthodoxy with real modern radicalism. During the 1920's and 1930's he was associated with socialist causes and for a while he offered a partial justification of the Russian Revolution on orthodox Christian grounds.

Fourthly, whatever the possibilities may be in later centuries, this is not one in which radical Conservatism is historically feasible. In spite of the "radical" elements in early Christianity, there was no doubt that an orthodox Christian society, whose ethic demanded the surrender of the selfish ego and absorption in the love of God, would be predominantly Conservative. But there is no indication today that a socialist society would be Conservative, that it would emphasize affection and self-denial above economic expansion. Until there is an equalitarian society which is simultaneously harmonious and self-restraining, radical Conservatism is, to say the least, premature. The Christian socialism of earlier decades has largely disappeared. In Niebuhr's case, although he never had any Utopian illusions about socialism, there has been a marked retreat from the "radicalism" of his early life in favor of more traditionalism, the only characteristic which all contemporary Conservatives have in common, at least to the point of giving lip service to it.

Will Herberg, a neo-orthodox Jewish sociologist, has called the appearance of the New Conservatism on the American scene the beginning of "the Great American Debate." We suggest that American Conservatism will never debate anything with anyone until it can agree on a spokesman. The very failure of American Conservatives to analyze clearly the differences among themselves, let alone resolve the dilemmas of each subgroup, makes it clear that they had better do a little "intramural" debating before they throw down the gauntlet. There is no single New Conservatism in America. Herberg may be able to delude himself into thinking he can agree simultaneously with Kirk, Rossiter, and Niebuhr. But Kirk is obviously uncomfortable about Rossiter; Rossiter and Viereck are lucid in their repudiation of Kirk; the Southern agrarians and Drucker do not live in the same world; Kirk is suspicious of Drucker; Rossiter thinks he can take him or leave him; Drucker doesn't understand any of them; Niebuhr keeps the entire group at arm's length; and while they all quote Niebuhr profusely, each manages to repudiate his position in some obscure corner of a book. Out of this collection of contending quarterbacks someone is supposed to develop a team called the "New Conservatives." For this chaos of mutually incompatible, self-contradictory, and amorphous Conservatism we are asked to accept the latest euphemism of "unity in diversity!" We should not wonder that they are looking so desperately for windmills against which to break their lances. Unless they can invent a grand battle as an excuse for the collective use of the term "New Conservatism," they will disintegrate into so many fragments to be scattered by the historical wind.

During the rest of the century, the Conservatives would do well to concentrate more on limiting their spokesmen. Reactionary Conservatism is an ideological monstrosity which can be neither consistent nor relevant for contemporary society. Its most pronounced tendency is to move towards an orthodox religious form of alienation. Corporatism is consistent but Utopian. Its easiest path lies in the direction which Drucker has already indicated—a piecemeal approach which makes realization of the goal no less impossible but gives the illusion of progress towards it. For all practical purposes, this becomes a kind of adjusted Conservatism. Radical Conservatism is at best premature, and if it cannot find refuge in either a confession of alienation or a willingness to adjust, it will have to remain suspended in parodox. The future of American Conservatism lies either with an admission of alienation or with "realistic" adjustment. The real choice before the New Conservative is whether he wants to be irrelevant or un-Conservative. For the twentieth century at least, the divorce between Conservatism and reality is permanent.

In Britain, the dominating group among Conservatives has necessarily chosen the path of adjustment, in order to remain near the centers of power. In America, where Conservatives play no role comparable to their British counterparts, there is no similarly impelling reason to follow one particular road. For whatever it is worth, the American Conservative is a freer agent in choosing his brand of illusion, though the "need to belong" will probably prevent most of them from being excessively "different."

VIII

The New Liberalism: No Enemies on

the Right

Since the contradictions of the New Conservatism are now evident, it might be supposed that we have arrived at the end of our task. This would, however, be a serious error. Only the weakness of existing forms of Conservatism has been demonstrated, not the untenability of Conservative ideology itself. If adjusted Conservatives admitted that the trends to which they adjust are not Conservative, they could go on to argue that the choice now is simply between some harmony or none. Alienated Conservatism could be consistent, even if unrelated to societal reality, if it could confine itself to criticism and leave society to its enemies, reasoning that the present world is irretrievably corrupt and that Conservatism must await a new generation of the future. Against these positions all the preceding arguments would be useless. The basic falsity of Conservative ideology itself has not yet been proved, because its primary value of harmony still stands.

Before proceeding, however, it is necessary to make what may seem a strange departure from the line which has been followed until now—Conservatism must first be defended against some of its Liberal critics. The purposes of this departure are twofold. First, by eliminating inadequate criticisms it will be possible to focus more clearly on the fundamental falsity of Conservatism. Secondly, it will reveal the obscurantism of the contemporary Liberal shift to its own brand of "conservatism." There are four types of arguments which we must consider.

The first type of inadequate criticism is the attempt to refute Conservative values by affirming the truth of Liberal values. This is a common criticism whose roots reach far back into history. Contemporary forms of this criticism include the affirmation that the meaning of "good" is always based on subjective interpretation, so the selection of a single criterion like "harmony" is gratuitous; or that since values are uniquely individualistic, it is important to allow for the "free clash" of many values; or that Conservatism ignores the importance of private interests. The difficulty with this line of reasoning is that it is meaningful only if the Liberal assumptions are accepted first. But the validity of these assumptions is the entire issue between Liberalism and Conservatism. To say that Conservatism elevates harmony above individualism is to state a fact, not a refutation. It is simply to say that it is Conservatism and not Liberalism. To argue that Conservatism selects a single value as supreme is a truism, and obscures the fact that Liberalism, like all ideologies, does precisely the same thing. In spite of its insistence on the subjectivity of value, Liberalism ultimately chooses individual freedom as objectively supreme. The Liberal assumption that there is no higher value than those which the individual consciously pursues is pluralistic empirically, but rests on a single abstract value, namely that desires are "good." The conflict between the free pursuit of desires and the minimizing of tensions by minimizing desires is the entire crux of the contradiction between Liberalism and Conservatism. The choice between them is obvious only to one who is already committed to one side or the other. In a sense, all ideologies really begin with "self-evident" assumptions. It is not a refutation to point them out in a particular ideology. We shall see that the more crucial question is not where ideologies begin but where they are forced to end.

A second type of inadequate criticism is to take specific Conservative ideas out of their total context and to subject them to empirical evaluation. A typical error is to equate Conservatism with aristocracy in any period of history. By contrasting the instabilities of aristocracy in modern history with the stability of American democracy, the Conservative position is presumably destroyed. The argument usually rests on the thesis that American democracy has achieved a stable order by balancing organized interests against each other. But as we have seen, an order of mutual conflict is not the same as Conservative harmony, and the mere absence of revolution does not prove the existence of harmony. If one is trying to attack Conservatism in this way, it must be shown that *Conservative* aristocracy (in the Homeric Age or the Middle Ages) was less harmonious (in the Conservative sense) than Liberal democracy in the era of the Greek city-state or the modern democratic state. On this basis, the attack is much less likely to succeed.

It is probably true that democracies necessarily have more active conflict than the aristocratic medieval societies, not so much because democracy allows conflicts as because democracy is historically a form of government adopted by societies already in a state of conflict as a result of the demand of lower classes for political power. For Conservatism, the use of force, either overt or through dependence on government authority to make new laws, is a sign of disappearing harmony. On this basis, force was obviously less necessary in the traditionalist, aristocratic societies of thirteenth-century Europe than in twentieth-century European democracies. Insofar as there may be contention for power within the aristocracy in a Conservative period, it should be noted that this is not really serious for Conservatism, unless there is also conflict with other social classes. As we saw earlier, such rivalry was really the only one Burke accepted, and even Plato was quite willing to see private violence among his guardians (though not over power) as long as it had no further ramifications.

A further fallacy which derives from taking Conservative ideas out of context is to reject the concept of the "best" on the grounds that it is arbitrary and has been given a variety of meanings by Conservatives. Some define it in terms of wealth, others of wisdom, others of "taste" or breeding, and still others in terms of moral standards. Surely, the critics suggest, we cannot expect all these always to occur together. But the point is that in consistent Conservatism, aristocracy is justified only when these qualities do occur together and when all are subordinated to the standard of harmony. As a matter of historical fact they were all characteristic of the medieval aristocracy, particularly if we include the clergy as part of the aristocracy. They were simultaneously the wealthiest, the wisest, the most moral, and the best bred, if these are all defined by Conservative standards.

Liberals object further that there are no clear criteria for selecting "best" rulers; that if there were, there would be no way of guaranteeing honest selectors; that there would not really be equal opportunities for developing the necessary qualifications; and that no aristocratic system really selects the most competent. All these objections are irrelevant for Conservatism. The "best" men for Conservatives are those capable of tensionless, moral self-control and of maintining a harmonious society. There is no abstract problem of "selection" for Conservatives. In contrast to Plato's *Republic,* the historical solution of Conservatism is an actual aristocracy which has already evolved a "gracious" culture and a tradition of communal harmony. The frequent assumption of hereditary "virtue" in Conservative aristocratic ideology does not refer to any particular skill or to superior intelligence but to the capacity for personal "graciousness" and love of the community. As for the actual process of training in harmony and hence in Conservative statesmanship, it is something presumably "built into" the nature of a proper aristocratic class. This is the meaning of Burke's entire defense of "natural" aristocracy, which does not mean that aristocratic membership need always depend on an objective examination, but that the proper aristocratic environment naturally produces Conservative results both for those who "inherit" aristocratic character and those who rise from below. The real "test" is whether the aristocratic character is actually "gracious" and whether the society it rules is actually harmonious. In this sense, aristocracy is the precondition rather than the result of "the test."

When the Liberal objects that businessmen may be as well informed about political affairs as aristocrats, and that they are therefore as qualified for political power, he has again taken the argument out of its Conservative context. If one accepts the Conservative assumption that true political knowledge must be rooted in the concept of harmony and that harmony is destroyed by the pursuit of wealth, then it follows that a man who is actively engaged in business should be disqualified from political power. This is not a conclusion which requires empirical proof of the businessman's political naïveté; and the fact that aristocracies may degenerate and fail to maintain harmony proves nothing, since inability to realize permanent perfection can be charged against all partisans.

The third type of inadequate criticism is the Liberal pragmatist argument that ideology must be "functional," that is, subject to a "practical" test. The actual meaning of this argument, as it is usually used today, is that ideological conclusions must be feasible in terms of existing societal forces and relations. Since a Conservative society and a Conservative aristocracy are not feasible today, they cannot be "tested," and Conservatism is therefore false, the argument goes. But although this is a valid test of consistency and has meaning in applying an ideology to a particular situation, it goes too far in assuming that decisive defeat in one period of history is permanent defeat. In actuality there is no ideology or set of values to whose decisive defeat we could not point in one period of history or another. Yet at a subsequent period the losers may have become victors. In the case of Conservatism, its defeat in the Roman Empire did not prevent its ascendancy in the Middle Ages. It is perfectly valid for the defenders of a particular theory to say in effect: It is apparently too late to expect men to understand that they have forfeited their only real hope for happiness or to make the effort necessary to achieve it; we must wait until they realize that they have been traveling towards a dead end before a new beginning can be made.   In the meantime, the pragmatic utility of an idea is likely to prove that the idea is corrupt rather than that it is true.   There have, after all, been times in the history of both animals and men when the course of development they were pursuing ended in disaster.   That there was no way out as the disaster approached does not prove that the course was a correct one.   The cases of the Roman Empire in the history of men and of the dinosaur in the history of animals are illustrative.

The fourth and last type of criticism is the most shallow, but its contemporary importance lies in the fact that its serves as an illusory bridge between Liberalism and Conservatism.   The central thesis in this criticism is that Conservatism is nothing more than the defense of existing institutions and traditions. Consequently, in twentieth-century America true Conservatism is simply a defense of Liberalism.   This means that only the most thoroughly "adjusted" Conservatism can be even partially legitimate.   In fact, Conservatism is simply defined out of existence as a separate ideology.

It is not surprising that many Liberals have turned defensive, particularly in the years since World War II, when the anti-Liberal tendencies of industrial society have become increasingly clear.   But it is rather curious that so many of the defensive Liberals should, at the same time, have found it desirable to claim sole title to the term "Conservatism."   The motivation seems to have been a desire to appropriate all the appeal that Conservatism has as an ideology while denying any Conservative basis for attacking Liberalism.   The historical weakness of American Conservatism has made this feat of ideological manipulation seem plausible, the more so since the popular American meaning of "conservatism" also refers simply to one's attitude towards change.   Furthermore, the equation of Conservatism and traditionalism has been strengthened by the fact that most of the New Conservatives have gone out of their way to emphasize the same idea. Indeed, this has been the most important characteristic of the New Conservatism, as compared with earlier Conservatism. It was almost certainly the traditionalism of defensive Liberals which caused the New Conservatives to focus on this idea, and the presumed "recrudescence" of Conservatism has in large part resulted from the fact that the Conservatives simply pounced upon the Liberal turn to traditionalism as a way of gaining a wider hearing than they have ever had in the twentieth century.

The result, as we have seen, has been a fantastic amount of Conservative obscurantism, in which Conservative values are smuggled in under a smoke screen of traditionalism. Nevertheless, the New Conservatives have, in varying degrees, combined traditionalism with legitimately Conservative criticisms of Liberalism and American society. This has forced the defensive Liberals to reinterpret Edmund Burke in the effort to show that traditionalism alone was the essence of his ideology and that a Conservative critique of existing institutions is impossible. In contrast to the slogan of French politics, defensive Liberals seem determined to have no enemies on the Conservative "right," even if they have to make it disappear by definitional fiat.

A striking example of this unjustifiably narrow interpretation of Burke and of Conservatism can be found in Daniel Boorstin's conclusions on "the genius of American politics." [1] Boorstin argues that Americans are preeminently the Conservatives of Western civilization, because we solve concrete problems and adhere to concrete institutions rather than to abstract ideologies. To demonstrate this theme, he points out the effect of the American environment in forcing Puritanism to shift from "theory" to practical problems. Then he emphasizes the Revolutionary arguments which focused on interpretations of the British constitution and the Civil War arguments which centered on American constitutionalism. But his whole analysis is based on the assumption that "concreteness" as opposed to "abstractness" is the essence of Burke's position and hence of Conservatism. Here is true irony. It is bad enough to take a single item out of the total context of a man's thought and identify it with the whole. But to lift one of the Liberal elements of Burke's liberal Conservatism and transform it into the core of Conservatism is to make Burke a convert. It was this very element which led Richard Weaver to conclude that Burke should not be the model for Conservatism at all.

Actually, as we saw earlier, Burke was not nearly as "concrete" and antitheoretical as he is often depicted. Furthermore, Boorstin, like Burke, uses "concreteness" to mean both traditionalism and a "realistic" approach to new problems. But if Burke's traditionalism has any discernible meaning it is that he favored existing institutions because he thought they really *were* Conservative, and because they seemed to retain medieval social traditions, as well as aristocratic political supremacy. Boorstin not only makes the mistake of identifying Burke and Conservatism with the absence of ideological values and of identifying Conservative traditionalism with Liberal traditionalism, but his concept of "concreteness" is so broad that it even includes pragmatic "problem-solving" and wrestling with nature. Unlike Burke's "realism," which meant compromise, caution, and conciliation in order to promote new harmonies, Boorstin's "realism" has nothing to do with Conservative values. The confusion leads to a virtual caricature of Conservatism. American religions, like American parties, he says, differ primarily on means but can agree on ends by stressing common denominators. The common denominator, in Boorstin's analysis, is that religions here become pragmatic solutions to social and psychological problems and are made subordinate to individual personality needs.[2] And our hostility to "theory" is proved by the fact that we continually remake society without plans![3] When Hartz argues that because America never had to fight against Conservative feudalism, its Liberalism has tended not to be self-conscious or clearly formulated, the argument makes sense and helps to explain much about American political thought. When Boorstin argues from the same premises that America is therefore Conservative and Burkean, we begin to wonder whether all verbal laws of gravity have now been suspended. But when real Conservatives such as Peter Viereck include Boorstin in their list of New Conservatives, we can understand how thoroughly the American tendency to cross ideological lines pervades contemporary culture. It is not simply that we are "practical" and willing to "adjust" our values to reality. The ease with which we obscure values enables us to pretend that we are merely "adjusting" them when we are, in fact, surrendering them. This applies to Liberals as well as Conservatives.

When the Liberal relies on Conservative arguments to defend his position, he is really abandoning Liberalism. A recent defensive Liberal argument frankly calls for such a shift as a defense against Communism:

The articulate exposition of a liberal ideology was necessary to convert others to liberal ideas and to reform existing institutions continuously along liberal lines. Today, however, the greatest need is . . . the defense of those [institutions] which already exist. This defense requires American liberals to lay aside their liberal ideology and to accept the values of conservatism for the duration of the threat. . . . To continue to expound the philosophy of liberalism simply gives the enemy a weapon with which to attack the society of liberalism. . . . As Boorstin, Niebuhr and others have pointed out, the American political genius is manifest not in our ideas but in our institutions.[4]

To the critic of Liberalism who points to racial inequality in America, the argument continues, the Liberal can reply with "conservative" arguments about the tensions caused by excessively rapid change and about the magnitude of the problems involved.

It is not necessary to spend much time on the misinterpretation of Burke which makes it possible for this Liberal to define Conservatism as nothing more than a defense of existing institutions, no matter what the institutions are—Liberal, authoritarian, or Communist. He simply points out that

Burke defended Liberal Whig institutions and that this defense included laissez-faire. The fact that Burke considered his advocacy of Liberal conceptions such as laissez-faire to be subordinate to his Conservative social values is completely ignored. It is presumed without further examination that when a man defends a particular society, he must always do so in terms of the predominant values of that society.

Much more important than this selective analysis is the fallacy of confusing a technique of action with a total ideology. Traditionalism, in the sense of resisting change and defending existing institutions, is a technique of action relative to a concrete situation; and techniques are never self-justifying. It is for this reason that, taken by itself, traditionalism is "displaceable" and can be used by any ideology. The same is true of other techniques—revolution, reform, or reaction. There have been revolutionary Liberals like Robespierre, Cromwell, and Jefferson; revolutionary Conservatives like Spengler; and revolutionary authoritarians like Machiavelli; as well as revolutionary radicals like Lenin. But neither traditionalism nor revolution can be evaluated in themselves. They can only have meaning if linked to values on the one hand and a concrete situation on the other.

It is an old and trite truism that the victorious revolutionaries of one age become the traditionalists of the next. It is equally obvious that the defeated traditionalists of one age must become the defenders of the successful revolution in the next, if they are nothing but defenders of existing institutions and traditions. To abandon values and rely purely on technique is to abandon all reason for using the technique. Advocacy of a single way of acting is in itself as contradictory as inertia. The same force of inertia which keeps bodies at rest also keeps them in motion. The advocate of tradition-in-itself must accept every successful change in history once the change becomes established reality. The traditionalist therefore turns out to be his own opposite. Once he cuts himself loose from values, his defense of established institutions becomes no defense at all. That change causes tensions because established institutions have an inherent inertia and power of resistance is true enough. But man's dislike of tensions has never stopped change from occurring, and is not much of a reason for trying to stop it. It is just as easy to argue that the tensions which occur during change are caused by those who resist change as it is to blame them on those who advocate the change. If the defensive Liberal is going to argue against change on the ground that it is upsetting, he must reject the whole history of Liberalism since the Reformation. In other words, he must reject the process which made possible the Liberal institutions he wants to defend.

This does not of course mean that it is never legitimate to defend existing institutions. But they must be defended on valuative as well as "practical" grounds. Institutions which are defended by ideological values, however, are always vulnerable to criticisms on the basis of the same values. This is an unavoidable result of the obvious fact that we do not achieve perfection, no matter which basic values we choose in judging reality. Far from being "unrealistic" because they are not realized completely at any given moment, ideological values are "realistic" precisely because they reflect the unfinished nature of reality. A Liberal can, therefore, defend his institutions only if he is concerned simultaneously with making those institutions more Liberal. If he abandons Liberal criticism and confines himself to defense, on the grounds that further development is dangerous, or that all effort must be concentrated on repelling hostile attacks, then he is abandoning Liberalism. But he is simultaneously abandoning the defense, for a nonvaluative defense is meaningless. This is not a matter of mere abstract logic. A society in which Liberal criticism begins to disappear is a society in which there is no room for further Liberal development. The mere fact that American Liberals in the past formulated their arguments in terms of defending existing institutions does not alter the fact that they interpreted these institutions with Liberal values which required

further Liberal development. When they concerned themselves with pragmatic "solving" of problems, the "solutions"
presupposed the acceptance of Liberal values. The fact that
American Liberals were often unclear in ideological articulation of their values does not mean that the values were not implicit in the programs. But when contemporary Liberals consciously abandon Liberal values, in favor of a blind defense of
reality, they are joining the adjusted Conservatives in leaving
the direction of that reality to their opponents. When they
omit the Liberal values in Liberal "pragmatism" and praise
the pragmatic solving of problems alone, they leave the door
wide open for an anti-Liberal pragmatism. On this basis,
Machiavelli too was a "pragmatist." It may be true that "the
genius of American politics" consists of its capacity to adjust to
historical changes easily, without admitting that it is changing.
But in itself this does not make its politics Liberal and it
certainly does not imply Conservatism.

Not only is defensive Liberalism given to obscurantism
about the nature of the American tradition, but it is just as
prone as Conservativism to use arguments about the traditions
of "Western civilization." If the Conservatives are likely to
see Conservative traditions in Western history, defensive Liberals have no trouble finding a Liberal tradition and in relying on it to bolster their position. Why imperialism, nationalism, and war should be any less a part of the "Western tradition" than freedom and democracy is never explained, and
since "bad" habits are nevertheless habits, there can never be
any reason for refusing to define as traditional those repeated
patterns of action which were not "good." If a tradition must
be "good," then its existence as a tradition is irrelevant. If the
fact of being a tradition is alone crucial, then there is no more
reason to reject the superseding of the Liberal tradition than
there was to reject the superseding of the Conservative medieval tradition by Liberalism.

It is almost unbelievable that Liberals should expose themselves to such elementary criticism. But these new Liberal

arguments have at least the merit of making explicit a fallacy which is too often hidden in contemporary reasoning. When Liberals acquiesce in curbs on individual freedom because they are a "practical necessity," they are no more likely than adjusted Conservatives to point out that this acquiescence to "necessity" is simultaneously a rejection of their own values. The "necessity" to which they bow is usually based on the priority of the need for stability and authority, and reality may well be pointed in this direction. But unless the extension of authority is coupled with the extension of freedom, the adjustment to reality is also the surrender of Liberalism. If this continues to be the direction of Liberal development, then Liberalism will have died without a *requiem*.

The frequency with which Liberals argue that the New Conservatism is wrong because it is critical indicates the extent of Liberal "adjustedness." The fact is that Conservative values not only permit but demand criticism in contemporary America, and the merit of these criticisms has increased in proportion to Liberal "adjustments." The tensions and confusions of modern society, the increase of manipulation, the extension of force and repression implicit in the increase of government authority—these and other problems which the Conservatives raise are worth raising, and the best Liberal analysts are well aware of them.

A further discussion of contemporary Liberal problems would be far beyond the scope of this book, and no general evaluation of Liberalism is intended here. However, two general conclusions follow from our whole analysis. First, contradictory ideologies like Liberalism and Conservatism can be combined only if the values of one are clearly dominant over those of the other. Secondly, an ideology which can adjust to changing realities only at the cost of obscuring its own values is an ideology which has surrendered those values. These conclusions should be the starting points of any meaningful study of contemporary American Liberalism.

IX

Values and History: the
Transition from
Ideology to Theory

Up to this point, the focus of our analysis has been on the *ideology* of Conservatism. We have seen that, in spite of historical variations, the unifying thread of Conservatism is its underlying value of harmony through minimizing individual desires and maximizing affection for the community. This ideal determines the Conservative attitude towards both reality and reason, for reality is evaluated in relation to harmony and reason is an instrument for directing reality towards increased harmony. The only techniques which are fully consistent with Conservative values are the defense of harmonizing traditions and exhortation to moral improvement.

The whole of Conservative ideology, however, stands or falls on the validity of its value of harmony. Yet though this value can be maintained even when there is no immediate hope of translating it into reality, it is incumbent on Conservatism to offer some proof that this is really man's supreme value. Almost invariably the Conservative argument is a negative one. It tries to prove that all other ideologies are prone to excesses which become self-defeating. The constant argument against Liberalism since Plato is that the pursuit of freedom above all else leads ultimately to chaos and to the imposition of repressive authority. Similar arguments are used against other values. Authoritarianism, for example, is seen as dependent on the justification of force alone as the instrument of stability, and since force generates counterforce it too is self-contradictory. After thus eliminating the other contenders, Conservatism is presumed to stand alone in the field.

But this reasoning is completely fallacious. No Liberal has ever advocated the total elimination of all values except freedom. Even anarchists assume that if authority is removed there will be other human values which will restrain completely "wanton" freedom. No authoritarian has ever rejected all values but force. He may affirm that overt force is necessary in certain periods of history, but will prefer that it remain latent and that stability be maintained without having to use it. He will not reject all freedom but only such freedom as conflicts with the need for authority and stability. If the Conservative retorts that this is all merely an admission that other theories find it necessary to mix their values, then we must ask whether this is not also true of Conservative values. What, after all, is harmony? It is not the total rejection of freedom, of the pursuit of pleasure, of authority, of force. On the contrary, it always admits the need for some measure of each of these. But the measure is limited by the supreme value of harmony itself, and it is this value which is the distinctive element of Conservatism. Harmony, like all ideological values, is a compound conception. It accepts all other human values, but subject to the need for minimizing (not eliminating) personal desires and for maximizing love of the community. This is no more than other ideologies do in reverse. Liberalism, for example, does not renounce all need for harmony and tranquillity. It merely affirms that if harmony comes into direct conflict with freedom, then it is the need for freedom which must be superior.

If we are to apply to Conservatism the arguments which it uses against others, then the question we must ask is whether harmony is not also self-defeating if carried to excess. Certainly all contemporary American Conservatives would not only agree that this is so, but frequently insist upon this observation of their own accord. Harmony and tranquillity are, by themselves, indistinguishable from stagnation. Burke pointed out that tranquillity is indistinguishable from death. Furthermore, we know as a matter of historical fact that periods of Conservative harmony do not last indefinitely and that they are followed sooner or later by periods of conflict. We shall see that the Conservative theory of history admits that harmony turns into its opposite just as easily as other values do theirs. Therefore, if all ideologies claim only supremacy and not exclusiveness for their values, and if exclusiveness and excess are self-defeating for all of them, how are we to judge between them? Since each of them begins from a different value assumption, the treatment of value theory as an independent realm can only end in stalemate and endless repetition of the same themes. Since any ideology can try to break out of the dilemma by claiming divine origin, the claim becomes useless. Unless there is some common ground for rational judgment, some common arena to include all the combatants, the battle of ideology becomes mere shadow-boxing in which the opponents never actually clash.

Unless we are to assume that ideology is an irrelevant construction of the mind, it is essential that values be grounded in history. *History is the real test of ideology,* because history is the actual battleground of the human values which ideology represents. Ideology is the affirmation of the superior importance for mankind of one value over others. But if the proposed values are really those of mankind, then history must first be explained in terms of those values. If, as authoritarianism maintains, power over nature and political integration of society are really man's most important values, then history must be explained in terms of overcoming the obstacles to these goals. For the Liberal it must be explained in terms of overcoming obstacles against the freedom to satisfy individual desires; for the Conservative, in terms of maximizing harmony. Until an ideology relates its values to an explanation of history, it remains a mere ideology, justifying partisan interest by an unsupported identification of its own values with those of mankind.

If an ideology tries to interpret history on the basis of its values, it is forced to assume that historical change occurs in a particular sequence. We shall examine how this applies to Conservatism. When the values are related to an explanation of historical change, however, ideology becomes "theory." It can then be "tested," and the "test" is its adequacy in accounting for historical change as compared with alternative theories. The mutual contradictions of ideologies can be resolved only on this level of historical theory.

This does not entitle anyone to use "history" as a short-cut argument to avoid examining the actual issues at stake. It is not valid to justify the existing conditions at a given moment on the grounds that the distribution of power throughout history always reflects the values of humanity. The defeated values of one age may be found in the seats of power of the next. The failure of the holders of power to realize the basic human values of society may be the cause of subsequent total decline. Since all ideologies agree that there are periods of decline, in which the existing reality is not desirable, no one can consistently argue that whatever exists is always good. Even if the successful accessions to power in history are considered to occur "inevitably," opposition to power and success must be considered equally inevitable. If the fact that one can see in history the continual rise of power of ruling classes justifies the thesis that the concern of political science or theory must be to promote political stability, then the fact that one may also see in history the continual fall of ruling classes can just as easily justify promoting revolution. There is no valid way of avoiding an examination of the actual process of historical change in evaluating a theory.

Ideological values are not simple statements of subjective preference. They are compound conceptions which include a recognition of all the basic human needs affirmed by other ideologies, but which advocate a particular ordering of these needs on the ground that such an order is objectively necessary for the maximum happiness of mankind. It is the objective element which is in dispute, and it is this element which is tested when we ask whether the values are consistent with the trends of reality in a given period. The transition to a general theory of historical change widens the scope of the test. The question of historical theory is not only whether the objective element of an ideological value is relevant to the reality of a contemporary period of history, but whether it is relevant to *any* period of history, including the one closest to its ideal.

If theory requires a comprehensive explanation of historical change, then only a few Conservatives qualify as theorists. Yet all of them are forced ultimately to accept the theory of Plato —that historical change is a cyclical process of moral degeneration—because this is the only explanation possible in terms of the value of harmony. Against this theory, there will be three major objections: First, the conception of moral degeneration is rationally inadequate. Secondly, the Conservative view of the sequence of historical change is empirically false. Finally, Conservatism not only grants its failure in the process of history, much worse, it has no rational way of redeeming itself from failure. By its own admission, its defeat is permanent. Having recognized the fact that its values have not been the values of mankind, it is forced to deny the validity of historical theory as the test of ideology. The Platonic "theory of Ideas," the Augustinian "City of God," and the recurrent claim of divine support for Conservatism are all attempts to escape from history. In the end, Conservatism is left fighting with shadows, locked with nothingness in an eternal combat for which it is free only to construct imaginary endings.

The Conservative Cycle: From Plato to the Stoics

It is sometimes said that the description of change in the *Republic* is merely logical and relative to Plato's ideal community rather than an attempt to chart the actual course of history. But the theory in the *Republic* is fully consistent with Plato's description of actual historical changes in other dialogues. The analysis in the *Republic* is only more abstract and pointed, but not different in kind. Furthermore, the conception in the *Republic*—that of history as a process of moral and social deterioration—is, by Conservative standards, a reasonably accurate description of the actual course of history. It is to this theory that Conservatism always returns, and it is with this theory that we must begin.

For Plato all change originates from a change in the capacity for moral self-control and affection for the community. In society, this change first appears as a transformation of social relations, especially the basis of prestige in the ruling class. During the earliest historical stages, social cohesion is maximal, and harmony is maintained by "true" kings or aristocrats who rule as "gods." In the course of time, however, there is a genetic deterioration in the character of the citizens, particularly in the ruling class. Though the emergence of private property is a factor in the initial process of degeneration, it is not really the primary factor. Private property is the result of societal discord, and discord first arises from social status resentment. Status resentment, which causes an altered conception of the basis of prestige, is in turn the result of degeneration in the psychic capacity for harmony.[1] The economic change is thus the consequence of moral and social change. It is one of Plato's recurrent themes that adequate moral fibre could resist economic temptations. Private property brings a new kind of conflict—conflict between classes—but this could be avoided by sufficiently strong moral character.

Psychologically, the first decline leads to the abandonment of Conservative "wisdom" as the supreme element of harmonious character. In societal relations, it transforms the ruling class into "timocracy"—rule by an uncultured aristocracy, motivated primarily by the direct quest for honor in itself rather than as the by-product of the superior goal of serving the community. The ruling class begins to use its military and political superi-

ority in order to acquire wealth and power and to satisfy its
desires for pleasure.[2]   It still remains more capable of personal
harmony and of preserving societal harmony than the classes
which share power later.   But its arrogance stirs resentment,
the desire for wealth leads to increasing accumulation and consumption, and this in turn leads to economic competition.[3]

Since that which is honored is cultivated and since wealth is
now honored,[4] a new stage of degeneration is reached when
wealth becomes the basis of prestige as well as political power.
The new ruling class (the upper middle-class "oligarchy") wants
above all to accumulate wealth, but in its thriftiness it denies
itself the satisfaction of material desires beyond its capacity to
maintain a harmonious self-control.   Its character therefore
necessitates continual self-repression and causes constant inner
conflicts.[5]   But as the rule of this class continues, its younger
generations have less and less capacity for even this kind of
self-control and they become increasingly extravagant.[6] This
produces a widening cleavage between the rich and the poor.
The final degeneration of the middle-class rule begins when the
values of the younger generation win out, and even temperance
is abandoned in favor of an ethic of luxury consumption and
freedom from all moral restraint.[7] Conflict now reaches a peak,
psychologically because material desires are insatiable and only
grow more intense with time,[8] societally because freedom leads
to disorder.   Parental and educational discipline are thrown
off, respect for age is abandoned, and a vulgar sex equality
emerges.[9]   Both the lower class and the lower middle class reject the rule of the "oligarchy" and set up a democratic
system.

But democracy brings increasing freedom, equality, social
variety, and disorder.[10]   Class conflicts grow more intense as the
poor and the spendthrift feed on the wealthy, who are driven
to seek a repressive authoritarian oligarchy for self-protection.[11]
This in turn leads the lower classes to resort to false accusations
and to seek a "tyrant" who will champion their cause. The
lowest depths are reached in the character of this tyrant, who,

once in power, discards those who put him there and rules only to satisfy his personal passions and desires. In him the wildest, hitherto submerged, animal passions of man become dominant. To the desire for unlimited wealth and power are added uncontrolled sexual and sadistic passions.[12] Being subject to the most violent psychic conflicts, he is the unhappiest of men, and to hold his power he must make society equally unhappy by projecting his personality upon the whole state. He always maintains a state of tension, he stirs up continual wars, he constantly purges potential enemies, and he rules oppressively.

This is as far as Plato carries the process in the *Republic*, but in the *Statesman* his "myth of Kronos" indicates that when rock bottom has been reached there is a new moral regeneration, caused by the direct intervention of God. Plato's general theory is thus that change occurs through a moral dialectic—once total harmony is abandoned, the tendency to excess of each moral system produces its own opposite. Excessive pursuit of honor leads to the desire to accumulate wealth; the accumulation of wealth leads to the spending of wealth; the concern for wealth in general necessitates the pursuit of political power; and excessive power causes total decline, which somehow produces regeneration.

One of Aristotle's major criticisms of Plato's theory is that it does not correspond to the empirical course of history. The order of change, he points out, need not follow that outlined by Plato. Tyranny may change into another tyranny or into oligarchy or democracy; oligarchy may change into tyranny; and democracy may change into oligarchy.[13] This general line of criticism is very substantial and damaging, but only if Plato's theory is interpreted as dealing with empirical details in any country, at any time. If, however, it is interpreted as dealing with very general stages of history, particularly in the leading societies, then the criticism becomes irrelevant. In a generally "oligarchical," that is, upper middle-class, period of history, the actual government at a given moment may not correspond exactly to the formal picture of an upper middle-class oligarchy. But the values of the upper middle class will nevertheless continue to be characteristic of the society as a whole. For example, the specific form and location of political power changed frequently from the sixteenth through the eighteenth centuries. By Aristotelian criteria, the British government during this period changed each century from a monarchy to an attempted democracy to an oligarchy. Within each century there were further changes both in degree and in kind. But it is nevertheless not inaccurate to characterize the entire period as upper middle-class and as corresponding in this sense to Plato's "oligarchy."

The order of succession in the *Republic* is, moreover, compatible with the actual course of Greek history. Plato's sequence can be summarized as follows: (1) a period of regeneration, (2) the ideal Conservative period which declines to timocracy, (3) a "Liberal" middle-class period which declines to democracy, (4) an authoritarian period of tyranny which leads to (5) the final period of decline, which God transforms into regeneration. The changes in Plato's civilization actually resembled the Platonic cycle: the "Heroic Age" of the early Greek tribes was followed by the "Homeric Age" of aristocracy, the commercial city-state, and the Alexandrian and Roman empires (foreshadowed in Plato's century by the rise of anti-democratic "tyrants"). Interestingly enough, Aristotle himself, when he describes change in terms of general historical periods, begins with very much the same sequence.[14]

Furthermore, in terms of Conservative harmony, the increasing material demands and decreasing socio-moral cohesion after the decline of the ideal Conservative period can only be described as a deepening degeneration. But the fact that there was some surface correspondence between Conservative theory and the process of history does not prove the Platonic case. On the contrary, the offhand impression is that it disproved his fundamental assumption. If man's moral capacity and his affection for others or for the community decrease with the passage of time, then the obvious conclusion is that Conservative harmony is not man's strongest value but his weakest. Therefore, no Conservative in history (with the possible exception of Henry Adams) has been able to stop with this view of history. Conservatives since Plato have been forced to deal with their theory of degeneration in terms which would not destroy their ideological postulates. To accomplish this purpose, their efforts have centered around two key theses. The first, with which we shall deal in the next chapter, is that their theory of historical causation cancels the damaging effect of the cyclical theory. The second, with which we shall be concerned here, is that the process of degeneration can be stopped at any time. Let us see how Conservatives, from Plato on, have fared in the attempt to break out of their own cycles of degeneration.

Plato himself takes the position that further change can be stopped at each successive stage. His first assumption is that reason can reverse the process. If men can be taught to understand that Conservatism is the only way out of their problems, then degeneration can be arrested. But in actual practice, it turns out that Plato would have to depend on the repressive use of political power. The first decline can at least be delayed by properly controlled breeding and tight cultural censorship.[15] The same policies could prevent the second change to middle-class oligarchy, and further degeneration from this stage could be avoided by sumptuary laws prohibiting extravagance, legal restrictions on the use of property, or the refusal by government to enforce contracts.[16] In his own day, the stage of "tyranny" was beginning to emerge from the decline of democracy. For this period, as we have seen, his original hope was that a tyrant like Dionysius II of Syracuse might put the *Republic* into effect. When this failed, Plato turned again to political repression. But the use of repressive power to effect regeneration is incompatible with his entire causal theory in which, as we shall see, moral changes are uncaused and can only develop from within the psyche. Only moral exhortation is consistent with the theory. In any event, neither Plato nor anyone else succeeded in arresting the process of degeneration, and the authoritarian period of imperial "tyranny" succeeded the Greek city-state.

The Middle Stoics accepted the Platonic theory of "natural" decline due to moral degeneration. But they superimposed on this theory the Aristotelian conception of political stability through "mixed government." This would presumably prevent the excesses which lead to decline. But they never explained how a political device could change the moral proclivity to degeneration and they only aggravated Plato's own contradiction in depending on political authority to solve the moral problem. The Late Stoics surrendered this political hope and admitted that the process of degeneration had been continuous. But they continued to believe that moral determination could solve the problem for the individual, if not for society, and many turned to a non-Christian conception of the "City of God" as compensation for failure. Those who most consistently accepted the implications of inevitability in the process of degeneration and could not bring themselves to believe in divine assistance for reversing the process did not write either ideology or theory. They committed suicide.

The Turn of the Cycle: St. Augustine to John of Salisbury

By the fifth century A.D., the age of St. Augustine, we arrive at the turn of the Conservative cycle, and the historical significance of his two "Cities" lies precisely in their symbolizing a position astride the end of one cycle and the beginning of another. The City of Man reflects the human proclivity to moral degeneration, and its movement is cyclical, from an early, relatively virtuous state to the later state of complete degeneracy. The conception of original sin is profoundly similar to the Platonic theory of historical decline through deterioration in the capacity for love and self-control.

The effect of the whole contrast with the City of God is to emphasize the emptiness of man's attempts to control his own history without God. The City of God is crucial because it offers divine redemption to men. It is not of interest to us here that for St. Augustine the conflict between the two Cities remains unresolved until the end of history. What is important is that for the new Christian civilization the transition from Graeco-Roman society to Christianity was a step forward for the City of God, and therefore a process of regeneration. This is really true even for St. Augustine, since the "binding of the Devil," which makes possible the formation of the Church, clearly means that man has a new opportunity for regeneration, essentially different and more hopeful than anything which occurred previously. Historically, the ambiguity of the battle between good and evil is, after all, bounded for St. Augustine by the fundamental advance which is embodied in the emergence of Christianity itself. If the regenerative nature of this advance for society as a whole was not emphasized in his works, it must be remembered that he was still living at the end of the old civilization, a civilization which he did not really want to see totally overthrown. But for those who lived in succeeding centuries, after the Roman Empire had clearly come to an end, the regeneration of society, as well as of individuals, must have become an increasingly strong belief. It is, indeed, clearly implied in the later concept of the Holy Roman Empire, for the qualifying adjective signifies just such a regeneration.

At any rate, in terms of Platonic theory, the centuries following the end of the Roman Empire may have seemed to be times of reversion to primitive harmony. Agrarian tribal societies, relatively uncorrupted by the temptations and internal conflicts of a mercantile society, were again dominant. New "aristocratic" warrior blood was infused into what was to become Europe. Custom rather than conscious law ruled again; and the Christian ethic of the surrender of self to God was superimposed on the strong, unsophisticated barbarian sense of religion and the supernatural.

Surely, however, this process of Conservative renewal cannot be interpreted as an expression of historical freedom or of moral determination. It occurred only after the previous cycle had run its course, at a time when the Platonic theory already expects total corruption to turn into its opposite of regeneration. Furthermore, in both Platonism and patristic Christianity, the precondition for renewal was the direct intervention of God. If this is the meaning of freedom, it is a meaning which is indistinguishable from necessity and inevitability. In Conservative historical theory, God is virtually obligated to regenerate man, at least after the collapse of a civilization.

Most important of all, insofar as the appeal of Christianity lay in the release which it provided for feelings of guilt, it contradicted the entire Conservative theory of change. Historically, forgiveness of sin meant a cancelling of the guilt caused by failure to fulfill the moral obligations of earlier society. If the sense of expiation was psychologically effective, then the result may well have been a subsequent increase in the capacity for love and moral self-control in relation to a new ethical code. But when Conservatives speak of moral regeneration in relation to their theory of history, they cannot consistently mean a regeneration which is preceded by a kind of release from earlier moral obligations. On the contrary, Conservative regeneration means an increase in the capacity to fulfill earlier norms, because they are more conducive to harmony than later ones. But it is precisely the inability to fulfill the old norms on the one hand and the inability to completely escape them on the other which causes guilt. When the Conservative Christian offered forgiveness of sin, he was admitting that regeneration required an escape from Conservatism. This raises the question of whether the precondition of moral "regeneration" is not always the obliteration of earlier moral ties, that is, whether Conservatism itself is not man's "original sin" —but more of this later.

The major inadequacy of ascribing the "regeneration" primarily to the ethical changes wrought by Christianity is that it ignores the shift from a slave economy to serfdom, as well as the bloody barbaric violence and cultural primitivism (the price for the local cohesion during this period). The role of the sword in spreading the influence of Christianity can all too easily be overlooked. Edmund Burke was well aware that this was not an age of Conservatism, and that it took centuries before the code of the barbarian warrior was "softened" by the code of chivalry. When Plato wants to teach virtue to his ideal republic through the legends from the corresponding "Heroic" tribal age of Greece, he is able to do so only after a thorough "purging" of Homer, that is, only after rewriting the history contained in the legends. Yet without the barbarian tribes which came to Europe, there is no indication that Christianity could have "regenerated" the ancient world.

One vital point remains about the relation between Christianity and Conservatism. In contrast to Graeco-Roman societies, the Christian foundation of European civilization introduced tensions which had not previously existed. It split man's allegiance to society by affirming his higher allegiance to God; and it built a conception of individual moral freedom and responsibility into the conscience of Western man. Whatever the justification for these ideas in terms of religion or other ideologies, they were, in purely Conservative terms, a degeneration from the whole of earlier civilization. If social cohesion and the renunciation of individual desires in favor of absorption in love of the community are the criteria of "good," then the whole "cycle" of Western European societies has been a step backwards from the civilization of Greece and Rome.

If the Late Middle Ages were the centuries of true Conservatism within Christian civilization, then it is interesting to note that for John of Salisbury they were already centuries of moral degeneration.[17] The general increase of luxuries, the moral corruption of the nobles, and the military weakness of his country were for him particularly important symptoms of this decline.[18] The time had already come for "the leader" to arrest the process of decline,[19] by serving as a moral example for others. But the later advances of the thirteenth century were due to opposite causes—the continued growth of towns and trade; the centralization of clerical and secular authority; and the more authoritarian Roman law.   Ideologically, these changes were accompanied by a shift from Plato to Aristotle, that is away from a Conservative ideology in favor of an ideology which emphasized the role of conscious, centralized authority in furthering the integration of society.   When contemporary Conservatives take the Middle Ages as their historical model for harmony, they usually find it expedient to treat Plato and Aristotle as two sides of the same Conservative coin.   But the fact that they are not the same and that medieval society found it necessary to abandon "pure" Conservatism before reaching its most advanced development suggests that Conservatism lacks an adequate explanation even for its "own" period of history.   At any rate, as the Platonic cycle foresees, medieval society declined and the period of maximum Conservative harmony was again superseded by a period of middle-class "oligarchy."

Thus far, the course we have traced in European history, like that of Graeco-Roman history, seems to correspond to the Platonic cycle.   The "regenerative" Dark Ages led to the Conservative Middle Ages, and the decline into a self-seeking "timocracy" led to the modern period of middle-class commercial capitalism, the third stage of the cycle.   But here we must pause, for while continental Conservatives may have looked upon the eighteenth century (the tail end of the commercial capitalist era) as a period of decline relative to the medieval era, Burke's attitude and his whole theory of change were by no means so simple.   It is necessary to examine Burke's position in some detail in order to understand the extent to which it was, in spite of its ambiguities, fundamentally similar to the Conservative theory of degeneration as we have outlined it.

The Attempt to Deny the Cycle: Edmund Burke

Burke's adoption of Liberal values made his theory of change fundamentally ambivalent.   Each time he was faced with a different kind of crisis his conceptions shifted.   But if we follow each of these shifts in order, we shall see that they led back finally to the Platonic theory.

The period of maximum appeal for Burke is not that of the early barbarian tribes nor even that of the Middle Ages. His actual ideal is the Whig settlement of the end of the preceding century, though he sees the medieval social system at the root of that settlement. It is this settlement which he fears the court of George III is trying to overthrow. Since freedom and prosperity are legitimate goals for him, provided they do not upset societal harmony, the transition from the medieval to the modern system is really one of advance, not of decay. If history is for him in part a process of decline in the moral capacity for harmony, it also includes what seems to be the contradiction of this conception—a process of progress, activated by the search for freedom and wealth. Does this then mean that the cyclical theory of decline is not the only tenable Conservative position? Burke pointedly rejects the decay theory as defeatist, on the old ground that one man often saves society.[20] Did he synthesize the concepts of moral decline and the progressive pursuit of freedom and wealth? Did he show that they were in fact not contradictory? Or was his rejection of the implications in the decay theory only the same kind of whistling in the dark which we have already found in Plato, the Stoics, and John of Salisbury, and which we find again in contemporary Conservatism? And was he finally forced to fall back on the same decay theory, because his attempt to combine Conservatism with Liberalism was really an illusion?

Burke's analysis of the American Revolution is a typical example of his tendency to combine a Conservative analysis of historical causes with explanations which would be acceptable to non-Conservatives. The natural drives of Americans, are in the direction of freedom, he says. This is due, among other things, to their great wealth, their Protestantism, their legalistic minds, their distance from England, and their growing population and strength.[21] Whether or not this listing is adequate, there is certainly nothing in it which a Liberal would reject. Burke's analysis, however, rested on two primary Con-

servative assumptions. The first was that the freedom which
the colonists sought was not abstract and "radical" but the
tangible hereditary rights of Englishmen. It is this element of
his thought which is continually emphasized by American Conservatives to prove both Burke's "realism" and the Conservative nature of the American Revolution. They point to the
historical evidence which indicates that the colonists did at first
want only what they considered to be their legitimate rights,
and that only under pressure of parliamentary opposition did
they resort to abstract claims of the "rights of man." This, they
say, is exactly the way Burke analyzed the whole problem.

As far as it goes, this vindication of Burke makes some sense,
but it does not go far enough, because it ignores the second and
most important Conservative assumption of Burke's argument.
Underlying all his discussions of the subject was the supposi-
tion that the interests of Britain and the colonies were fundamentally in harmony within the framework of the British Empire. He specifically states that the colonies "would *never* have
raised these questions" of freedom if Parliament had not forced
them to do so, "for their interests and inclinations were not in
that direction." [22]   To this, the Conservative may respond that
Burke eventually came around to the idea of a kind of dominion status for the colonies; but it is essential to understand that
Burke never wanted the kind of dominion status which is
found in the British Commonwealth today, a status which is
tantamount to total independence. His most advanced position, expressed after the Revolution had gotten under way, was
an offer of limited independence which still clearly included
the dominance of Great Britain. He begins by saying:

We seek only to pursue the objects of government by joint counsels.
. . . Even if we get no revenue from you, your commerce with us
and your support in war and peace will compensate and make us a
powerful combination.[23]

And he immediately adds:

Of course, a large portion of wealth and power must go to the pre-
siding state as it must bear the greatest burdens. . . . We assume

you will not allow yourself, under proper circumstances, to be se-
duced into alienation from dependence on Britain, since it is
doubtful whether you can preserve your liberty apart from its
original fountain. Only England can give you the benefits of a
free constitution, since you are not likely to be capable of such a
constitution in an independent state for ages. . . . Any outstanding
issues can be settled provided we achieve a spirit of forgiveness and
you one of manly obedience.[24]

It may be objected that Burke is simply expressing an eighteenth-century view on the subject and that at a later period
real dominion status would have been compatible with his
liberal Conservatism. But this is to assume that there is no
limit to the extent to which Burke could consistently display
his willingness to adjust to change. It would require considering him to be another "adjusted" Conservative, an interpretation to which he sometimes lends himself and which leads to
a practically contentless ideology, as we have seen. But he is
quite explicit in stating that his entire attitude towards America
would have been different if he had thought that the colonists
were really seeking independence, or even just an increase of
freedom, instead of legitimate rights of Englishmen within a
British Empire.[25] Actually this means that Burke's entire
analysis of the relations with America can be vindicated only
if it is assumed that America would never have sought real
independence had the British government been more conciliatory in the eighteenth century.

If American Conservatives are prepared to support this contention, they have certainly avoided making the attempt to do
so. The only relevance of the fact that Burke lived in the
eighteenth century was that he could avoid seeing the serious-
ness of his dilemma on this entire subject. Unlike the test to
which the French Revolution subjected his theory, he could go
on thinking that the American Revolution had vindicated
what he had claimed all along and that it would never have
occurred if the British government had heeded his warning.
Even if we focus on his later comments about America, we can
see, as he did not, the historical dilemma in his position. After

the Revolution, he consoled himself with the thought that America could be included among the European powers arrayed against France, because she still retained the marks of her origin [26] and had respectable leaders like George Washington.[27]   But, in apparent reference to the Jeffersonians, he warned against the "mischievous" Jacobin "faction" in the United States.[28]   If Burke had lived to see nineteenth-century America, he would have had to conclude that it too had gone the way of revolutionary France.   Indeed, we shall see shortly that the liberal Conservative distinction between the American and French Revolutions, which began with Burke, is based on both theoretical contradictions and historical illusion.

A problem similar to that of British relations with the American colonies arises in connection with Burke's analysis of India.   Here again, he charged the British government, and especially Warren Hastings, with oppressiveness, exploitation, and destruction of native traditions.   These charges sound like his criticism of American policy, except that they are applied to policy in a backward, foreign Conservative society instead of a colonized Liberal one.   His crucial assumption is that the British could have held power in India even if they had adopted the fair and conciliatory policies which he advocated. For example, he rejects Hastings' argument that his use of force conformed to the practice of Asia with the retort that he should have conformed to the "true constitution" of the land,[29] meaning apparently that which its traditions should have been.   He refuses to believe that the natives would not have provided the necessary supplies without force if the British had dealt fairly with them.[30]   He seems to assume somehow that there is no problem inherent in getting a backward people to accept foreign domination.   But the verdict of contemporary historians such as G. M. Trevelyan is that Burke was wrong in his evaluation and that against both internal and external (French) resistance, force was unavoidable if Britain was to hold India.[31] After centuries of imperialist history, who today can doubt the truth of this conclusion, especially in relation to India?   Per-

haps then Burke was willing to see Great Britain get out of
India. One might infer this from an early generalization that
imperialism is a sop to the pride of the lowly, who seek to have
others inferior to them.[32] But this was not in fact Burke's position on India. We are, he said, in India "by the grace of God,"
and we must now "make the most of it." [33] Far from being the
astute, realistic analyst that his standard-bearers claim, his recommendations on India rested on the contradictory assumption
that England could simultaneously hold a vast foreign empire
and pursue a conciliatory, Conservative policy towards it.

Burke's characteristic attitude towards change in domestic
British affairs is to combine reform and conservation. On the
surface he sounds like a Liberal when he refuses to accept the
thesis that "public repose should never be disturbed," [34] and
when he points out that those "who loll at their ease are usually averse to reformation." [35] But his acceptance of change
and reform is limited by his primary thesis that British harmonies must be preserved. One might suppose then that a
Burkean could have gone on accepting British reforms during
the nineteenth century, even after these reforms had produced
an undeniably Liberal system. But this would be a serious
perversion of Burke's actual position. It has been shown at
some length that his attitudes towards parliamentary reform,
broadening of the suffrage, and political parties would have
made acceptance of the nineteenth-century system impossible
for him. The real significance of his acceptance of change was
the assumption that the process of change would not alter the
fundamental Conservative harmony which he thought he saw
in British society. But such change did in fact occur in the
nineteenth century. One cannot therefore generalize about
his acceptance of change; it was limited to a very specific and
rather short period of history. The actual effect of his Liberal
attitude towards change was to negate his Conservatism. But
as in all the situations we have discussed so far, Burke was able
to evade the basic contradiction of his theory because it was
not yet historically clear to him. It was the French Revolu-

tion, however, which finally forced him to see the nature of the contradiction.   It is to this crucial Burkean problem that we must now turn.

His first analysis of the causes of the French Revolution is to be found in the *Reflections on the Revolution in France.*   He does not try to place his analysis within the framework of the whole course of Western history.   Instead his analysis is confined specifically to eighteenth-century France.   In this restricted framework his key causal factors are nevertheless legitimately Conservative, for aside from a general change in "moral opinion," he sees the primary cause of the French Revolution to be the failure of the nobility to satisfy the upper middle class by giving it social status.   This is compatible with the Platonic theory, which also ascribes to status resentment the initial conscious motivation of actual societal change, while moral degeneration is the underlying but unconscious cause of change in the individual.   Oppression by the king, Burke says, cannot be considered the cause of the Revolution because the king ruled mildly.[36]   Nor was a faulty economy or deteriorated culture the cause.[37]   The nobility was still honorable, spirited, and cultured.[38]   The real difficulty was the existence of socio-economic conflict between the nobility and the middle class. The system of inheritance and the retention of large land tracts by the crown and Church prevented the integration of the aristocracy and the middle class.   But most important was the continual snobbery of which the aristocracy was guilty.[39] Having been made to feel inferior, the middle class struck at the aristocracy through the king and the Church [40] and sought to acquire prestige through political power.[41]   The same status resentment was to be found among the new middle-class intellectuals, who served as a kind of link between the rich and poor and were able to direct the lower-class envy of wealth against the aristocracy instead of against the upper middle class.[42]

Since Burke was aware of the growing wealth and numbers of the middle class, the striking thing about this analysis is that logically it should have led to the conclusion that the Revolution was inevitable and justifiable. Burke's basic critique of the Revolution was that it was total and social instead of cautious and political, as he considered the English Revolution to have been. But prestige and status are social problems, and there is no way to change them except through fundamental social transformation. After having dwelt at some length on the problem, he dismisses it as a mere "error of opinion" which "could easily have been corrected." [43] Surely this not only excessively optimistic but amazingly superficial, especially for a Conservative. How does an entire social class go about "easily correcting" a social prejudice which is centuries old? Since he is well aware that much of the British aristocracy had its origin in the upper middle class which had purchased confiscated Church lands in the sixteenth century, he should have concluded that this was one of the factors which caused the altered status ethic of the British landed class. Combined with the further awareness that primogeniture in Britain had aided the intermarriage of landed class and middle class, this should have led him to conclude that similarly revolutionary socio-economic changes would be necessary to produce any solution for the status problem in France. Furthermore, since the relations between the two classes in Britain had become especially close after the political revolutions of the seventeenth century, and since the liberalization of British opinion and ideology (including Conservatism) was also of long standing, the difference between the two countries were so great, even on the basis of Burke's own analyses, that only far-reaching changes could possibly have eliminated them. And this is not to mention a host of other historical differences, many of which we discussed much earlier.

Burke frequently comments on the relative mildness of British problems as compared with those of other countries. Even British "tyrants" such as Cromwell and Henry VIII were mild in comparison with the French revolutionary leaders. He might have concluded that this mildness was due to the fact that societal changes in Britain were spread over three centuries against relative weak resistance. Since the same changes had been thwarted in France for a similar period of time, they could therefore only occur with relatively more violence and totality. But Burke reached none of these conclusions. For all his supposed insistence on the distinctiveness of different societies, he failed to follow the implications of these differences; and this failure led him in the end to a virtual obliteration of comparative analysis. In the *Reflections* he recommends that France follow the example of Britain directly. Somewhat later he apologizes for the misleading implications of this recommendation and calls on France to adjust to its own special problems, for example, by allowing the king greater power than the British monarch. But except for this stress on the king's power, he is still really asking France to reproduce what is essentially the British system of the eighteenth century without having experienced the British changes of the sixteenth and seventeenth centuries.

Burke's analysis of status resentment is quite out of keeping with much of the *Reflections,* in which the causes of the Revolution are often reduced to a selfish, conspiratorial grab of money and power on the part of the middle-class leaders. But while a conspiratorial analysis might have been passably adequate for explaining the conflict with the court in England, it is hardly acceptable for a phenomenon like the French Revolution. Nor does he enlighten us when he concludes that the excessive concessions of the French king were important factors in the subsequently uncontrolled nature of the Revolution. Certainly the character of the king was an important empirical factor, but it was hardly fundamental. To make things worse, he is quite prepared to admit that the French aristocracy was much more dissolute and blind to the danger of "licentious philosophy" than the British, and that the French clergy was culpable in allowing considerable agnosticism in their ranks.[44] If the French ruling class had already deteriorated morally, if the powerful middle class was goaded by status resentment, and if the king was incompetent, where was the foundation for the moderate, harmonious solution which Burke sought? *

Burke must have realized the dilemma in which his status analysis placed him, because he retracted it in his next treatment of the Revolution. Within a year of the publication of the *Reflections* he had sharply reversed himself. The merchants and intellectuals of France, he now found, had in fact been highly honored, and the purchase of titles of nobility had been too easy rather than too difficult.[45] What seems to have disturbed him most about the Revolution was not simply that power in France had passed to wealth, but that it had been transferred to the lower middle class for the first time in modern European history. If he were going to adhere to the thesis that status resentment was the cause of change, he would have to conclude that the lower middle class also wanted higher status. (In Plato's theory this does, in fact, follow as a matter of course once the upper middle class has come to power). What frightened Burke most about all this was that it could be applicable even to Britain. It was, after all, not the entire middle class which had status in Britain. He hastened to admit that at the present "we take few peers from trade and send few into trade." Therefore, "English merchants may also be incited to discontent" as in France if we follow the status assumption through. Under the circumstances, he now wanted to make it clear that "where there is a crown and a hereditary nobility, new wealth cannot ever rank first or even near the first." [46]

What then was the real cause of the Revolution? Burke had frequently spoken of the importance of "interest" as a cause, even a justification, of change, but his use of this concept had always been limited by the assumption of the superiority of harmony. Now that he could no longer assume this superiority, it was dangerous to talk of interest at all, unless the con-

* We might note that here at last Burke has clearly drawn the line beyond which he would refuse to be conciliatory or to adjust to change, and the line lies at the point where the middle class becomes dominant in the society.

cept was first reinterpreted. Therefore, he no longer confined it to economic interest, which had previously been his meaning when he used the term. Interest now included opinion,[47] and the primary motivation of the Revolution was the abstract doctrine which the Liberals had propagated with religious fervor.[48] This was compatible with his insistence in the *Reflections* that the real revolution had been in "manners and moral opinion." [49]   But if ideology was so all-powerful, especially when fed by real "abuses," then the rest of Europe was also susceptible to it, and in fact he now pointed to the existence of "seeds of revolution" in Germany, Spain, the Papal States, and Russia.[50]

Superficially, the emphasis on "moral opinion" seems to rest on real Conservative theory, but actually its use by Burke and almost all contemporary American Conservatives is misleading. When they speak of the primary force of "ideas," they cannot mean what non-Conservatives mean by rational ideas or ideology.   It is not intellectual forces in themselves which are decisive for Conservatives, because this would mean that all ideas are equally powerful and primary and it would make Conservative harmony impossible at any time.   More important, it would make rational ideas rather than social and moral relations the arena in which the conflicts of history are fought. Burke indeed seems to take this position when he says there is no limit to the power of men who have control of the communications channels of a country,[51] and Kirk likes to cite this statement as an example of the relevance of Burkean analysis for contemporary problems like totalitarianism.   But this is shallow Conservatism.

When Conservatives speak of ideas, they mean moral ideas. However, they cannot mean that the ideas are more vital than the actual state of morality, for this would imply that all morality is manipulable and subject to indefinite change.   For them the ideas really reflect the actual state of morality.   If abstract Liberal ideology leads to a revolution, the Conservative can only conclude that the moral state of the society has already declined so seriously that it is irreparable.   That

Burke was aware of this implication in his second analysis of the French Revolution can be inferred from his resignation at the end of it. The man who had lightly dismissed the decay theory inherent in his own values now backed into that very theory, though with the typical obscurantism of the post-Revolutionary liberal Conservative. Exhausted by the attempt to make sense out of the Revolution, he sinks into a mood of despair. These are virtually the last words in his *Thoughts on French Affairs:*

I have done with this subject. . . . If a great change is to be made in human affairs, the minds of men will be fitted to it. . . . Every fear, every hope will forward it; and then they who persist in opposing this mighty current in human affairs will appear rather to resist the decrees of Providence itself than the mere designs of men. They will not be resolute and firm, but perverse and obstinate.[52]

In the next few years Burke's pessimistic mood about the course of the Revolution continued. In the same letter in which he rejected the decay theory as an excuse for inactivity, he deplored the apparent inability of the European aristocracies and monarchies to take the actions which he considered necessary to fight the Revolution. "What can be done," he cried, "against the resolution of the great to accomplish their own ruin?"[53] He never asked himself whether this very will to self-destruction was not itself a clear sign of the decay which he rejected. Nor did he try to reconcile this inability to act even in the face of a supreme danger with his earlier dismissal of the status problem as a defeat which "could easily have been corrected" by the French rulers without revolution.

When the Revolution had first broken out, Burke had scoffed at British fear of France's potential strength. Britain, this "anti-abstract" and supposedly realistic thinker asserted, could look forward to a long period of French weakness under these meddling, upstart leaders because "the law of gravity" prevents that which has degenerated from rising as rapidly as it has fallen.[54] A few years later he confessed his error. Who could have foreseen, he asked in despair, that a total revolution would be caused by mere intellectuals? Who could have known that with a complete absence of known talent France would be able to govern with unprecedented authority and supply treasuries and armies "by fear alone?" [55]

Entangled by now in a jungle of dilemmas and contradictions, Burke tried in his last years to make a new start in analyzing the causes of the Revolution. In the *Second Letter . . . on the Regicide Peace* he seems suddenly to shift his causal analysis and to accept the primacy of economic motivations. Before the Revolution, he now finds, French leaders had observed that France was falling behind in the race for trade and expansion. They admired the energy of the ancient republics and decided that France's solution was to become a republic. This decision was supported by American success in establishing a republic for their large country. The French king did not have the energy necessary for effective resistance. (Contemporary monarchies in general suffer from inability to pursue single goals effectively, because they allow a wide measure of freedom).[56] Burke still insists that the Revolution was preceded and prepared by a more important moral revolution, in which the "chain of subordination" between "the great" and the populace had been broken. But the moral change had accompanied the growth in the wealth and power, as well as the "great energies and impatient talents," of the middle class. The lower classes had come under its influence and the intellectuals had become its allies. Finally, the development of the modern press had made every government into one largely "democratic" in spirit and prepared for "great changes." The movement than gathered such great momentum that there was no longer any way of stopping it, and though Louis XVI meant to make partial concessions, he ended by yielding totally.[57]

It is bad enough that this analysis justifies the Revolution even more than the previous ones. Much worse is the fact that it opens for Burke the most disastrous question of all. If the French Revolution was caused by the advance of the middle class in its quest for wealth, what would save Great Britain from a similar revolution? Burke in effect asks himself this very question, and his answer is that Britain is saved by its great wealth.[58] A moment's reflection will make clear the astounding nature of this admission. If the whole system of British balance and harmony depended finally on its wealth, then material forces and values were stronger than those of harmony and morality. Most important, Burke's whole ideology becomes an illusion, for the British system was then not one which permitted the pursuit of Liberal goals within a fundamentally Conservative framework, but on the contrary, one which retained Conservative characteristics for the moment because it was so preeminently successful in its Liberalism. If the direction of British history was already Liberal, should one not have expected that it would continue (as in fact it did) even beyond the Burkean point of acceptable change, to the clear dominance of the entire middle class? Does this mean that Britain did not have to go through a Liberal revolution in the eighteenth century only because she had in fact already gone through such a revolution? Does it not mean also that America could appear for the moment to be "Conservative" in its Revolution, as compared to that of France, because she did not have to go through a Liberal revolution at all, because she was, as Louis Hartz and Elmer Davis say, "born free?"

Burke's dilemma is now complete and inescapable. No matter where he turns, the conclusion is unavoidable that his combination of Liberalism and Conservatism rested on an illusion which was possible only for a fleeting moment of history. If material forces and goals are dominant, then the French Revolution was not only inevitable but a positive historical advance. If social and moral forces and goals are dominant, then the French Revolution was a degeneration but one which could not have been stopped and one which would have its impact even on England. The supposed success which contemporary Conservatives claim for Burke in altering the course of European history rests on another of those confusions which by now we can expect of them. The most that can be claimed is that he roused Britain to defend its particular brand of Liberalism and capitalism against that of France. Even this claim must depend on the absurd notion that without Burke England would not have challenged France's bid for world leadership. In the goal which really mattered for Burke—stemming the further advance of Liberalism in both Europe and Great Britain—he was a total failure. When Kirk, in a kind of intellectual desperation, ascribes to Burke Britain's success in adjusting to change without violence, he is making a claim which would have been no consolation to Burke. It also forces him to ignore completely the extent to which Burke's liberal Conservatism was itself the product of British history and society and not simply a force from heaven which launched a new Conservative tradition for the country.

Unable to avoid choosing between the Liberal and the Conservative views of history and change because he could not remain neutral in the French Revolution, Burke finally makes the only choice really possible for him. Still repeating bravely that he does not think empires fall "of their own weight" but unable to bring himself to open acceptance of the historical theory of moral decay inherent in his own Conservatism, he takes the only escape route he can find. In what is virtually his last real judgment on the Revolution, he confesses,

Our moral sense is confounded by what has happened to good people in France, and we sink into silent adoration of the inscrutable dispensations of God.[59]

Only a few months earlier he had admitted that it is because we are unable to trace clearly the causal process of decline that we are "obliged" to attribute it to mere chance or to the "hand of God." [60] Who can doubt that Burke has really arrived at the Platonic theory of degeneration or that this was his predestined fate from the beginning?

New Elements in the Cycle: The New Conservatives

To turn now to the theories of change of contemporary American Burkeans is an anticlimax. If liberal Conservatism was already an impossible contradiction by the time Burke died, the later Burkeans have in effect been living on borrowed time. The only interesting point to note about our twentieth-century reactionary and adjusted Conservatives is that almost all of them now accept the concept of the general social and moral deterioration of civilization. Henry Adams obviously adhered to this idea in his theory of the degeneration of "energy." It was also accepted by Babbitt, More, and Cram. It was implicit in all the discussions of the Southern agrarians and explicit in the writings of Agar,[61] though he has not integrated it with his recent "adjustment." Hallowell writes the theoretical history of Europe by its light, though he has "adjusted" this history with his Aristotelianism. Even Kirk accepts cycles of degeneration and regeneration as inevitable "once reverence is lost."[62] Only Rossiter and Viereck have nothing to say about moral cycles. But all of them, whether reactionary or adjusted, still sing the same song about how much can be done by moral determination to prevent decline. After two thousand years of Graeco-Roman history and well over a thousand years of Western history, in which Conservatives have continually admitted decline from the preceding age, in spite of the determination of earlier Conservatives to arrest the process, they still go on playing the same pointless game. Perhaps it is because their "realistic" aim is generally to preserve the harmonies and values of the most recent rather than the more remote past that they are able to blind themselves to the vacuum in which they live intellectually. Whatever the reason, the process continues merrily on its way.

There is little attempt among contemporary Conservatives to examine their theory of change in any detail. Russell Kirk occasionally tosses out analyses which are presumably examples of Conservative "realism." On no evidence but the old unexamined assumption that one great moral leader changes the course of history, he concludes that if Canning had lived a little longer he might have prevented the complete repeal of the pro-agrarian Corn Laws in the nineteenth century and saved a "balanced economy" for England.[63] Since Canning did not

live long enough and since Kirk only says he "might" have
changed later history, he runs little risk of conclusive refutation. When he deals with clear Conservative failure like that
of Calhoun, he is prepared to admit that the forces of materialism were too strong even for this supposedly competent thinker.
But when the subject is even a little obscure Kirk is quick to
claim victory, even though it may be hollow. Ignoring all the
dilemmas of Burke's politics, he hails Burke's great success in
saving Britain from Jacobinism. He might as meaningfully
have acclaimed Yugoslavian Orthodoxy for saving the country
from Stalinism if the victory of English over French Liberalism
in Britain is such a real consolation for him.

By the time Kirk comes to Disraeli, however, he finds it a
little more difficult to claim the latter's political successes as
unequivocal by Conservative standards. Therefore, he con-
tents himself with the fantastic assertion that Disraeli succeeded
because of the power of his Conservative ideas and not because
of his economic and political reform program.[64] But his worst
rationalization occurs when he pounces upon David Riesman's
mention of the high birth rate in primitive traditionalist societies. The reason such Conservative societies have high birth
rates, Kirk says, is that their members have superior characters
and are not bored like modern men. Their high death rates on
the other hand are due only to the "accident" that they lived in
a prescientific age.[65] This convenient reasoning enables Kirk
both to ignore the high birth rate of the Liberal nineteenth
century and to give Liberalism no credit at all for the advances
of modern medicine, while pretending that the Conservative
advocacy of adjusting to nature instead of controlling it has
nothing to do with the medical backwardness of Conservative
societies. At any rate, Kirk issues the Burkean call to prepare
for great "Providential changes" often enough to make it clear
that even he does not really think he has escaped Burke's fate.

The only new idea of permanent significance for Conservative theory is Peter Drucker's admission that the desire for
rising standards of living can no longer be resisted by any

people and that economic expansion is now built into industrial society. This admission has extremely profound consequences for Conservatism. If economic expansion depends on the continual stimulation of desires for commodities, as is the case in contemporary America, then the Conservative minimization of tensions has become an illusion. Even if this is not the case, the fact that managers (the "natural aristocracy" of industrial society) must be concerned constantly with expansion and with the initiation of change makes it impossible for them to develop the harmonious, tensionless, graceful personalities which Conservatism assumes to be the product of leisure, tradition, and an unharried life. If we accept the further Conservative assumption that such personalities are necessary for the capacity or inclination to think of society in terms of harmony, then we must conclude that industrial managers are less qualified to fulfill Conservative goals than any previous "aristocracy" in history. If additional evidence is needed, William Whyte's study of the "organization man" makes it clear that the current stereotype of the tranquil, well-rounded executive is at best an unrealized hope.[66] Drucker once described trustees of investment funds as well-educated, moderately wealthy and conscious of their moral obligations. This sounds somewhat more like the Conservative ideal than the characteristics which he thinks managers should have. But trustees of investment funds would never be accepted as an aristocracy in industrial society. Even if we assumed that there may be a political aristocracy in the industrial society of the future, such an aristocracy would, like the managers, still have to be responsible for the over-all economic expansion of the society. Nor can the Conservative dismiss lightly the impact of permanent, "built-in" industrial change on tradition. And for the average citizen the prospects for the conquest of nature, for space travel, for weather control, for mastering the basic sources of energy, are so overwhelmingly appealing that the Conservative attitude towards nature cannot possibly remain feasible for future societies.

It is bad enough that Conservatism is continually defeated within the "cycle" of a civilization. But it is far worse that the process of degeneration and defeat which it is forced to recognize in the course of a single civilization is equally evident in the changes from one civilization to the next. If harmony is measured by the identification of the individual with the societal totality, by maximum cohesion and minimum tensions or conflicts, then the tribe was probably more harmonious than the society of antiquity, ancient society more than Christian civilization, and Christian civilization more than the industrial world which has now made its appearance and which will undoubtedly be the basis of future societies. The defeat of Conservatism has been a constant of history all along, but it has become more decisive with each age. Now that man is on the threshold of changes comparable to the beginning of civilization itself, Conservatism is in danger of becoming a kind of ideological fossil. Even if it is going to adjust itself to an industrially and technologically expanding society, it must find some limit beyond which it denies the legitimacy of increasing material satisfactions, unless it is to surrender one of its key values. Neither Drucker nor the others indicate where this limit might lie. But even if they find it, Conservatism will have traveled far along the road to perdition since the primitive Golden Age.

Conservative theory must now make room not only for industrial progress but also for modern individualism. The effect of these new elements on the cyclical theory of degeneration can be seen in Niebuhr's formulations. The fundamental ambivalence of history, he says, lies in man's capacity to break the harmonies of nature.[67] As the simpler, more complete harmonies are shattered, man must use his reason to create new, artificial harmonies. Man is thus capable of initial historical periods of creativity. But sooner or later original sin asserts itself through sensuality or pride, and men think they can perfect the process of history without divine aid.[68] Hence there is the inevitable stage of decline, an inevitability, however, based somehow on human freedom and sin, not on natural necessity. For Niebuhr, as for St. Augustine, the over-all process of history remains ambiguous to the end. But for St. Augustine the ambiguity lay in the simultaneous strengthening of the Church and of the enemies of the Church. The process of regeneration would be matched by one of persecution. For Niebuhr the ambiguity has a different meaning. On the one hand, human civilizations are leaving a cumulative heritage of technological and rational progress, more inclusive ends, and more complex human relations. On the other hand, the periods of disorder and conflict grow more intense as human civilization grows more complex.[69] The only ultimate hope for man lies, therefore, in Christian eschatology. In the final judgment and redemption, God will fulfill the process of history, since history cannot fulfill itself.[70] Human progress will not be negated, but only God can make this progress compatible with total harmony, because this is the essential achievement which history itself cannot reach.

If Conservatives are willing to accept this theory, their future will be assured. Though Niebuhr himself has in the past made very different use of his own theory, Conservatives can, in time to come, react in their traditional way to each crucial advance that anti-Conservatives make by escaping from harmonies of the past. They can do nothing to further the advances themselves, but after progress occurs they can continue their historical career of lamentation at each step in the subsequent Conservative degeneration. This will keep them busy until the end of history. By then, man may have come within an inch of universal mastery but will presumably have failed to achieve a corresponding degree of harmony. At that all-important moment, when neither Conservatives nor anti-Conservatives know how to solve the problem, Conservatism will finally perform the consummate act which will vindicate its long historical suffering—it will pass the problem on to God!

X

The Conservative
Theory of Change:
Upside-Down History

The Conservative view of history as a series of cycles in which the early periods of harmony are succeeded by cumulative degeneration is not merely a figment of the imagination. If all the relevant terms are given Conservative definitions, this cyclical theory is a tenable reflection of the actual course of history. If harmony depends on a minimum of economic expansion, then the earliest periods of Graeco-Roman and of Western European civilization were more harmonious than those which followed. If morality depends on the minimizing of individual desires, and if social cohesion is maximal when it is unconscious, traditional, and anchored in relatively fixed classes or estates, then the later periods of civilization are periods of moral and social degeneration. Few would disagree that the twentieth century has brought moral confusion and a serious weakening of social cohesiveness. By Conservative standards it is true that things have been getting worse since the Middle Ages, and there is no foreseeable prospect of improvement.

But far from being a support for the Conservative ideology, this theory of history offers every reason for rejecting Conservatism. If harmony is constantly giving way to other values, then the obvious conclusion is that Conservatives speak not for mankind, but for its tail end. Instead of condemning history on the basis of Conservative values, we should reject Conservatism on the basis of history. The fact that no Conservative ideologist has ever been prepared to rest his case on the cyclical theory alone makes it clear that, consciously or otherwise, all of them are aware that the theory is self-defeating. It is for this reason that they are forced ultimately into the realm of Mystery, where they delude themselves into thinking that they are immune from rational criticism. Our final task is to follow them into the dark corners of Conservatism and to show that even their final refuge is nothing but illusion.

Theoretical Inadequacy of the Conservative Theory of Moral Change

Ever since Plato, Conservatives have sought in an Original Mystery the explanation of the failure of Conservatism. For Plato, the loss of early harmony was caused by improper breeding, by departure from the unknowable astronomical laws governing the seasons for mating. The result was a drop in the capacity of men for affection and moral self-control. The patristic conception of original sin served the same theoretical purpose as the Platonic conception of Mating-Out-of-Season. But it pushed the Mystery back to the "Golden Age" before the dawn of history, when man first asserted his own ego instead of obeying God's commandments. The later historical tendency to moral degeneration was a consequence of original sin.

It is unnecessary to dwell on the obvious irrationality of these explanations for Conservative failure, or on the fact that the Garden of Eden story, in which the Fathers of the Church saw the first "Revelation" of original sin, was interpreted differently by Judaism. The theories of improper mating and of original sin are not really crucial in themselves, for purposes of evaluating Conservatism. If Plato or the Fathers of the Church had stopped with these explanations, they would have done nothing to escape from the central problem which we have traced. If a mysterious First Cause is responsible for the historical defeat of Conservative values, then the defeat is as inevitable as it would be if everyone agreed that Conservative values are false. The only qualification we would have to add to the irrelevance of Conservatism for historical man would be a perennial sense of guilt. But on the other hand, if moral degeneration were inevitable, we might as easily conclude that sin should be enjoyed while it lasts, or that it cannot, under these circumstances, be sin at all.

The truth is, of course, that Conservatives have never been able to rest with a theory, even of Mystery, which would lead to a conclusion of inevitable degeneration. Although Conservatives have asserted an initial presumption towards degeneration, resulting from the nonrational First Cause, they have always added that the way is open to resist decline. For Plato, resistance depended on rational conviction that Conservatism offered the only solution to current problems. For Christian Conservatives, it depended on the grace of God. For Conservatives at all times, it has included some element of moral determination on the part of mankind. Without these qualifications, which leave the way open for stopping degeneration, the whole Conservative theory would fall to the ground. But with them, Conservatism is forced to further conclusions which negate the effect of the original qualifications, in spite of increasing resort to Mystery.

The Platonic position that reason alone can cause a fundamental change in the values of a society is one which few people would hold today, and it is particularly indefensible as the instrument of regeneration in the direction of Conservatism. Conservative theory, with its emphasis on the primacy of morality, demands that love and the moral will be the human origin of regeneration, and, except for Plato, this has always been its position.* Even before the development of Christian doctrine, the Stoics had rejected the thesis that reason could by

---

* The orthodox Christian conceptions of the predestined election of the few and the total dependence of a regenerate moral will on grace deepened the sense of Mystery, but they did not alter the fact that only individual men were directly regenerated. It was not through a change in societal relations that grace was bestowed on mankind.

itself lead the way back to Conservatism, and no Conservative theorists in Western civilization have accepted it.

If the moral will is the origin of regeneration, it must also be the origin of degeneration. It is essential that this point be understood clearly, because it is often obscured in Conservative formulations. The Conservative cannot accept the thesis that changes in individual morality are caused by changes in societal relations, without destroying his entire ideology. If moral change is a consequence of societal change, then there is no reason to condemn men for failing to fulfill a moral code which is related to earlier periods of history. Conservatives must, therefore, assert that, far from being an effect of history, inner moral change is the first human cause of each historical change. This is, in fact, the persistent Conservative position, but its meaning is often glossed over. It does not mean simply that economic expansion, for example, is preceded by the desire for increased wealth. This would be a mere truism. The primacy of moral change means that each transformation of history must be a separate causal unit, in which an uncaused drop or increase in the individual capacity for affection and moral self-control causes all other manifestations of change in individuals and in society. In Freudian terms, economic expansion is caused by a sudden scarcity of libidinal energy, according to Conservatism. But Conservatism has no rational way of accounting for the moral changes which occur throughout an entire society or civilization within a relatively limited period of time. The theory of uncaused moral change must conclude that the changes originate simultaneously in large numbers of individuals either because of pure chance, or because God intervenes actively at every important point of change, or because degeneration is predetermined *unless* God intervenes to reverse the process through regenerative grace. In any case, the irrational web of Mystery comes to pervade the entire structure of Conservatism and its conception of historical change.

But, given the continuation of the cycle of degeneration throughout the course of Western civilization, the conception becomes shaky, even as a matter of obscurantist "faith." Plato's hopes for regeneration obviously did not materialize during the course of ancient civilization. Neither reason nor moral determination prevented the continued decline and ultimate disintegration of his civilization. The advantage of the Augustinian conception of history, which based the promise of regeneration on the grace of God, was that, applied to the beginning of the new Western civilization, it seemed to fulfill its promise. But the validity of the patristic theory of history becomes highly suspect when viewed in relation to the subsequent course of history. As long as Christianity accompanied a period of regeneration, it seemed as though God's grace was "available" and the patristic doctrine made some sense. But the subsequent course of Western civilization, even in Conservative descriptions, has followed the same process of degeneration as did ancient civilization. In fact, industrialization has, by Conservative standards, made the contemporary period even worse than the corresponding period in the earlier cycle. From this historical viewpoint, the Conservative can only conclude that God's grace has *not* changed the course of history, that the process of degeneration remains as inevitable now as it was in Graeco-Roman civilization.* If God's grace has a Conservative purpose, then the supply is limited and running dangerously low; and at a time of increasing scarcity of grace, it becomes increasingly difficult to place moral responsibility on the individual's free will for failing to fulfill the Conservative goals. The inevitability behind original sin, and with it the negation of the whole Conservative theory, looms ever larger. Simultaneously, God's grace fades ever further. Neo-orthodoxy has already pushed divine regeneration ahead to the end of history. In the meantime, whatever its validity for other interpretations of Christianity, original sin has become a

* The provision in the Augustinian formulations for the future strengthening of the forces of evil in the City of Man was coupled with the promise of the progress of the City of God. By Conservative standards only the City of Man advanced.

dangerous support for the Conservative Christian. Yet without it, the Conservative affirmation of the primacy of moral change and the exhortation to moral effort still lead back to the same conclusion of inevitable defeat.

Historical Falsity of the Conservative Theory of Social Change

If the Conservative resort to Mystery forces it ever onward to new Mysteries, none of which solves its underlying dilemmas, there is one sphere where it is finally forced, in spite of itself, into the light of rational historical theory. Here the problem is not merely the persistent inability to formulate a doctrine which satisfactorily resolves its glaring contradictions, but outright falsification of history; and with the exposure of this falsification, the Conservative edifice collapses, Mysteries and all.

The Conservative theory that historical changes originate with a change in the individual's capacity for affection requires the further theory that, within the realm of societal relations, social changes occur first and cause economic, political, and intellectual changes. This follows because social relations are within society what the capacity for affection is within the individuals, that is, they are the externalization of affection. The primacy of social change within society has, in fact, been at the root of Conservatism ever since Plato. But again, it is important to understand clearly what this theory means. It does *not* mean that social forces "interact" with other forces in society. It does *not* mean that an undesirable economic change endangers the existing socio-moral code. The Platonic-Conservative position requires that social change be viewed *always* as a first cause which need not have occurred. This implies that industrialization, for example, is the consequence of earlier changes in the family system, the status system, and the moral code. On the other hand, it must be denied that industrialization is the cause of later social changes. For Plato, private property was the effect of the original moral degeneration, not the cause. The same was true of the Stoics and the Church Fathers. In the Platonic theory, all subsequent change was preceded by a change in the status system, and at any given point the effect of economic or political changes could have been stopped. The primacy of social change is the cornerstone of Conservative theory, for if it is not true, then the Conservative hope can never be other than illusory. If a particular social system is the consequence of economic or political causes, then, as Burke admitted, a given code of honor is as transient as "summer flies." Even worse, morality then cannot be the foundation of political power, and Conservative harmony is the result of special historical conditions which cannot be recaptured without a recurrence of the antecedent conditions. Conservatism, in short, becomes simply the rationalization of early periods of civilization rather than a valid theory of human values.

The question of whether social relations change first in the sequence of historical change runs immediately into the contemporary American doctrine that all causal elements in a given situation "interact," that each element is both cause and effect, that changes occur in many relationships simultaneously, and that causation is therefore "multilinear." There is an overwhelming amount of empirical data to support this position. Psychological factors such as "confidence" are now known to be elements in economics. An election will be influenced by money, but it will also depend on traditional predispositions, social prestige, the character of candidates, or events in some distant part of the world. On the other hand, the results of an election will probably influence all the factors which influenced it, including the characters of the men elected. The theory of multiple causation and interaction is in itself a partial refutation of the Conservative theory, because to admit that changes in social relations are to any extent the effects of other changes is to weaken the Conservative case by a corresponding extent. But this is not refutation, and if one does not go beyond the theory of interaction, then Conservatism can still claim that social changes are somehow the most decisive.

If the theory of interaction merely asserted that a given event has multiple causes and that effects become the causes of new effects, then it would be neither very new nor very significant. Few theorists in history have ever said that every event has a single cause or that every cause has a single, discrete effect. What is new in the way some social scientists handle the concept of interaction is their conclusion that one should not speak of cause and effect at all, but rather of changes in "functional" interrelations, and that causation has no identifiable sequence. The fallacy behind this conclusion is the assumption that all historical changes are of equal importance, that there is no difference between a quantitative and a qualitative change. It is easy to point out that in the shift from medieval to modern society there was a continual configuration of changes which affected all aspects of societal relations. If there were economic and political changes in the fifteenth century, it is equally true that there were social and intellectual changes. It has become a commonplace since Max Weber's *The Protestant Ethic and the Spirit of Capitalism* to point out that changes in the social ethic began even before the breakup of medieval society, that these changes pointed in the direction of capitalism and of the later Protestantism which facilitated the progress of capitalism. But none of these formulations addresses itself to the vital question of the sequence in which the various aspects of societal relations broke qualitatively and finally with the Middle Ages, the order with which the new systems became dominant. When the question is posed in this way, it is not nearly as difficult to answer as some of the "interactionists" would have us believe, and it is particularly easy when applied to the Conservative thesis about the primacy of social change. If the Conservative position is true, then we must be able to find not merely that some changes occurred in the social ethic very early in the transition to modern society, but that during the "modern" period (let us say, from 1400 to 1800) the Liberal social ethic broke with the medieval ethic *and* became dominant before the corresponding break in the economic, political, and intellectual realm.

When this question is applied to England, the most advanced nation during the relevant period, it becomes impossible to find any support for the Conservative theory. As R. H. Tawney has shown, the full development of the capitalist social ethic did not begin until the end of the seventeenth century. From the fifteenth century, when commercial capitalism began to dominate European economies, until the eighteenth century there was continual resistance, even in the "Protestant ethic," to accepting the pursuit of wealth as legitimate in itself.

When the age of the Reformation begins, economics is still a branch of ethics, and ethics of theology; . . . the legitimacy of economic transactions is tried by reference, less to the movements of the market, than to moral standards derived from the traditional teaching of the Christian church. . . . The secularization of political thought, which was to be the work of the next two centuries, had profound reactions on social speculation, and by the Restoration the whole perspective, at least in England, has been revolutionized. . . and the idea of a rule of right is replaced by economic expediency as the arbiter of policy and the criterion of conduct. . . .
. . . . Thus the conflict between religion and those natural economic ambitions which the thought of an earlier age had regarded with suspicion is suspended by a truce which divides the life of mankind between them. The former takes as its province the individual soul, the latter, the intercourse of man with his fellows in the activities of business and the affairs of society.[1]

But during the entire period when the social ethic was resisting change, the economy was expanding as a result of the new productive system, in spite of the fact that this expansion was probably retarded by the social resistances. In the meantime there were also basic advances in scientific method and a change in the dominant ideology. The Liberalism of the seventeenth century was fundamentally contradictory to the medieval ideology in spite of the carry-over of particular medieval

terms and ideas. Furthermore, the modern state and the absolute monarchy which emerged in the sixteenth century represented a complete break with the medieval system; and by the
end of the seventeenth century, the capitalist merchant class,
which already held economic power, was secure in the seats of
political power.* The change in social ethics which corresponded to these other changes did not occur until last. The
major characteristic of a social system is not that it initiates
change but that it resists and changes only under prolonged
pressure. Even in the eighteenth century, Burke could still
see strong vestiges of the medieval system of "manners,"
chivalry, and the code of honor. But he could see no traces of
the medieval economy in modern British capitalism.

The transition from medieval to modern society is perhaps
the most crucial change in history for Conservative theory, and
the falsity of the theory when applied to this period of change
is alone enough to destroy the foundation of Conservatism.
But it is very likely true of all major historical changes that
the social system is the last rather than the first to break decisively with the preceding period. In the period of the mercantile Greek city-state (c.700-c.300 B.C.), the transformations
to a commercial money economy, a territorial political system
which consciously legislated law, and a democratic ideology
were all completed before the traditional communal ethic fully
gave way to a correspondingly complete individualistic social
ethic. In the Late Middle Ages (c.1000-c.1400), the model for
Western Conservatism, the shift from the intensely self-denying

* The recent controversy among British historians about the class origins
of the seventeenth-century Civil War does not affect the present thesis. H. R.
Trevor-Roper makes the unorthodox claim that it was an economically declining
gentry which spearheaded the Civil War in order to unseat the already dominant merchant class and the office-holding nobility, both of which were protected by the monarchy. But since he emphasizes that the gentry challenge
failed, it would remain true that power was in the hands of the upper middle
class by the end of the century. The qualification that this power was shared
by yeoman farmers and a land-owning class which often depended on capitalist
agriculture and whose upper segment had family ties to the commercial class
does not affect the present position. See H. R. Trevor-Roper, *The Gentry,
1540–1640* (Cambridge: Cambridge University Press, 1953).

Platonic-Augustinian moral code to the far more permissive Aristotelian-Thomistic morality did not occur until the late thirteenth century, long after the crucial economic change to the town economy and the guild system which distinguished the late medieval economy from the early manorial system. It is well worth repeating here that the "Conservative" medieval society was not nearly as Conservative as its later apologists would have us believe. The twelfth century, which was for the Conservative John of Salisbury a period of degeneration and moral corruption, was followed by the flowering of medieval civilization in the thirteenth century, and it was this later period which became the true ideal of later Conservatism. Yet, the dominant ideology by the end of the thirteenth century was Thomism, whose basic Aristotelian values were not Conservative but authoritarian, though a Conservative form of authoritarianism. When contemporary Conservatives move promiscuously between their own ideology and Thomism or Aristotelianism, they seem completely unaware of the admission of inadequacy implicit in their confusion.

The untenability of the Conservative theory applies also to the contemporary period. Obviously there have been profound and continual economic changes throughout the twentieth century. But the basis of contemporary economic relations was established by the Industrial Revolution, which began just before the beginning of the nineteenth century, and by the industrial corporation, which was developed by the end of that century. All the economic changes of Western civilization in the twentieth century still rest on these foundations of the previous century. The present century is, however, preeminently a period of political change, the final result of which has not yet emerged (though the outlines will perhaps be clear by 1984). Much of the current political development has already crystallized—the growth of administrative services, the advance of centralization, and the strengthening of the executive branch, for example. But the social system, as the Conservatives themselves have emphasized time and again, is in a state of increasing chaos. The older family system and the older moral code have been seriously weakened, but nothing has taken their place yet. The most striking characteristic of the "other-directedness" which David Riesman describes and of the "organization man's" "Social Ethics," which William Whyte delineates, is that the new morality has no content, that it consists only of a direction, a readiness to obey the norms set by "others," or by the "organization." It is as though the "Social Man" for whom Peter Drucker holds out so much Conservative hope were waiting for the Economic, Political, and Ideological Man to tell him what to do. Yet even readiness for future moral change, the distinguishing trait of the new ethic, is far from being socially dominant in contemporary society. Our historical distance from the commercial, individualistic society of the sovereign Liberal nation-state can, in economic and political terms, already be measured in decades. But the emergence of a new social system still lies somewhere in the future.

It may be objected that this discussion is a cavalier treatment of so broad a subject as the nature of social change, but this would misrepresent the present intention. The common contemporary thesis that we do not know enough about history to prove or disprove general theories about it is a half-truth. Certainly, history is a fantastically complex study insofar as it includes all the multi-sided activities of man. Certainly, there are vast gaps in our historical data. But the answers to many of the most crucial problems of theory depend on the way the relevant questions are formulated. The contention here is that if the foregoing formulation of the test of Conservative theory is correct, there is no question that the data are available for drawing valid conclusions. Furthermore, the present task is not to support any particular theory of social change, but simply to disprove the Conservative hypothesis that social change is primary in the history of society. The persistent inadequacy of Conservatism lies in the fact that its advocates have never formulated their theory in a way which could be tested; they have continually sought refuge in the obscure and the mysterious. The point here is that the Conservative Mysteries are the result not of profundity but of the fact that a rational presentation of Conservative theory is so clearly untenable. Conservatives have *never* presented the slightest shred of relevant rational evidence that their theory is true, because the evidence is not available. But the counterevidence is within easy reach.

The analyses of Peter Viereck provide a typical example of Conservative obscurantism. But they also help demonstrate that the falsity of Conservative theory can be revealed by proper formulation of the relevant questions without depending on the availability of new information. Viereck applies the Platonic-Burkean concept of status resentment (which for some reason he traces only from Nietzsche) to American politics. The American "masses," he says, have always wanted to be "quality folk," but they have also resented the superior status symbols of the American elite, especially the New England "aristocracy" of old wealth. The Populist revolt was the crystallization of this resentment, and its targets of urban business, England, international finance, and Jews were all symbols associated in some way with its real enemy—the New England status elite. The Populist prejudices against recent immigrants on the other end of the social scale were also expressions of the need for status superiority. But their most important motivation was correctly captured in the refrain which Vachel Lindsay ascribes to the backers of Bryan: Smash Plymouth Rock!

From Populism, Viereck traces the later development of the status motivation to the Progressive Party of La Follette, reactionaries of the 1930's such as Coughlin and Lemke, and the McCarthyites of the 1950's. The participants in these movements changed somewhat in the course of time, and some of their slogans changed, but the underlying status resentment against the New England target remained the same. Catholics and other immigrant groups were added to the movement, especially after the rankling resentment caused by the 1928 election. The bitterest hostility of McCarthyism was directed not against Communists but against status symbols like "the boys in the striped pants." The transfer of animosity from the "Wall Street conspiracy" to the "Communist conspiracy" was incidental and caused only by shifting historical circumstance. The constant factor was the identification of New England "aristocratic" symbols (including Harvard) with each of the conspiracies.

Viereck also finds a general restlessness in the suburbs. Here too he thinks that the status motivation is crucial, though in reverse, so to speak. The suburbanites have risen so fast in the socio-economic scale since the war that they have necessarily felt insecure in their new status, and this social insecurity easily lends itself to political reaction.[2]

This is a reasonably interesting analysis of certain concrete historical and contemporary developments. But Viereck is not simply offering descriptive data. His repeated emphasis on status motivation is part of a conscious attempt to support the Conservative position on the primacy of social and moral causes in history. In a negative sense, his central aim is to disprove any theory which would make economic relations causally more important than social relations; and he makes periodic generalizations about the inferior importance of economics. But the generalizations are so formulated that there is no relation whatsoever between them and his concrete analyses.

Instead of confining the generalizations to distinct though related categories like social relations and economic relations, both of which are aspects of societal organization, he pits economics against "values" and "ideas."[3] In so doing, he completely shifts his ground and obscures the issue. "Values" are synonymous neither with morality nor with social relations. Values are human purposes and purposes are not confined to any one kind of relationship. The disputes of theory and ideology are not over the question of whether there are such things as human purposes, but over the relative importance of particular categories of value. Obviously economics depends on "values," the particular purpose of economics being the production and consumption of material goods. The "value" behind social relations is human affection. If Viereck means to say that man is not motivated only by the need for material goods, that he "does not live by bread alone," then he will have a difficult time finding anyone to disagree with such a platitude. To say that historical change is based on changes in the content of human values is to say that history is concerned with men and not chimpanzees. To say that men have more than one kind of basic values is not even to distinguish them from the chimpanzees.

When Viereck jubililantly concludes that economics is secondary because it depends on organization and because organization depends on values,[4] he is saying less than nothing. Organization is one of the essential elements in the concept of society itself. The question in dispute is the relative importance of social organization and economic organization in historical change, not the difference between organization and nonorganization.

The term "ideas" is equally irrelevant to the central issue. If "ideas" refer to ideology—a conscious, rational conception of how society should be organized and how control should be distributed—then the claim that ideas are historically primary has nothing to do with Conservatism at all, and Viereck looks no further into the possible primacy of ideology anyway. If the term refers simply to the existence of mental images, then obviously it is, like values, a concomitant of all human activity. If it refers to the whole range of culture, then the argument has shifted away from the conception of society altogether. Culture includes science and it would be little consolation to Conservatism to prove that science changes societal relations.

Viereck even thinks he can prove that the economic collapse of 1929 was not the real cause of the depression of the 1930's by pointing to the prior existence of psychological revulsion against materialism and the economic system.[5] But, aside from the fact that he offers no proof that this psychological resentment was really widespread, he is again shifting, this time from the societal category of economics to the realm of psychology, which deals with man's inner state rather than his external relationships. In none of these confusions of terminology does Viereck address himself to the real issue which he has raised—the relative historical importance of economic and social relations.

Only in his concrete analyses does he implicitly delineate something of the central problem, and then he completely fails to support the Conservative position. The emphasis on the mere existence of status resentment proves nothing. Hofstadter also underscores the importance of status motivations, not only for Populism but for the entire Progressive movement of the early twentieth century. But he points out that the technological revolution in international transportation and the consequent fall of farm prices on the world market were the most immediate causes of the change in farmers' social attitudes. The more fundamental cause of the farmers' emphasis on social status, Hofstadter says, was the fact that they could no longer claim to be necessary for economic progress in an increasingly industrialized world.[6] By omitting these factors, Viereck makes it seem as though the social changes preceded the economic changes in agriculture and caused the political transformation into Populism. But the concept of "resentment" itself presupposes an antecedent cause. This brings us to another basic confusion in Viereck's reasoning.

It is no support for the Conservative case even to prove that status resentment precedes economic or political changes. The Conservative theory demands demonstration that a *new* status system precedes a *new* economic and political system. Plato's theory maintains that status resentment leads directly to the development of a new code of prestige, a code which represents a deterioration from the old one. "Resentment" in itself is not a historical change in the relevant sense but a historical resistance against changes which have already occurred. Without the existence of prior changes, there is nothing to resent. Even Burke's discussion of status resentment in France is irrelevant to the crucial issue. Only his claim that a transformation of the moral code preceded all other societal causes of the French Revolution is addressed to the vital point. And insofar as this meant what Burke never recognized it to mean— that the emergence of middle-class morality preceded the emergence of commercial capitalism and the nation-state—the claim was patently false. When Viereck speaks of the status resentment of the farmers, the analysis floats in historical mid-air unless it is discussed in relation to the development of industrial society. When he speaks of the status insecurity of the suburbanites, resulting from their excessively rapid rise in the social scale, the very terms of his causal order make it clear that the postwar economic expansion which made this rapid rise possible was the precondition of the insecurity.

Viereck's real task is to show, for example, that the new ethic of consumption, which replaced the old Protestant ethic of production and thrift and which endangered the prestige position of the farmers, was the cause rather than the effect of industrialization, that it was historically prior to the economic changes. Plato at least does not balk at making his corresponding claim clear. For him, the degeneration to a social ethic which honors consumption is the cause of the expansion of production which brings surplus and luxury. But obviously Viereck could not maintain today that the new ethic of consumption was the cause rather than the effect of industrialization, because this social change is a recent one whereas the economic change is over one and a half centuries old. Furthermore, the new social ethic is far from dominant even now, while the industrial corporation has dominated the economy since before the beginning of the twentieth century, and the rapid increase of productivity has been going on since the beginning of the Industrial Revolution. If Viereck has done nothing to advance the case of Conservatism, he has at least done a reasonably thorough job of making it difficult to understand what the issue is in the first place.

Peter Drucker also tries to maintain the primacy of morality and other social factors in the process of change. But his contention that fascism was caused by the moral failure of Liberal capitalism is nullified by his later thesis that the basic problem of the modern age has been the incompatibility between the older forms of "mercantile society" and the new reality of "industrial society." His insistence that the "real revolution" was not in machinery but in human relations does not enable him to deny that the technological and economic changes occurred first and that these changes caused the ethical and social crises rather than the reverse. His claim that "resignation and withdrawal" can lead at any time to regeneration is contradicted by his admission that coercive authority was the instrument of transition from the moral values of one period of history to those of another; and his citing of Burke's effect on nineteenth-century Britain as an example of such "regeneration" [7] is just another bit of fictitious Conservative "history."

The obscuring of the crucial problem of historical theory by irrelevant, contradictory formulations is not confined to contemporary Conservatism. We have seen the confusions in Burke's analysis. John of Salisbury avoided the subject altogether, and the patristic discussions of history were beclouded by the injection of theology. The clearest, though far from adequate, formulation of Conservative theory was Plato's, but Plato made no attempt to support his historical generalizations. To repeat the earlier conclusion, the crucial problem in the testing of the Conservative theory of history lies in the formulation of the issue, rather than in the availability of data. Conservatives have never formulated the issue clearly, because to do so is to reveal Conservatism for what it is, an illusion based on an imaginary theory of history.

The present argument, that social change is not primary in the history of societal development, should not, however, be construed to mean that social change is unimportant or that a social system inevitably gives way to each political, economic, and ideological change. On the contrary, social resistance can be of major importance. The persistence of Catholicism and medieval social mores after the decline of medieval society affected the whole subsequent history of countries such as France. But it is precisely this characteristic of resistance which underscores the essential passivity of social relations in the process of historical change. No country in the world has been able to resist industrialization in the twentieth century. But a great number of countries still cling to socio-moral systems of the past. When a Conservative like Russell Kirk warns against industrializing backward areas because of the impact which it will have on the social traditions, he seems totally oblivious of how far he has gone in destroying Conservatism altogether. A socio-moral system can resist historical change or it can adjust to it, but there is no evidence that it initiates change. Marx's charge against Hegel is far more applicable to Conservatism, the validity of its theory depends on a capacity to read history standing on one's head.

The Foundation of Conservative Contradictions

Conservatism sees man's capacity for moral self-denial as dependent on the capacity for love and affection. The realm of psychology as a whole, the inner relations of man, is for Conservatism causally prior to the realm of society, the external relations of men. Changes in human psychology presumably cause changes in society, and changes in the capacity for love and affection cause changes within the human psyche. There is, however, no ascertainable cause for changes in the capacity for affection. They result either from mysterious laws of genetics or from sin and the intervention of God. It is on this psychological theory that the whole Conservative system of values depends. An examination of the relevant psychological data is beyond the scope of this book. But the falsity of the Conservative theory of history in itself implies the falsity of its psychological theory.

Social relations within society correspond to the sphere of affective emotions within the psyche; the one is the externalization of the other. If affection changes first psychologically, then social relations change first societally—this has been the legitimate assumption of Conservatism. But the fact that social relations do not change first in society creates the virtually insuperable presumption that affection does not change first in human psychology. Furthermore, as we have already said, the whole thesis that changes in the characters of individuals are the causes of changes in society requires the irrational assumption that history consists of a constant stream of uncaused or supernatural first causes. The only tenable conclusion we can reach from the historical and theoretical evidence is therefore that social change is the consequence of other changes in society, and that psychological change as a whole and change in the capacity for affection in particular are the consequences of societal change. It could be maintained that societal change can, in turn, be explained most rationally as due to altered relations between man and nature, but it is not necessary for our critique of Conservatism to pursue this question further.

There is a final reason for rejecting Conservatism—only with an alternative theory can we understand the continual contradictions of Conservative ideology. Conservatives have never had an adequate explanation for the internal tensions, cleavages, and inconsistencies of their own ideology. The best they have offered is that Conservatives, like everyone else, are prone to error and sin. Far more frequently, they have simply failed to recognize their ideological problems at all. It will be argued here that the historical contradictions of Conservatism are the inherent results of its own theoretical fallacies. Since the values on which Conservatism is based are not man's strongest and most active but his weakest and most passive aspirations, the forces on which Conservatism relies are not in the forefront of history but in its rear guard. The contradictions of Conservatism are the tensions between the charging spearheads of history and its dragging Conservative tail.

The essential passivity of Conservatism is manifest not only in the passive historical role of social relations and in the Conservative inability either to avoid continual defeat in history or to account rationally for it, but it is also evident in the Conservative ideology itself. The key concepts of Conservatism lack meaningful, identifiable content, and they are relevant only in historical retrospect. We have seen several times that the idea of "natural aristocracy" has no practicable meaning except in reference to an existing aristocracy. Similarly, Conservatism has never been able to offer feasible concrete criteria for societal harmony, until harmony has already been embodied in an actual tradition. And no Conservative has ever been able to tell us how to create a tradition; he is intelligible and consistent only when he tells us how to preserve an existing one, and even in this he always fails.

The passivity of the Conservative societal conceptions—aristocracy, harmony, and tradition—are rooted in the passivity of its psychological conception of morality. According to Conservatism, the rules of morality are derived from conscience, which in turn is based on the capacity for affection. If this were true, then Conservatives should be able to delineate the proper rules of morality through a conception of "natural law," without reference to historical changes in society. Yet this is what Conservatism has never been able to do, though it has persistently claimed that it could. The content of Roman "natural law" was very different from that of medieval "natural law," and the relationship of each to its corresponding historical conditions is too striking to be ignored. The acceptance of the right of an authoritative Church to decide on the norms only substitutes one society for another; it does not prove that morality can be derived from conscience and love directly. The contemporary Conservative likes to offer the Ten Commandments as a summary of human conscience and morality which is independent of history. But since the Commandments are always discussed in the abstract, completely out of their Biblical context, to cite them is to say no more than that society needs rules of behavior if it is to survive and that man needs rules which objectify his affective relations. But this is a mere matter of definition and proves nothing for Conservatism. If the injunction against stealing or adultery can refer to *any* property or family system which society may evolve, then it is still society which makes the changes. If the injunctions are supposed to refer to a particular system, it obviously cannot be the primitive system in the Bible, and if they refer to other particular systems, then we are back to the problems of "natural law" and the question of how we can know from an abstract view of conscience whether or not a concrete moral code is good.

As a matter of fact, Conservatives themselves have continually adjusted their moral conceptions to historical change. The Conservative of antiquity was certain that the morality of the ancient world was "true," and the Christian Conservative is equally certain that Christian morality is true. Undoubtedly the tribal Conservative, if he thought about it at all, felt the same way of his own morality. Why should anyone doubt that the Conservative of the future will consider the new morality of industrial society to be "natural?" But if Conservative morality is, in general, based on the existing civilization, it is, in particular usually based on an earlier period of that civilization. If John of Salisbury looked back to patristic morality, Burke often looked back to medieval morality, and the contemporary Conservative looks back to middle-class morality.

What then is the "objective" content of the Conservative conscience? The history of Conservatism itself shows that when man looks to his conscience he finds the rules of the historical past. When Conservatives admit this by emphasizing mere traditionalism, they are denying the whole idea of an objective "natural law." Yet, without a "natural law" of some kind, to distinguish good from bad moral traditions, Conservatism becomes a blind inertia. The foundation of the whole Conservative structure is thus built on the sands of passivity to change. But if conscience is passive in the sense that it does not initiate change, it is also resistant in the sense that its adjustment to

change is never complete. It was one of Freud's great contributions to show that early relations of affection and early
norms of conscience are amazingly persistent throughout life.
The contradictions of Conservatism stem from the fact that it
rests on forces which are both passive to changes it cannot
control and resistant to changes it cannot stop.

The Conservative assumption that affection for others has
been historically antithetical to the quest for satisfaction of
individual needs is one of its few truths, and it is borne out by
the fact that there is some correspondence between its cyclical
theory and actual history (though not for Conservative reasons).
This is why Conservatism demands that affection be coupled
with a conception of tranquillity which seeks to avoid tensions
and conflicts by surrendering individual needs, particularly for
material goods. But the direction of history has been precisely
the opposite of Conservatism; and it is for this reason that
Conservatives are always forced to find their models in the past,
whether the immediate or the remote prehistoric past. Obviously, since not all the alternative, anti-Conservative theories
can be true, they too suffer from varying degrees of historical
contradiction. But it is the dubious distinction of Conservatism that it is always inconsistent except in the most limited
periods "at the beginning," and that even when it appears
consistent the achievement occurs in spite of its own theory,
not because of it.*

The norms of conscience do not originate within the individual but from his external relationships in society. They
change not because the capacity for affection changes but because the material, intellectual, and power imperatives of
society change. This is true even of the periods which approximate Conservative harmony. Did not Burke admit that blind
settlements of force had preceded the supposedly harmonious
period of the Late Middle Ages? The most that he really
claimed for medieval harmony was that it "softened" (and, we

---

* It should be clear by now that our historical "types" of Conservatism are
really summaries of its record of perennial defeat.

might add, obscured) the element of force, because men learned to impose upon themselves what had originally been imposed on them by outside repression. Do not Plato and Drucker find the coercive basis of harmony to be their ultimate dilemma? What is harmony then but the retention of changes which have been forced on conscience by societal relations? Was the slow rate of economic expansion and intellectual change in the Middle Ages due to its superior morality and capacity for affection or to the fact that the period followed a relapse into barbarism? Is there any reason to believe that medieval man could have resisted economic expansion any more than modern man? If so, how are we to account for the inability of cohesive, backward societies (even those still in a tribal age) to resist the allure of greater material comforts? The Conservative ignores all this or fails to draw the necessary conclusions. He can consistently explain his presumably harmonious periods only with the claim that man somehow "regenerated" himself through some spontaneous causation for which there could be no active causal agent except God. If he recognizes the centuries of force and bloodshed which were the price of "harmony," he nevertheless dismisses them as irrelevant and begins his calculations of significant historical time from the harmonious "Golden Age," even if he can only identify the harmony in retrospect.

But every passing moment of time, every change in society or culture, widens the contradictions in his own empty concepts, because neither he nor his ideas can do anything but resist or adjust to changes which originate elsewhere, because a theory which has no roots in historical reality is a theory which contradicts the sequence of time itself. In his need to cling to the morality of the supposedly harmonious past through an ever-changing present, the quest for tranquillity ends in guilt. In his need to cling to past traditions, the quest for harmony ends in conflict. If, like Burke, he adjusts to one period of change, he cannot adjust to the next. When a historical trauma shatters his whole inner world, his fixation on

empty traditions which no longer refer to harmonious relations and his repetition of meaningless incantations about the
"harmonies" of chivalry only make change more explosive and
the possibility of real societal harmony ever more remote. If
he is prepared to adjust to all changes which he cannot stop
(and this really means he proposes no qualification at all), he is
still propelled by blind inertia, even if, like the "adjusted"
Conservatives, he appears to be "progressive," or if he takes the
trouble to go through the ritual which he grandiosely calls
"withdrawal and regeneration." If, like Kirk, he insists that
the latest changes be stopped somehow, he must succeed in
deluding himself that without these changes, harmony and
traditional morality would spring out of their own accord—a
regeneration out of historical season. If, like Plato or Drucker,
he finally admits that the past is of no use to him and tries at
last to seize the historical initiative, it is only to find that he
must remain motionless unless he appeals to the use of coercion, which would defeat him before he starts and which he
is unwilling to recognize as the condition of his ideal periods of
"harmony." Small wonder that he rejects any theory of historical progress or human perfectibility. If the Conservative
values were truly the supreme goals of history or men, who
could disagree with these conclusions, conclusions which are
preordained in the premises? When Conservatism solemnly
confides to the world that man is inescapably evil, it is merely
using different terms to say not only that in history Conservatism is inescapably defeated, but that it finds contradiction
no matter where it turns. Small wonder that it periodically
surrenders to "God's inscrutable will."

Conservative theology is not really an initial postulate of
faith on which it bases its theory. It is the conclusion to which
Conservatism is driven because of the failure of its theory and
the insolubility of its contradictions. When neo-orthodoxy
frankly presents its theology as a conclusion which is "necessary" in order to make life meaningful, it is far more correct
than that Conservatism which claims to start from theology.
But why not make life meaningful by changing the value

premises of Conservatism rather than by inventing a Conservative God? How meaningful is the concept of a God who taunts man by making it impossible for him either to find happiness or to follow the divine commandments? What meaning can free will have in a historical world where degeneration and the continual defeat of "the Good" are predestined? What meaning can there be in the offer of free choice to the individual when his world as a whole has no such choice? Russell Kirk brushes off Henry Adams' agnosticism with the easy comment that he was pessimistic because he could not muster enough faith to believe in God. This is the usual Conservative reversal of causation. Adams could not believe, because pessimism was inescapable, especially in the new industrial world, once he had begun with Conservative premises. He could not believe because he drew back in horror from a God who could be so sadistic as to make life into a meaningless taunt. "God might be . . . a Substance," he exclaimed, "but he could not be a Person!" [8] Why is this any less "necessary" a conclusion of Conservative theory than the conclusion that God will somehow make everything right? *

If Conservatism cannot avoid contradiction and alienation from history, then it offers nothing to historical man except submission to necessity, resignation to defeat. But total resignation becomes aimless activity; total necessity becomes pointless freedom. Here is the final contradiction. If Conservatism will be defeated in spite of anything the Conservative may do, then it cannot matter what he does. If there is no tenable objective standard for the Conservative, then he might as well adopt more subjective standards, those of class, position, personality, whim. What difference does it finally make whether he lives in a forgotten past or adjusts to a changing present, whether he is reactionary or radical, whether he makes the most of the present or sulks in it, whether he seeks refuge in imaginary utopias or divine heavens or total pessimism? What

---

* It should be emphasized that this is not an attack on Christianity but on the application of a Conservative interpretation of Christianity, or any other religion, to societal history.

difference does it make if he is Kirk or Viereck, Tate or Rossiter, Drucker or Agar, Santayana or Henry Adams?   The end is the same in any case, and Conservatism may as well enjoy the orgy of paradox and amuse itself by calling this the flowering of free thought and diversity.

The day may not be far off when the Conservatives of Western civilization, like those of antiquity, will find in death the final solution of the ideology of "love" for the burdens of history.   Russell Kirk has already made the interesting claim that tranquillity in the hour of death is man's greatest potential happiness.[9]   But the view that lifeless existence provides a model of harmony superior to that of human life has been implicit in Conservatism from the beginning.   The Conservative conception of nature has seen it neither as an object of human desire nor as the source of danger to man.   Certainly Conservatism has not viewed nature as the source of fantastic quantities of locked-in energy, awaiting release by science in order to make possible increasing human control over the whole of nature.   On the contrary, it has abstracted from nature the "Idea" of cohesion and quiescence; and man's proper attitude towards this harmonious nature is not to upset it by appropriating pieces of it, not to fight it, above all not to disturb its pattern and release its energy, but to conform to its model, to adjust to it, to "hand it back to God the way we got it."   Henry Adams speaks the authentic language of Conservatism when he sees the accepted hierarchies of nature as inverted hierarchies of harmony.   Human life is necessarily less harmonious than lower forms of life because reason constantly leaves open paths which lead to disturbances and pretensions to power.   The situations in which animals can engage in aimless tranquillity are limited only by relatively infrequent periods of instinctual stimulus or unavoidable objective dangers.   But man's reason is a constant stimulus to his energies, directing them not only to existing objects but to objectives yet unknown.   Yet, even lower forms of life are discordant compared to the harmonies of inorganic matter, and it is the relations of matter, symbolized by the lifeless pattern of the heavens, which has been the supreme model for Conservatism, the antithesis of man's original sin. When Adams concludes that the evolution of the universe, which has now culminated in man's unprecedented rational achievements, is really a process of the degeneration of "energy" and that the Second Law of Thermodynamics is the essence of the entire process, he reflects the true outlook of Conservatism. The defeat of Conservatism is not confined to human history. Apparently it began with the beginning of life, and (who knows?) perhaps with the beginning of the universe. In Conservatism, as in Freudian psychology, love and death become blood brothers.

It has been intimated in this book that the term "Conservatism" is largely a misnomer for the ideology which developed through Edmund Burke, because it implies that this ideology consists of the mere resistance to change of any kind; and this has not been the conscious intention of Conservatives. Perhaps the objection to this term should now be retracted. Whatever its form at a given moment, the most profound and permanent tendency of the ideology which began with Plato is the attempt to conserve the past. It is true that resistance to historical change can often be found outside the ranks of Conservatism, but in no other position is this resistance the basis of the theory from the very outset. Other ideologies shift to an attempt to arrest change only under limited conditions. Conservative resistance is built into the theory itself.

But inability to effect changes beyond a limited point is probably the ultimate cause of the decline of civilizations. Graeco-Roman civilization was never able to outgrow its slave system and its communal mores. The historical significance of Christianity was that it helped accomplish what the older civilization could not do for itself—cancel the guilt attendant on the inability to fulfill the older morality, while providing a basis for the rejection of slavery. Even then the transition to a new level of civilization did not occur until after the end of the old civilization. In our own case, there is, so far, little indication that we shall be able to effect fundamental revisions in our moral code, even though we are no longer able to live by that code.   If Western civilization declines at some future date, it is far more likely to be due to Conservatism than to original sin.

There is little room for ambiguity in passing judgment on Conservatism.   It has never been able to break out of the cyclical theory in which it admits its own defeat; and it has never found a tenable, consistent way of accounting for the defeat. Its version of historical change reverses the causal sequence of reality and makes inevitable the permanent contradictions for which it has no rational explanation of its own.   The falsity of the Conservative theory of history is also the falsity of its system of values.   Conservatism does not speak for mankind but only for bewildered individuals and groups which are left behind by historical development.   Ever since Plato, it has been the ideology of classes which lack the capacity to keep up with economic expansion.   Most often it has been the ideology of landed aristocracy, less often of an old middle class or a failing professional class.   If it is today sometimes offered to expanding classes, there is no reason to believe that the offer will be accepted.   The Conservative must now be content with spiritual consolation, and the ideologist who wants to defend contemporary society must abandon the Conservative premises of man's past.   In any case, Conservatives and Conservatism never belong in the foreground of history.   We know, without Conservatism, that affection is a vital need of man and that there are limits to bearable tensions, though there are times when so few are concerned with these problems that critical Conservative warnings may be of considerable value, even if not for Conservative reasons.   But to offer mankind Conservative harmony as its supreme goal, on the assumption that social and moral forces are decisive in history, is to offer an illusion; and to burden man with a superfluous sense of guilt for failing to achieve an illusion is to make a grim joke of a history which has too long borne unnecessary tragedies.

Notes

INTRODUCTION

1. Louis Hartz, *The Liberal Tradition in America* (New York: Harcourt, Brace & Co., 1955).

I: HISTORICAL FORMS OF CONSERVATISM

1. Plato, *Laws*, tr. by A. E. Taylor (London: J. M. Dent & Sons, 1934), 897. All references to Plato's writings are based on the standard pagination.

2. Plato, *Republic*, tr. by B. Jowett (New York: Modern Library, 1941), 441–43.

3. *Ibid.*, 372–73, 420, 423.   4. *Ibid.*, 377–78, 391–403, 434.

5. *Ibid.*, 423–24.

6. See his discussion of the "Myth of Kronos" in Plato, *Statesman*, tr. by J. B. Skemp (New Haven: Yale University Press, 1952), 271–72, and the similar discussion in *Laws*, 679–85.

7. *Republic*, 425–27.   8. *Ibid.*, 374–76, 412–13.

9. *Ibid.*, 475–76, 486, 503–5, 526–31.

10. *Ibid.*, 330, 373, 421–23, 415–17.   11. *Ibid.*, 431.

12. *Ibid.*, 378, 599–601.   13. *Ibid.*, 550, 473, 500–2.

14. *Ibid.*, 462–63, 457, 415–17.   15. *Ibid.*, 412–14.

16. *Statesman*, 292–93.   17. *Ibid.*, 309–10.

18. *Laws*, 846.

19. George H. Sabine, *A History of Political Theory* (New York: Henry Holt & Co., 1955), pp. 141–44, 148–51.

20. Cicero, *De re publica, de legibus*, tr. by C. W. Keyes (Cambridge: Harvard University Press, 1928), pp. 213, 469. Also Sabine, *A History of Political Theory*, pp. 151–67.

21. Sabine, *A History of Political Theory*, pp. 174–80.

22. "Discourses of Epictetus," in W. J. Oates, ed., *The Stoic and Epicurean Philosophers* (New York: Random House, 1940), p. 422.

23. *Ibid.*, p. 358. The pervasive weariness of life is obvious throughout "The Meditations of Marcus Aurelius," in Oates, ed., *The Stoic and Epicurean Philosophers.*

24. St. Augustine, *The City of God*, tr. by M. Dods (2 vols., New York: Hafner Publishing Co., 1948), Book XIV, Chap. xv.

25. *Ibid.*, Book V, Chap. xii; Book II, Chap. xviii, xix.

26. *Ibid.*, Book XIX, Chap. xiv, xvi.

27. *Ibid.*, Book XII, Chap. iii; Book XIX, Chap. xvi.

28. *Ibid.*, Book XIX, Chap. xiv.

29. *Ibid.*, Book XIX, Chap. xxvii.

30. *Ibid.*, Book XXII, Chap. xxiii; Book XIX, Chap. xvii.

31. *Ibid.*, Book XX, Chap. xxx.

32. *Ibid.*, Book II, Chap. xviii, xix.

33. *Ibid.*, Book IV, Chap. iii.

34. Reinhold Niebuhr, *The Self and the Dramas of History* (New York: Charles Scribner's Sons, 1955), p. 101.

35. John of Salisbury, *The Statesman's Book*, tr. by J. Dickinson (New York: Alfred A. Knopf, 1927), Book VI, Chap. ii, pp. 182–83.

36. John of Salisbury, *Frivolities of Courtiers and Footprints of Philosophers*, tr. by J. B. Pike (Minneapolis: University of Minnesota Press, 1938), Book I, Chap. iv, p. 26.

37. *Ibid.*, Book III, Chap. i, p. 154.

38. *Ibid.*, Book VIII, Chap. xiv, pp. 391–93.

39. John of Salisbury, *The Statesman's Book*, translator's introduction, pp. xviii, xxv.

40. *Ibid.*, Book VIII, Chap. xx.

II: EDMUND BURKE: THE CONTRADICTIONS OF LIBERAL CONSERVATISM

1. *A Vindication of Natural Society*, in *The Writings and Speeches of Edmund Burke* (12 vols., London: Bickers & Sons, n.d.), I, 1–66. I have used this early nineteenth-century edition of Burke's collected works exclusively, and in subsequent notes to this chapter all volume and page references are to this edition, not to the individual titles cited.

2. *A Philosophical Enquiry into the Origin of Our Ideas of the Sublime and Beautiful*, I, 165, 190–94, 232–33.

3. *Ibid.*, I, 200.

4. *Ibid.*, I, 131–44, 146–60,, 107, 216, 167, 94–95, 186.

5. *Ibid.*, I, 215.

6. *A Vindication of Natural Society*, I, 62.

7. *Thoughts on the Cause of the Present Discontents*, I, 439; *Thoughts and Details on Scarcity*, V, 135–36; *Reflections on the Revolution in France*, III, 367, 369, 371.

8. *A Letter to . . . the Sheriffs of Bristol, on the Affairs of America,* II, 229–30; *Reflections on the Revolution in France,* III, 409.

9. Burke called this a definition of the "state," but, as he himself admitted, he often used this word to mean "society." *A Letter to Sir Hercules Langrishe on . . . the Roman Catholics of Ireland,* IV, 243.

10. *Reflections on the Revolution in France,* III, 359–60.

11. *Thoughts on the Cause of the Present Discontents,* I, 458.

12. *Reflections on the Revolution in France,* III, 298, 308.

13. *Thoughts and Details on Scarcity,* V, 135, 139–42, 163–64; *A Letter to Samuel Span* and *A Letter to [Merchant] Company,* II, 253, 260.

14. *Letters . . . on the Proposals for Peace, with the Regicide Directory of France,* V, 300; *Reflections on the Revolution in France,* III, 276, 298, 332.

15. *Reflections on the Revolution in France,* III, 358.

16. *Thoughts on the Cause of the Present Discontents,* I, 436.

17. *A Letter to . . . the Sheriffs of Bristol, on the Affairs of America,* II, 243.

18. *Reflections on the Revolution in France,* III, 297.

19. *A Letter . . . to a Noble Lord, on the Attacks Made upon Him and His Pension,* V, 224. Italics added.

20. *Reflections on the Revolution in France,* III, 175.

21. *Fragments of a Tract [on] the Laws against Popery in Ireland,* VI, 353–54.

22. *Thoughts on the Cause of the Present Discontents,* I, 436; *Thoughts on French Affairs,* IV, 342; *A Letter to a Noble Lord,* V, 200–202.

23. *Reflections on the Revolution in France,* III, 356, 366, 443.

24. *Ibid.,* III, 334–36.

25. *Thoughts on French Affairs,* IV, 327.

26. *Reflections on the Revolution in France,* III, 276, 377, 286–88.

27. For example, see *Thoughts on the Cause of the Present Discontents,* I, 436–37.

28. *Reflections on the Revolution in France,* III, 346.

29. *A Philosophical Enquiry into . . . the Sublime and Beautiful,* I, 180.

30. *Reflections on the Revolution in France,* III, 457.

31. *Ibid.,* III, 457.

32. *Speech . . . on . . . Conciliation with the Colonies,* II, 121.

33. *Reflections on the Revolution in France,* II, 302.

34. *Thoughts on the Cause of the Present Discontents,* I, 436.

35. *An Appeal from the New to the Old Whigs,* IV, 165; *Letters on . . . Peace with the Regicide Directory of France,* V, 380.

36. *Reflections on the Revolution in France,* III, 292, 477.

37. *An Appeal from the New to the Old Whigs,* IV, 174–76.

38. *Ibid.,* IV, 170–72, 166.

39. *Fragments of a Tract [on] the Laws against Popery in Ireland,* VI, 20–22.

40. *Reflections on the Revolution in France,* III, 241–42, 313, 559.

41. *A Vindication of Natural Society,* I, 32–34.

42. *Ibid.,* I, 36.   43. *Ibid.,* I, 41–43.

44. *Ibid.,* I, 48.

45. *Reflections on the Revolution in France,* III, 398. The criticisms of democracy can be found in III, 296, 355. It should be noted that Burke used the terms "mixed government" and "balanced government" interchangeably. The distinction here is not between these two terms, but between Burke's earlier and later definitions of them.

46. *An Appeal from the New to the Old Whigs,* II, 93.

47. *Reflections on the Revolution in France,* III, 473.

48. *A Letter to a Member of the National Assembly,* IV, 50.

49. *Reflections on the Revolution in France,* III, 277.

50. *Observations on the Conduct of the Minority,* V, 49.

51. *A Letter to a Member of the National Assembly,* IV, 47–49, 51.

52. *Reflections on the Revolution in France,* III, 469, 395, 279.

53. *Thoughts on the Cause of the Present Discontents,* I, 505.

54. *An Appeal from the New to the Old Whigs,* IV, 152, 162.

55. *Observations on a Late Publication Intituled "The Present State of the Nation,"* I, 371–72; *Reflections on the Revolution in France,* III, 282.

56. *A Letter to Sir Hercules Langrishe on . . . the Roman Catholics of Ireland,* IV, 256.

57. *Speech on Shortening the Duration of Parliaments,* VII, 78.

58. *Thoughts on the Cause of the Present Discontents,* I, 458, 517; *Speech on Shortening the Duration of Parliaments,* VII, 73.

59. *Reflections on the Revolution in France,* III, 490–91.

60. *Speech . . . on Mr. Fox's East India Bill,* II, 459.

61. *Observations on . . . "The Present State of the Nation,"* I, 419.

62. *Thoughts on the Cause of the Present Discontents,* I, 473, 528.

63. *Speech at . . . Bristol . . . Previous . . . to Election,* II, 370.

64. *Reflections on the Revolution in France,* III, 296–97.

65. *Letters on Peace with the Regicide Directory of France,* V, 491–92.

66. *Thoughts on the Cause of the Present Discontents,* I, 531.

67. *Ibid.,* I, 530.

68. *A Vindication of Natural Society,* I, 49.

69. *Thoughts on the Cause of the Present Discontents,* I, 526, 531.

70. *Ibid.,* I, 535.   71. *Ibid.,* I, 533.

72. *Ibid.,* I, 529, 526.

73. *Observations on "The Present State of the Nation,"* I, 419.

74. *Letters on Peace with the Regicide Directory of France,* V, 425.

75. *Observations on the Conduct of the Minority,* V, 7–63.

76. *Thoughts on the Cause of the Present Discontents,* I, 488–89.

77. *Reflections on the Revolution in France,* III, 253, 256.

78. *A Letter to Sir Hercules Langrishe on . . . the Roman Catholics of Ireland,* IV, 293.

79. *Speech to the Electors of Bristol,* II, 95–97.

80. *Speech on Conciliation with the Colonies,* I, 491–92.

81. *Speech . . . on Reform in the House of Commons,* II, 357.

82. *Speech to the Electors of Bristol,* II, 95–97.

83. *Reflections on the Revolution in France,* III, 481.

84. *Thoughts on the Cause of the Present Discontents,* I, 471–72, 477, 448.

85. *Reflections on the Revolution in France,* II, 342, 510.

86. *Ibid.,* III, 257, 269; *Speech on the Middlesex Election,* VII, 63; *Speech to the Electors of Bristol,* II, 98.

87. *A Letter to . . . the Sheriffs of Bristol, on the Affairs of America,* II, 196, 225.

88. *Thoughts and Details on Scarcity,* V, 133–34.

89. *Letters on Peace with the Regicide Directory of France,* V, 466–69.

90. *Fragments of a Tract* [on] *the Laws against Popery in Ireland,* VI, 340.

91. *Speech on Reform in the House of Commons,* II, 331.

92. *A Letter to a Member of the National Assembly,* IV, 24.

93. *Speech on the Acts of Uniformity,* VII, 11.

94. *Speech on . . . a Petition of the Unitarian Society,* VII, 47, 30.

95. *Thoughts on the Cause of the Present Discontents,* I, 436.

96. *A Short Account of a Late Short Administration,* I, 265–68.

97. *Observations on . . . "The Present State of the Nation,"* I, 403.

98. *Speech on Conciliation with the Colonies,* II, 145–46, 150.

99. *Ninth Report on the Affairs of India,* VIII, 257–59.

100. *A Letter to . . . the Sheriffs of Bristol, on the Affairs of America,* II, 234.

101. *Thoughts on the Cause of the Present Discontents,* I, 447, 459.

102. *Speech at Bristol Previous to Election,* II, 402.

103. *Speech at Bristol on Declining the Poll,* II, 428–29.

104. *Speech at Bristol Previous to Election,* II, 422.

105. *Reflections on the Revolution in France,* III, 312.

106. *A Philosophical Enquiry into . . . the Sublime and Beautiful,* I, 128.

107. *A Letter to Sir Hercules Langrishe on . . . the Roman Catholics of Ireland,* IV, 266–67.

108. *Speech . . . on Powers of Juries . . . in Libels,* VII, 105–27.

109. *Speech on Mr. Fox's East India Bill,* II, 442.

110. *Thoughts on French Affairs,* IV, 349.

111. *Speech on a Petition of the Unitarian Society,* VII, 41.

112. *Thoughts on the Cause of the Present Discontents,* I, 477.

113. *Speech on Reform in the House of Commons,* II, 280.

114. *Speech on American Taxation,* II, 71–73.

115. *Speech on Conciliation with the Colonies,* II, 108.

116. *Speech on American Taxation,* II, 29–30.

117. *A Letter to Sir Hercules Langrishe on . . . the Roman Catholics of Ireland,* IV, 249.

118. *A Letter to a Member of the National Assembly,* IV, 8.

119. *Remarks on the Policies of the Allies,* IV, 462–65.

120. *An Appeal from the New to the Old Whigs,* IV, 92.

121. *A Letter to Sir Hercules Langrishe on . . . the Roman Catholics of Ireland,* IV, 272.

122. *Reflections on the Revolution in France,* III, 528, 531.
123. *Ibid.,* III, 451.   124. *Ibid.,* III, 267, 271.
125. *A Vindication of Natural Society,* I, 50.
126. *An Appeal from the New to the Old Whigs,* IV, 23.
127. *Speech . . . on the Dormant Claims of the Church,* VII, 141.
128. *Reflections on the Revolution in France,* III, 253.
129. *Letter on the Protestant Ascendancy in Ireland,* VI, 412.
130. Plato, *Republic,* 520.   131. *Ibid.,* 420–21.
132. *Ibid.,* 547–49.
133. *Thoughts on the Cause of the Present Discontents,* I, 440.
134. *Thoughts on French Affairs,* IV, 337–42.
135. *Reflections on the Revolution in France,* III, 400–405.
136. *Speech in the Debates on the Army Estimates,* III, 227.
137. F. W. Coker, *Organismic Theories of the State,* in *Studies in History, Economics, and Public Law,* Vol. XXXVIII, No. 2.   (New York: Columbia University Press, 1910).

III: CONSERVATISM IN AMERICA

1. Richard Hofstadter, *The Age of Reform: From Bryan to FDR* (New York: Alfred A. Knopf, 1955), p. 45.
2. Louis Hartz, *The Liberal Tradition in America* (New York: Harcourt, Brace & Co., 1955), p. 43.
3. *Ibid.,* pp. 5-6.
4. Clement Eaton, *A History of the Old South* (New York: Macmillan, 1949), pp. 47, 56-58, 61-66; Francis B. Simkins, *The South, Old and New* (New York: Alfred A. Knopf, 1947), pp. 25-26.
5. Wilbur J. Cash, *The Mind of the South* (Garden City, N.Y.: Doubleday & Co., Anchor Books, 1956), pp. 24, 34; J. G. Randall, *The Civil War and Reconstruction* (Boston: D. C. Heath & Co., 1953), pp. 34–36, 22, 24–25, 67, 73; Eaton, *A History of the Old South,* pp. 67, 210–12, 230, 291, 373, 445-46, 450; Simkins, *The South, Old and New,* pp. 39, 58, 73.
6. Cash, *The Mind of the South,* p. 34; Eaton, *A History of the Old South,* pp. 53–54, 212, 256, 317, 231, 243, 410; Randall, *The Civil War and Reconstruction,* p. 9; Simkins, *The South, Old and New,* pp. 28, 54–55.   (Simkins' comment that ownership of a plantation and slaves was the real criterion of a "gentleman" is especially revealing of the capitalist foundation of Southern "aristocracy.")
7. Eaton, *A History of the Old South,* pp. 396, 424, 463, 469–70; Simkins, *The South, Old and New,* p. 51; Randall, *The Civil War and Reconstruction,* pp. 21–22; Cash, *The Mind of the South,* p. 45.
8. The aristocratic disdain of trade was much less evident in the colonial South.   See Eaton, *A History of the Old South,* pp. 54-55, 400, 467; Randall, *The Civil War and Reconstruction,* pp. 21–22; and Cash, *The Mind of the South,* p. 87.
9. Eaton, *A History of the Old South,* pp. 404, 412, 418–20, 422; Cash,

The Mind of the South, pp. 36–38. By 1860, Southern railroad mileage was only half that of the North.

10. The 1850's were a prosperous decade for the South because of high cotton prices. But the prosperity was bought at the price of continuing soil erosion and the continued postponment of industrialization, which tended to make advances only during wartime (1812) and agricultural depression (1838–50). By 1860, the South was producing only one tenth, by value, of the manufactured goods of the country, although in colonial times it had been almost on a par with the North. Eaton, *A History of the Old South,* pp. 231, 256, 275, 278, 407, 424, 432, 442; Simkins, *The South, Old and New,* p. 49; Randall, *The Civil War and Reconstruction,* pp. 21–22, 67–69.

11. Cash, *The Mind of the South,* pp. 59–60; Eaton, *A History of the Old South,* pp. 71, 86; Simkins, *The South, Old and New,* pp. 63–65; Randall, *The Civil War and Reconstruction,* p. 25.

12. Cash, *The Mind of the South,* pp. 66–70, 85, 97; Eaton, *A History of the Old South,* pp. 77–79; Simkins, *The South, Old and New,* pp. 54, 65, 76.

13. Cash, *The Mind of the South,* pp. 77–79; Simkins, *The South, Old and New,* pp. 23, 58, 107–8; Randall, *The Civil War and Reconstruction,* pp. 114–15, 117. Whatever the validity of the conclusions he draws, the thesis of Ulrich B. Phillips that the racial problem was "the central theme of Southern history" seems perfectly valid. Without this factor, there is no way of accounting for the trend away from Liberalism and towards Conservatism in the ante-bellum South's "agrarian way of life." See Phillips, *The Course of the South to Secession* (New York: Appleton-Century, 1939), pp. 151–65.

14. Richard Hofstadter, *The American Political Tradition* (New York: Alfred A. Knopf, Vintage Books, 1954), pp. 79–83.

15. Cash, *The Mind of the South,* p. 77; Eaton, *A History of the Old South,* p. 207; Simkins, *The South, Old and New,* pp. 13, 36; Randall, *The Civil War and Reconstruction,* p. 25.

16. C. Vann Woodward, *Origins of the New South, 1877–1913* (Baton Rouge: Louisiana State University Press, 1951), pp. 20–21, 152, 179, 183–84; Simkins, *The South, Old and New,* pp. 283–89.

17. Woodward says the use of violence increased in the "New South." Woodward, *Origins of the New South,* pp. 158–60.

18. Woodward, *Origins of the New South,* pp. 157–58.

19. Hartz, *The Liberal Tradition in America,* p. 224.

20. *Ibid.,* pp. 220–22.   21. *Ibid.,* p. 219.

22. Austin Ranney, *The Doctrine of Responsible Party Government* (Urbana, Ill.: University of Illinois Press, 1954), Chap. 3.

23. Maurice Duverger, *Political Parties: Their Organization and Activities in the Modern State,* tr. by B. and R. North (New York: John Wiley & Sons, 1954).

24. Oswald Spengler, *The Decline of the West,* tr. by C. F. Atkinson (2 vols., New York: Alfred A. Knopf, 1926–28), II, 448–51.

25. C. Wright Mills, *The Power Elite* (New York: Oxford University Press, 1956), Chap. 2.

26. *Ibid.*

27. Hofstadter, *The Age of Reform*, pp. 135–56.

28. *Ibid.*, p. 139.   29. *Ibid.*, p. 232.

30. *Ibid.*, p. 143.

31. Bernard I. Bell, *Crowd Culture* (New York: Harper & Bros. 1952).

32. A Lawrence Lowell, *Public Opinion and Popular Government* (New York: Longmans, Green & Co., 1926), Chap. 5.

33. A. L. Lowell, *Public Opinion in War and Peace* (Cambridge: Harvard University Press, 1923), Chap. 7.

34. A. L. Lowell, *Essays on Government* (Boston: Houghton Mifflin Co., 1889), pp. 11–14.

35. H. A. Yeomans, *Abbott Lawrence Lowell* (Cambridge: Harvard University Press, 1948), pp. 407–8.

36. Hofstadter, The *Age of Reform*, p. 140; Mills, *The Power Elite*, p. 34.

IV: THE ILLUSION OF A SOUTHERN CONSERVATIVE REVIVAL

1. Harvey Wish, *Society and Thought in Modern America* (New York: Longmans, Green & Co., 1952), pp. 17–18. C. Vann Woodward, *Origins of the New South, 1877–1913* (Baton Rouge: Louisiana State University Press, 1951), pp. 179, 184; Francis B. Simkins, *The South, Old and New* (New York: Alfred A. Knopf, 1947), p. 284.

2. Wilbur J. Cash, *The Mind of the South* (Garden City, N.Y.: (Doubleday & Co., Anchor Books, 1956), pp. 135, 195–96, 161–62, 133; Simkins, *The South, Old and New*, p. 284; Woodward, *Origins of the New South*, pp. 208–10. Woodward points out that even after the Civil War the planters had a definite economic and political stake in smoothing over race relations.

3. V. O. Key, *Southern Politics in State and Nation* (New York: Alfred A. Knopf, 1950), pp. 19–20, 25–27; Simkins, *The South, Old and New*, pp. 448, 454.

4. *Ibid.*, Chaps. 3, 6, 8, 12, 5, 9, 4, 10.

5. Marian Irish, "Recent Political Thought in the South," *American Political Science Review*, XLVI (1952), 121–41.

6. Herbert Agar, *Land of the Free* (Boston: Houghton Mifflin Co., 1935), p. 129.

7. Twelve Southerners, *I'll Take My Stand* (New York: Harper & Bros., 1930), pp. 74–75, 77.

8. Allen Tate, "View of the Whole South," *American Review* (1934), 411–32.

9. *I'll Take My Stand*, pp. 173–74.

10. *Ibid.*, pp. 74–75.   11. *Ibid.*, pp. 209–10.

12. *Ibid.*, pp. 92–93.   13. *Ibid.*, pp. ix–xv.

14. *Ibid.*, pp. 346, 350.   15. *Ibid.*, p. 260.

16. Donald Davidson, *The Attack on Leviathan* (Chapel Hill: University of North Carolina Press, 1938), p. 138.

17. Tate, "View of the Whole South," *American Review* (1934), 411–32.

18. Agar, *Land of the Free*, p. 166.

19. Agar and Tate, eds., *Who Owns America?* (Boston: Houghton Mifflin Co., 1936), pp. 191–92.

20. *Ibid.*, pp. 162, 183, 184.

21. *Ibid.*, pp. viii–ix.

22. *Ibid.*, pp. 82, 93, 133, 248.

23. *Ibid.*, pp. 166–67.

24. *Ibid.*, p. 173.

25. *Ibid.*, p. 250.

26. *Ibid.*, pp. 70–72; 7–10.

27. *Ibid.*, p. 63.

28. *Ibid.*, p. 164.

29. Davidson, *The Attack on Leviathan*, *passim*.

30. *Ibid.*, p. 251.

31. Agar and Tate, eds., *Who Owns America?*, pp. 130–33.

32. Davidson, *The Attack on Leviathan*, pp. 51–55.

33. Agar and Tate, eds., *Who Owns America?*, pp. 123, 132–33.

34. Herbert Agar, *The People's Choice* (Boston: Houghton Mifflin Co., 1933).

35. *Ibid.*, pp. 53–55.

36. *Ibid.*, p. 275, 276, 313.

37. Agar, *Land of the Free*.

38. *Ibid.*, pp. 5, 6, 22, 95, 46, 138, 152–53, 36, 163.

39. *Ibid.*, p. 196.

40. *Ibid.*, p. 192.

41. Herbert Agar, *Pursuit of Happiness* (Boston: Houghton Mifflin Co., 1938), pp. 18–19.

42. *Ibid.*, pp. 27, 26, 21, 28, 114, 126, 118.

43. *Ibid.*, pp. 194–96, 197–99.

44. Herbert Agar *et al.*, *The City of Man* (New York: Viking Press, 1941).

45. *Ibid.*, pp. 33, 56–58, 89–92, 78–79.

46. Herbert Agar, *A Time for Greatness* (Boston: Little, Brown & Co., 1942).

47. *Ibid.*, pp. 14–16.

48. *Ibid.*, pp. 267–69.

49. *Ibid.*, pp. 79, 106–7, 246–47, 269, 277.

50. Richard M. Weaver, "The Tennessee Agrarians," *Shenandoah*, Summer, 1952, pp. 3–10.

51. *I'll Take My Stand*, p. xvi.

52. Davidson, *The Attack on Leviathan*, p. 142.

53. *I'll Take My Stand*, p. 82.

54. *Ibid.*, p. xiv.

55. Richard Hofstadter, *The Age of Reform: From Bryan to FDR* (New York: Alfred A. Knopf, 1955), pp. 30–33, 50–52, 36–38.

56. *Ibid.*, pp. 37–43.

57. *Ibid.*, p. 20 and Chap. 2.

58. *Ibid.*, pp. 110-11.

59. C. Wright Mills, *White Collar* (New York: Oxford University Press, 1951), Chap. 1.

60. Louis Hartz, *The Liberal Tradition in America* (New York: Harcourt, Brace & Co., 1955), pp. 160–63.

61. Clinton Rossiter, *Conservatism in America* (New York: Alfred A. Knopf, 1955), pp. 206–7.

V. THE NEW CONSERVATISM: FROM REACTION TO ALIENATION

1. Samuel Lubell, *The Revolt of the Moderates* (New York: Harper & Bros., 1956), Chap. 8.
2. John C. Ransom *et al*, "Agrarianism Today," *Shenandoah*, Summer, 1952, pp. 14–33.
3. Donald Davidson, *The Attack on Leviathan* (Chapel Hill: University of North Carolina Press, 1938), p. 55.
4. Russell Kirk, *The Conservative Mind: From Burke to Santayana* (Chicago: Henry Regnery Co., 1953), 7–8.
5. *Ibid.*, p. 26.
6. Richard M. Weaver, *Ideas Have Consequences* (Chicago: University of Chicago Press, 1948), p. 19.
7. *Ibid.*, p. 18.
8. Kirk, *The Conservative Mind*, p. 30.
9. Kirk, *The Intelligent Woman's Guide to Conservatism* (New York: Devin-Adair Co., 1957), p. 20.
10. *Ibid.*, p. 24.
11. Kirk, *A Program for Conservatives* (Chicago: Henry Regnery Co., 1954, p. 4.
12. Kirk, *The Intelligent Woman's Guide to Conservatism*, p. 26.
13. *Ibid.*, p. 15.
14. Kirk, *A Program for Conservatives*, p. 8.
15. *Ibid.*, pp. 200–201.
16. *Ibid.*, pp. 167–68.
17. *Ibid.*, p. 51.
18. *Ibid.*, p. 243.
19. *Ibid.*, p. 237.
20. *Ibid.*, p. 227.
21. Kirk, *Beyond the Dreams of Avarice* (Chicago: Henry Regnery Co., 1956), pp. 68, 63.
22. Kirk, *The Conservative Mind*, pp. 190, 297, 41.
23. *Ibid.*, pp. 131, 134, 218, 328.
24. Kirk, *A Program for Conservatives*, pp. 120–22, 140, 115–17.
25. Kirk, *The Intelligent Woman's Guide to Conservatism*, p. 46.
26. Kirk, *A Program for Conservatives*, pp. 110, 112, 138, 167.
27. Kirk, *Beyond the Dreams of Avarice*, p. 127.
28. Kirk, *A Program for Conservatives*, pp. 92, 95.
29. Kirk, *Beyond the Dreams of Avarice*, p. 13.
30. Kirk, *The Intelligent Woman's Guide to Conservatism*, p. 39; *The Conservative Mind*, p. 222; *The Intelligent Woman's Guide to Conservatism*, p. 39; *A Program for Conservatives*, p. 243.
31. Kirk, *The Conservative Mind*, pp. 177–78.
32. Kirk, *Beyond the Dreams of Avarice*, p. 55.
33. Kirk, *A Program for Conservatives*, pp. 156–57.
34. Kirk, *Beyond the Dreams of Avarice*, p. 66; *The Conservative Mind*, p. 157.
35. Kirk, *The Conservative Mind*, pp. 214, 206.
36. Kirk, *A Program for Conservatives*, pp. 169, 153, 207, 190, 185.

37. Kirk, *The Intelligent Woman's Guide to Conservatism*, p. 69.

38. Kirk, *A Program for Conservatives*, pp. 60–61; *The Conservative Mind*, p. 40.

39. Kirk, *Academic Freedom* (Chicago: Henry Regnery Co., 1955), p. 190.

40. Kirk, *A Program for Conservatives*, pp. 65, 59, 66.

41. Kirk, *Beyond the Dreams of Avarice*, pp. 156, 153, 48.

42. Kirk, *Academic Freedom*, pp. 188–89; *Beyond the Dreams of Avarice*, p. 49.

43. Kirk, *Academic Freedom*, pp. 42, 17, 116.

44. *Ibid.*, pp. 189, 160, 122, 126.

45. Kirk, *Beyond the Dreams of Avarice*, p. 44; *The Conservative Mind*, p. 199.

46. Kirk, *A Program for Conservatives*, pp. 257, 270.

47. *Ibid.*, pp. 160–61, 264; *The Conservative Mind*, p. 296; *Academic Freedom*, p. 190.

48. Kirk, *The Conservative Mind*, pp. 260–61.

49. Kirk, *A Program for Conservatives*, p. 118; *Beyond the Dreams of Avarice*, pp. 171, ix, 137.

50. *Beyond the Dreams of Avarice*, pp. ii, x, 55.

51. Weaver, *Ideas Have Consequences*, passim.

52. *Ibid.*, pp. 119, 166–67, 187.

53. Richard M. Weaver, *The Ethics of Rhetoric* (Chicago: Henry Regnery Co., 1953), p. 29.

54. *Ibid.*, p. 74.

55. Alan Valentine, *The Age of Conformity* (Chicago: Henry Regnery Co., 1954).

56. Anthony Harrigan, "Iis Our Administration Conservative?", *Catholic World*, April, 1954, pp. 24–28; "The Realities of the American Situation," *Catholic World*, March, 1957, pp. 458–64.

57. Anthony Harrigan, "Masters of the Market," *Catholic World*, April, 1957, pp. 410–15.

58. Frederick L. Wilhelmsen, "The Conservative Vision," *Commonweal*, June 24, 1955, pp. 295–99.

59. Frederick L. Wilhelmsen, "The Alienated Professor," *Commonweal*, April 6, 1956, pp. 9–12.

60. Frederick L. Wilhelmsen, "Contemporary Criticism in the Georgian Manner," *Commonweal*, June 13, 1956, pp. 375–76.

61. Frederick L. Wilhelmsen, "The Alienated Professor," *Commonweal*, April 6, 1956, pp. 9–12.

VI: THE NEW CONSERVATISM: BURKE READJUSTED

1. John Hallowell, *Main Currents in Modern Political Thought* (New York: Henry Holt & Co. 1950), pp. 22, 693.

2. *Ibid.*, pp. 661, 671, 688–91.   3. *Ibid.*, pp. 690–91.

4. *Ibid.*, pp. 697–98, 375.

5. *Ibid.*, pp. 111–15; John Hallowell, *The Decline of Liberalism as an Ideology* (Berkeley: University of California Press, 1943, pp. 5; 137n.

6. John Hallowell, *The Moral Foundations of Democracy* (Chicago: University of Chicago Press, 1954), pp. 109–10, 103n., 114.

7. Hallowell, *Main Currents in Modern Political Thought,* pp. 625, 444, 652.

8. Hallowell, *The Moral Foundations of Democracy,* pp. 109, 81, 121, 49–50; *Main Currents in Modern Political Thought,* pp. 157–58.

9. Hallowell, *Main Currents in Modern Political Thought,* p. 15.

10. Hallowell, *The Moral Foundations of Democracy,* pp. 52, 116, 106–7.

11. *Ibid.*, pp. 35–37, 122, 56, 59–60.

12. Herbert Agar, *A Declaration of Faith* (Boston: Houghton Mifflin Co., 1952), pp. 199, 178–80.

13. Herbert Agar, *The Price of Union* (Boston: Houghton Mifflin Co., 1950), pp. 117, 558–60.

14. *Ibid.*, pp. 263, 637; Agar, *A Declaration of Faith*, pp. 135, 186.

15. Agar, *A Declaration of Faith*, p. 138.

16. *Ibid.*, p. 168; Agar, *The Price of Union*, pp. 56, 292, 405, 437, 636.

17. Agar, *The Price of Union*, pp. 45–46, xiv–xv, 52, 66–67, 202, 495, 655, 514, 687.

18. *Ibid.*, pp. xiv, xvii 689, 345, 85n, 56.

19. *Ibid.*, pp. 269, 354, 690, 688, 347.

20. Peter Viereck, *Shame and Glory of the Intellectuals* (Boston: Beacon Press, 1953), pp. 39, 197.

21. Viereck, *Conservatism Revisited* (New York: Charles Scribner's Sons, 1949), p. 29; *Shame and Glory of the Intellectuals,* p. 83.

22. Viereck, *Conservatism Revisited,* p. 15; *Shame and Golry of the Intellectuals,* pp. 129, 201; *The Unadjusted Man* (Boston: Beacon Press, 1956), pp. 327, 80.

23. Viereck, *Conservatism Revisited,* pp. 137, 150n; *Conservatism: From John Adams to Churchill* (New York: Van Nostrand Co., Anvil Books, 1956), pp. 108:9.

24. Viereck, *Conservatism Revisited,* p. 15; *Conservatism: From John Adams to Churchill,* p. 19; *Shame and Glory of the Intellectuals,* p. 221.

25. Viereck, *Conservatism Revisited,* pp. 28, 16–17, 108.

26. Viereck, *Conservatism: From John Adams to Churchill,* p. 13; *The Unadjusted Man,* pp. 238, 104.

27. Viereck, *The Unadjusted Man,* pp. 39–40; *Shame and Glory of the Intellectuals,* p. 8.

28. Viereck, *The Unadjusted Man,* pp. 42, 239.

29. *Ibid.*, p. 9; *Shame and Glory of the Intellectuals,* pp. 47, 49, 59, 60.

30. Viereck, *The Unadjusted Man,* p. 43; *Shame and Glory of the Intellectuals,* pp. 122, 276, 135.

31. Viereck, *The Unadjusted Man,* pp. 28, 16, 51.

32. *Ibid.*, pp. 67–69; *Shame and Glory of the Intellectuals,* pp. 227, 225.

33. Viereck, *The Unadjusted Man,* p. 91; *Shame and Glory of the In-*

tellectuals, pp. 122, 65.

34. Viereck, *The Unadjusted Man,* p .331.

35. *Ibid.,* pp. 40–41; *Shame and Glory of the Intellectuals,* pp. 13, 247.

36. Viereck, *Shame and Glory of the Intellectuals,* pp. 192, 194, 202; *The Unadjusted Man,* pp. 27, 34, 218–19.

37. Viereck, *The Unadjusted Man* pp. 82–83, 86; *Shame and Glory of the Intellectuals,* p. 255.

38. Viereck, *The Unadjusted Man,* p. 340.

39. Viereck, *Conservatism: From John Adams to Churchill,* p. 107; *Shame and Glory of the Intellectuals,* p. 64; *The Unadjusted Man,* p. 44.

40. Viereck, *Shame and Glory of the Intellectuals,* p. 277.

41. Viereck, *The Unadjusted Man,* pp. 135, 244, 245.

42. *Ibid.,* pp. 151, 220.

43. Clinton Rossiter, *Conservatism in America* (New York: Alfred A. Knopf, 1955), p. 300.

44. *Ibid.,* pp. 217, 239, 160, 67, 77, 71–73, 86, 89–95.

45. *Ibid.,* p. 245.   46. *Ibid.,* pp. 186, 260, 278, 257.

47. *Ibid.,* pp. 264–65, 258.   48. *Ibid.,* pp. 263–64.

49. *Ibid.,* pp. 78, 280.   50. *Ibid.,* p. 270.

51. Clinton Rossiter, *Constitutional Dictatorship* (Princeton: Princeton University Press, 1948), pp. 7, 6, 12–13, 27.

52. Clinton Rossiter, *The American Presidency* (New York: Harcourt, Brace & Co., 1956), pp. 86, 90, 93–94; italics mine.

53. *Ibid.,* pp. 138, 163, 38–42.

54. *Ibid.,* pp. 151, 155 57, 136; *Conservatism in America,* p. 264.

55. Rossiter, *Conservatism in America,* pp. 295, 296.

56. Rossiter, *The American Presidency,* pp. 143, 144, 154, 29.

57. *Ibid.,* p. 154.   58. *Ibid.,* p. 154.

59. Rossiter, *Conservatism in America,* p. 58.

60. *Ibid.,* p. 100.

61. John C. Ransom, *Poems and Essays* (New York: Vintage Books, 1955), pp. 135–45.

62. Rossiter, *Conservatism in America,* p. 253.

63. *Ibid.,* p. 252.   64. *Ibid.,* p. 284.

65. *Ibid.,* p. 287.   66. *Ibid.,* p. 51.

67. Clinton Rossiter, "The Legacy of John Adams," *Yale Review,* June, 1957, p. 531.

68. David Riesman *et al, The Lonely Crowd* (New York: Doubleday & Co., Anchor Books, 1953), p. 37.

VII: THE NEW CONSERVATISM: CORPORATIST UTOPIA

1. Peter F. Drucker, *The End of Economic Man* (New York: John Day Co., 1939), pp. 21, 39, 37.

2. *Ibid.,* pp. 108–9, 101–3.

3. Peter F. Drucker, *The Future of Industrial Man* (New York: John Day Co., 1942), pp. 24, 25, 29–30, 37–38, 39.

4. *Ibid.,* pp. 54–58, 74, 75, 78–79, 81, 84.

5. *Ibid.,* pp. 263, 224, 256–57.

6. George Santayana, *Reason in Society* (New York: Charles Scribner's Sons, 1929), pp. 128–30, 131–33.

7. George Santayana, *Dominations and Powers* (New York: Charles Scribner's Sons, 1951), pp. 374, vii–viii.

8. Drucker, *The Future of Industrial Man,* p. 55.

9. *Ibid.,* pp. 150, 152, 184, 177, 255.

10. *Ibid.,* pp. 184–88.

11. *Ibid.,* pp. 274, 278–80.   12. *Ibid.,* p. 267, 291.

13. Drucker, *The New Society* (New York: Harper & Bros., 1950), pp. 13–14.

14. Drucker, *Concept of the Corporation* (New York: John Day Co., 1946), p. 213.

15. Drucker, *The New Society,* pp. 247, 252, 192.

16. *Ibid.,* pp. 183–84, 216–18, 220–21.

17. *Ibid.,* p. 172.   18. *Ibid.,* pp. 161, 305–6.

19. *Ibid.,* p. 351.

20. Drucker, *Concept of the Corporation,* p. 113; *The New Society,* pp. 151, 153.

21. Drucker, *The New Society,* pp. 50–51, 66, 46.

22. *Ibid.,* pp. 71–72.   23. *Ibid.,* p. 282.

24. *Ibid.,* pp. 171–73.   25. *Ibid.,* pp. 158, 348.

26. *Ibid.,* pp. 283–92, 306.

27. *Ibid.,* pp. 199, 232–38, 243–44, 251.

28. *Ibid.,* pp. 318-24, 175–77.   29. *Ibid.,* pp. 115–16, 257–62.

30. *Ibid.,* pp. 222, 267–75, 289; *Concept of the Corporation,* pp. 36, 96.

31. Drucker, *The New Society,* pp. 118–20, 131–42, 241–42, 276, 325–30, 332–34, 340–42.

32. Drucker, *America's Next Twenty Years* (New York: Harper & Bros., 1957), pp. 4, 6, 8, 10, 19–28, 36–39, 47–50.

33. *Ibid.,* pp. 67–68; *The New Society,* pp. 36–37, 312–13, 338.

34. Drucker, *America's Next Twenty Years,* pp. 94–113.

35. Drucker, *Concept of the Corporation,* pp. 242–44, 297.

36. Robert A. Nisbet, *The Quest for Community* (New York: Oxford University Press, 1953); Drucker, "A Key to American Politics: Calhoun's Pluralism," *Review of Politics,* October, 1948, pp. 412–26.

37. Drucker, *The New Society,* p. 154.

38. *Ibid.,* p. 352.

39. Drucker, *The Future of Industrial Man,* p. 282.

40. Drucker, *The New Society,* p. 201.

41. *Ibid.,* p. 335.   42. *Ibid.,* p. 182.

43. *Ibid.,* p. 197; italics mine.   44. *Ibid.,* p. 315.

45. Drucker, *The Future of Industrial Man,* p. 177.

46. *Ibid.,* p. 293.

47. Drucker, *The New Society,* p. 291.

VIII: THE NEW LIBERALISM: NO ENEMIES ON THE RIGHT

1. Daniel J. Boorstin, *The Genius of American Politics* (Chicago: University of Chicago Press, 1953).

2. *Ibid.,* pp. 140–43.   3. *Ibid.,* p. 179.

4. Samuel P. Huntington, "Conservatism as an Ideology," *American Political Science Review,* LI, No. 2 (June, 1957), 472–73.

IX: VALUES AND HISTORY: THE TRANSITION FROM IDEOLOGY TO THEORY

1. Plato, *Republic,* tr. by B. Jowett (New York: Modern Library, 1941), 546–47.

2. *Ibid.,* 548–49.   3. *Ibid.,* 550.
4. *Ibid.,* 551.   5. *Ibid.,* 554–55.
6. *Ibid.,* 555.   7. *Ibid.,* 555, 557.
8. *Ibid.,* 560–61.   9. *Ibid.,* 557–58.
10. *Ibid.,* 558.   11. *Ibid.,* 564–65.
12. *Ibid.,* 571–75.

13. Aristotle, *Politics,* tr. by B. Jowett (New York: Modern Library, 1943), 1316.

14. *Ibid.,* 1286b.   15. Plato, *Republic,* 546, 424.
16. *Ibid.,* 555–56.

17. John of Salisbury, *The Statesman's Book,* tr. by J. Dickinson (New York: Alfred A. Knopf, 1927), Book VI, Chap. xiv, p. 223; Chap. xxiv, p. 251.

18. *Ibid.,* Book VI, Chap. xiv, p. 223; Chap. xxiv, p. 251.

19. John of Salisbury, *Frivolities of Courtiers and Footprints of Philosophers,* tr. by J. B. Pike (Minneapolis: University of Minnesota Press, 1938), Book VII, Chap. iv, p. 225.

20. Edmund Burke, *Letter to Wm. Elliot,* in *The Writings and Speeches of Edmund Burke* (12 vols., London: Bickers & Son, n.d.), V, 124.   In all subsequent citations of Burke in this chapter (through note 60), the volume and page references are to this edition, which I have used exclusively, not to the separate titles.

21. *Speech . . . on . . . Conciliation with the Colonies,* II, 122, 126, 127, 131.

22. *Letter to the Marquis of Rockingham,* VI, 179.   Italics added.

23. *Address to the British Colonists,* VI, 185, 187.

24. *Ibid.,* VI, 187, 191–92.

25. *An Appeal from the New to the Old Whigs,* IV, 99–100.

26. *Letters . . . on the Proposals for Peace, with the Regicide Directory of France,* V, 423.

27. *Ibid.,* V, 53, 55.   28. *Ibid.,* V, 423.

29. *Charge . . . against Warren Hastings . . . ,* IX, 465.

30. *Ninth Report on the Affairs of India,* VIII, 257.
31. G. M. Trevelyan, *History of England* (3 vols., Garden City, N. Y.: Doubleday & Co., Anchor Books, 1952), III, 125.
32. Burke, *Speech at . . . Bristol . . . Previous to Election,* II, 417.
33. *Speech . . . on Mr. Fox's East India Bill,* II, 465.
34. *Speech . . . on Powers of Juries . . . in Libels,* VII, 121.
35. *Speech on the Act of Uniformity,* VII, 5.
36. *Reflections on the Revolution in France,* III, 340.
37. *Ibid.,* III, 400–405.　　　38. *Ibid.,* III, 413.
39. *Ibid.,* III, 376.　　　40. *Ibid.,* III, 377.
41. *Ibid.,* III, 380.　　　42. *Ibid.,* III, 381.
43. *Ibid.,* III, 415.　　　44. *Ibid.,* III, 414, 430.
45. *Thoughts on French Affairs,* IV, 325–26.
46. *Ibid.,* IV, 327.　　　47. *Ibid.,* IV, 321.
48. *Ibid.,* IV, 319.
49. *Reflections on the Revolution in France,* III, 337.
50. *Thoughts on French Affairs,* IV, 332, 337–39, 342.
51. *Ibid.,* IV, 328.　　　52. *Ibid.,* IV, 377.
53. *Letter to Wm. Elliot,* V, 119.
54. *Speech in the Debates on the Army Estimates,* III, 215.
55. *Remarks on the Policies of the Allies,* IV, 469–70.
56. *Letters on the Proposals for Peace with the Regicide Directory of France,* V, 368–73.
57. *Ibid.,* V, 380.　　　58. *Ibid.,* V, 374.
59. *Ibid.,* VI, 42.　　　60. *Ibid.,* V, 235.
61. Herbert Agar, *Land of the Free* (Boston: Houghton Mifflin Co., 1935), pp. 13–16.
62. Russell Kirk, *The Conservative Mind: From Burke to Santayana* (Chicago: Henry Regnery Co., 1953), p. 59.
63. *Ibid.,* pp. 114–15.　　　64. *Ibid.,* p. 237.
65. Russell Kirk, *A Program for Conservatives* (Chicago: Henry Regnery Co., 1954), p. 110.
66. William H. Whyte, Jr., *The Organization Man* (Garden City, N. Y.: Doubleday & Co., Anchor Books, 1956), Chaps. 10, 11, 12.
67. Reinhold Niebuhr, *The Irony of American History* (New York: Charles Scribner's Sons, 1952), p. 157.
68. Reinhold Niebuhr, *The Nature and Destiny of Man* (2 vols, New York: Charles Scribner's Sons, 1943), II, 302–6.
69. *Ibid.,* II, 315.　　　70. *Ibid.,* II, 291.

X: THE CONSERVATIVE THEORY OF CHANGE: UPSIDE-DOWN HISTORY

1. R. H. Tawney, *Religion and the Rise of Capitalism* (New York: Mentor Books, 1947), pp. 228–29.
2. Peter Viereck, *The Unadjusted Man* (Boston: Beacon Press, 1956), pp. 113–17, 167, 171, 175, 180, 193, 196, 205, 213–15, 217.

3. Peter Viereck, *Shame and Glory of the Intellectuals* (Boston: Beacon Press, 1953), p. 195; *Conservatism Revisted* (New York: Charles Scribner's Sons, 1949), p. 123.

4. Viereck, *Conservatism Revisited*, pp. 194–95.

5. *Ibid.*, p. 113; Viereck, *The Unadjusted Man*, p. 326.

6. Richard Hofstadter, *The Age of Reform: From Bryan to FDR* (New York: Alfred A. Knopf, 1955), pp. 33, 50–51.

7. Peter Drucker, *The End of Economic Man* (New York: John Day Co., 1939), p. 265.

8. Henry Adams, *The Education of Henry Adams* (New York, Modern Library, 1931), p. 297.

9. Russell Kirk, *A Program for Conservatives* (Chicago: Henry Regnery Co., 1954), p. 19.

Bibliography

Adams, Henry. The Education of Henry Adams. New York: Modern Library, 1931.

Agar, Herbert, et al. The City of Man. New York, Viking Press, 1941.

—— A Declaration of Faith. Boston: Houghton Mifflin Co., 1952.

—— Land of the Free. Boston: Houghton Mifflin Co., 1935.

—— The People's Choice. Boston: Houghton Mifflin Co., 1933.

—— The Price of Union. Boston: Houghton Mifflin Co., 1950.

—— Pursuit of Happiness. Boston: Houghton Mifflin Co., 1938.

—— A Time for Greatness. Boston: Little, Brown & Co., 1942.

—— and Allen Tate, eds. Who Owns America? Boston: Houghton Mifflin Co., 1936.

Aristotle. Politics. Translated by B. Jowett. New York: Modern Library, 1943.

Augustine, St. The City of God. Translated by M. Dods. 2 vols. New York: Hafner Publishing Co., 1948.

Bell, Bernard I. Crowd Culture. New York: Harper & Bros., 1952.

Boorstin, Daniel J. The Genius of American Politics. Chicago: University of Chicago Press, 1953.

Burke, Edmund. The Writings and Speeches of Edmund Burke. 12 vols. London: Bickers & Son, n.d.

Cash, Wilbur J. The Mind of the South. Garden City, N. Y.: Doubleday & Co., Anchor Books, 1956.

Cicero. De re publica, de legibus. Translated by C. W. Keyes. Cambridge: Harvard University Press, 1928.

Coker, Francis W. Organismic Theories of the State. Studies in History, Economics and Public Law, Vol. XXXVIII, No. 2. New York: Columbia University Press, 1910.

Davidson, Donald. The Attack on Leviathan. Chapel Hill: University of North Carolina Press, 1938.

Davidson, Donald. "I'll Take My Stand: A History," *American Review*, V (1935), 301–21.

Drucker, Peter F. America's Next Twenty Years. New York: Harper & Bros., 1957.

— Concept of the Corporation. New York: John Day Co., 1946.

— The End of Economic Man. New York: John Day Co., 1939.

— The Future of Industrial Man. New York: John Day Co., 1942.

— "A Key to American Politics: Calhoun's Pluralism," *Review of Politics*, October, 1948, pp. 412–26.

— The New Society. New York: Harper & Bros., 1950.

Duverger, Maurice. Political Parties: Their Organization and Activities in the Modern State. Translated by B. and R. North. New York: John Wiley & Sons, 1954.

Eaton, Clement. A History of the Old South. New York: Macmillan Co., 1949.

Hallowell, John. The Decline of Liberalism as an Ideology. Berkeley: University of California Press, 1943.

— Main Currents in Modern Political Thought. New York: Henry Holt & Co., 1950.

— The Moral Foundations of Democracy. Chicago: University of Chicago Press, 1954.

Harrigan, Anthony. "Is Our Administration Conservative?" *Catholic World*, April, 1954, pp. 24–28.

— "Masters of the Market," *Catholic World*, April, 1957, pp. 410–15.

— "The Realities of the American Situation," *Catholic World*, March, 1957, pp. 458–64.

Hartz, Louis. The Liberal Tradition in America. New York: Harcourt, Brace & Co., 1955.

Hofstadter, Richard. The Age of Reform: From Bryan to FDR. New York: Alfred A. Knopf, 1955.

— The American Political Tradition. New York: Alfred A. Knopf, Vintage Books, 1954.

Huntington, Samuel P. "Conservatism as an Ideology," *American Polital Science Review*, LI, No. 2 (June, 1957), 454–73.

I'll Take My Stand, by Twelve Southerners. New York: Harper & Bros., 1930.

Irish, Marian. "Recent Political Thought in the South," *American Political Science Review*, XLVI (1952), 121–41.

John of Salisbury. Frivolities of Courtiers and Footprints of Philosophers. Translated by J. B. Pike. Minneapolis: Univ. of Minnesota Press, 1938.

— The Statesman's Book. Translated by J. Dickinson. New York: Alfred A. Knopf, 1927.

Key, V. O. Southern Politics in State and Nation. New York: Alfred A. Knopf, 1950.

Kirk, Russell. Academic Freedom. Chicago: Henry Regnery Co., 1955.

— Beyond the Dreams of Avarice. Chicago: Henry Regnery Co., 1956.

—— The Conservative Mind: From Burke to Santayana. Chicago: Henry Regnery Co., 1953.

—— The Intelligent Woman's Guide to Conservatism. New York: Devin-Adair Co., 1957.

—— A Program for Conservatives. Chicago: Henry Regnery Co., 1954.

Lowell, A. Lawrence. Essays on Government. Boston: Houghton Mifflin Co., 1889.

—— Public Opinion and Popular Government. New York: Longmans, Green & Co., 1926.

—— Public Opinion in War and Peace. Cambridge: Harvard University Press, 1923.

Lubell, Samuel. The Future of American Politics. New York: Harper & Bros., 1952.

—— The Revolt of the Moderates. New York: Harper & Bros., 1956.

Mannheim, Karl. Ideology and Utopia. Translated by L. Worth and E. Shils. New York: Harcourt, Brace & Co., 1954.

Mills, C. Wright. The Power Elite. New York: Oxford University Press, 1956.

—— White Collar. New York: Oxford University Press, 1951.

Niebuhr, Reinhold. The Children of Light and the Children of Darkness. New York: Charles Scribner's Sons, 1944.

—— The Irony of American History. New York: Charles Scribner's Sons, 1952.

—— The Nature and Destiny of Man. Vol. II. New York: Charles Scribner's Sons, 1943.

—— The Self and the Dramas of History. New York: Charles Scribner's Sons, 1955.

Nisbet, Robert A. The Quest for Community. New York: Oxford University Press, 1953.

Oates, J. W., ed. The Stoic and Epicurean Philosophers. New York: Random House, 1940.

Odgard, H. P. Sin and Society: Reinhold Niebuhr as Political Theologian. Yellow Springs, Ohio: Antioch Press, 1956.

Phillips, Ulrich B. The Course of the South to Secession. New York: Appleton-Century, 1939.

Plato. Laws. Translated by A. E. Taylor. London: J. M. Dent & Sons, 1934.

—— Republic. Translated by B. Jowett. New York: Modern Library, 1941.

—— Statesman. Translated by J. B. Skemp. New Haven: Yale University Press, 1952.

Randall, J. G. The Civil War and Reconstruction. Boston: D. C. Heath & Co., 1953.

Ranney, Austin. The Doctrine of Responsible Party Government. Urbana, Ill.: University of Illinois Press, 1954.

Ransom, John C. *et al.* "Agrarianism Today," *Shenandoah,* Summer, 1952, pp. 14–33.
—— Poems and Essays. New York: Vintage Books, 1955.
Riesman, David, *et al.* The Lonely Crowd. New York: Doubleday & Co., Anchor Books, 1953.
Rossiter, Clinton. The American Presidency. New York: Harcourt, Brace & Co., 1956.
—— Conservatism in America. New York: Alfred A. Knopf, 1955.
—— Constitutional Dictatorship. Princeton: Princeton University Press, 1948.
—— "The Legacy of John Adams," *Yale Review,* June, 1957, pp. 528–50.
Sabine, George H. A History of Political Theory. New York: Henry Holt & Co., 1955.
Salisbury, John of, *see* John of Salisbury.
Santayana, George. Dominations and Powers. New York: Charles Scribner's Sons, 1951.
—— Reason in Society. New York: Charles Scribner's Sons, 1929.
Simkins, Francis B. The South, Old and New. New York: Alfred A. Knopf, 1947.
Spengler, Oswald. The Decline of the West. Translated by C. F. Atkinson. 2 vols. New York: Alfred A. Knopf, 1926–28.
Spitz, David. Patterns of Anti-Democratic Thought. New York: Macmillan Co., 1949.
Tate, Allen. "View of the Whole South," *American Review* (1934), 411–32.
Tawney, R. H. Religion and the Rise of Capitalism. New York: Mentor Books, 1947.
Trevelyan, G. M. History of England. 3 vols. Garden City, N. Y.: Doubleday & Co., Anchor Books. 1952.
Trevor-Roper, H. R. The Gentry, 1540–1640. Cambridge University Press, 1953.
Twelve Southerners. I'll Take My Stand. New York: Harper & Bros., 1930.
Valentine, Alan. The Age of Conformity. Chicago: Henry Regnery Co., 1954.
Viereck, Peter. Conservatism: From John Adams to Churchill. New York: Van Nostrand Co., Anvil Books, 1956.
—— Conservatism Revisited. New York: Charles Scribner's Sons, 1949.
—— Shame and Glory of the Intellectuals. Boston: Beacon Press, 1953.
—— The Unadjusted Man. Boston: Beacon Press, 1956.
Weaver, Richard M. The Ethics of Rhetoric. Chicago: Henry Regnery Co., 1953.
—— Ideas Have Consequences. Chicago: University of Chicago Press, 1948.
—— "The Tennessee Agrarians," *Shenandoah,* Summer, 1952, pp. 3–10.
Whyte, William H., Jr. The Organization Man. Garden City, N.Y.: Doubleday & Co., Anchor Books, 1956.

Wilhelmsen, Frederick L. "The Alienated Professor," *Commonweal*, April 6, 1956, pp. 9–12.

—— "The Conservative Vision," *Commonweal*, June 24, 1955, pp. 295–99.

—— "Contemporary Criticism in the Georgian Manner," *Commonweal*, June 13, 1956, pp. 375–76.

Wish, Harvey. Society and Thought in Modern America. New York: Longmans, Green & Co., 1952.

Woodward, C. Vann. Origins of the New South, 1877–1913. Baton Rouge: Louisiana State University Press, 1951.

Yeoman, H. A. Abbott Lawrence Lowell. Cambridge: Harvard University Press, 1948.

Index

Academic freedom: defined by Kirk, 150

Adams, Brooks: closeness to reality, 94

Adams, Henry: traditionalist, 94; symbolizes shift to sweeping criticism from Mugwump laissez-faire, 98; death, 101; charge that modern society has no moral image of love, 132; agnosticism, 138, 311; anti-Semitism, 185; secular Conservative, 207; theory of organic industrial philosophy, 223; theory of degeneration of "energy," 281; view of hierarchies of nature as inverted hierarchies of harmony, 312

Adams, John: hero to Agar, 113; view that vote be restricted to property owners, 114; considered by Kirk the native model for Conservatism, 140

Adams, John Quincy: resistance to party system, 115

Adams family: denunciation of slavery, 81; political oscillations, 94; rejection of Southern society, 142

Adjusted Conservatism, 186, 239; adjusted to increased scope of political authority, 98; revival, 159

Adjusted Conservatives, 96–98; acceptance of democratic Liberalism and industrialization, 97; argument on New Deal, 100; realistic about religious revival, 147; acceptance of change, 171; criticisms of American society, 177; false assumptions in historical comparisons, 180; prepared for more authoritarian future, 199; Rossiter's extreme and explicit form, 200; impossible position, 203; separation of theory and practice, 204; and Middle Stoics, 235

Advertising: anti-Conservative influence, 85, 228

Aesthetics: Burke's work on, 34–35

Affection: Conservative theme, 35; importance of, 41; individual's capacity for, 289, 291; see also Communal affection; Love

Agar, Herbert: early distributist tie to Southern agrarians, 107; on race problem, 109; ideology, 112–18; member of group publishing statement of principles for wartime America, 116–17; interpretation of "concurrent majority," 125; shift to adjusted Conservatism, 132; accepts American system of pressure groups and party compromise, 159; adjustment to American politics, 168–74; confusion in moral standards, 170; analysis of American parties, 173; theory of degeneration, 281

"Agrarian myth," 121

Agrarians, Southern, *see* Southern agrarians

Southern agrarians on, 126; revolutionizes nature of American society, 128; destruction of tradition, 143; and dehumanization of man in Hallowell's analysis, 164; Viereck's views on, 179; Santayana's vs. Drucker's views, 212; effect on process of degeneration, 290; causes, 291

Industrial Revolution: moral and political fragmentation of the world attributed to, by Agar, 168; foundation of 20th-century economic changes, 296

Industrial society: Rossiter's acceptance of, 188; subordination of social function to economic function, 219

Inflation: justifiable limits on scope of government action on, 192; Drucker's solution, 223

Inflationary pressures: relief through automation, 223

Inherited property: and Burke, 58; *see also* Old wealth

"Intellectual": term, 9*n*

Intellectual conflict: Kirk's acceptance of, 150

Intellectual elite, 101; Kirk's solution to degeneration of American society, 149

Intellectual power: qualification for, 10

Intellectuals: influence as "conscience" of society, 181

Interaction, *see* Multiple causation and interaction

Ireland: in Burke's analysis of imperial relations, 54

Irish Catholics: discrimination against, 57

Isolationism, 122

Ives, Irving: example of "natural aristocrat" for Viereck, 183

Jefferson, Thomas: Liberal leadership, 72; hero to Agar, 113; reference to, by Southern agrarians, 124; Kirk's reference to, 140; institution of private property unchallenged by, 187; revolutionary Liberal, 248

Jeffersonian agrarianism, 107

Jeffersonianism, 111

Jeffersonian Liberalism: effort to weld with Southern Conservatism, 110

John of Salisbury: *Policraticus*, 25; Conservative ideology, 25–30; critical of corrupting influences of the cities, 26; favorable evaluation of society, 27; lack of solution for problems of day, 28–29; criticisms of aristocracy, 64; view of Late Middle Ages as period of moral decline, 265–66; avoidance of historical analysis, 303

Justice: Aristotle's definition, 165

Ketteler, Wilhelm Emmanuel von: criticism of Liberalism, 207

King, *see* Monarch

Kirk, Russell: cited, 128; ideology, 133–54; *The Intelligent Woman's Guide to Conservatism*, 134–35, 137, 138; concept of justice, 139; social and economic ideology, 143–49; representative of contemporary Conservatism in its most contradictory position, 148; criticism of his ideology, 157; attitude toward the Negro, 193; Drucker's plan in opposition to, 234; examples of Conservative "realism," 281; theory of degeneration, 281; warning against industrializing backward areas, 304; on Henry Adams' agnosticism, 311; claim that tranquillity in death is man's greatest potential happiness, 312

Kohn, Hans: member of group publishing statement of principles for wartime America, 116–17

Labor shortages: America, 69

Labor unions: Conservative, to Viereck, 179; effects of, 217; *see also* Unionism

La Follette, Robert M.: Progressive Party, 298

Laissez-faire Liberalism: equated with Conservatism, 186

Laissez-faire policy: advocated by Burke, 53; rejected by Rossiter as anti-Conservative, 187

Landed aristocracy, 11; England, 72

Landed property: basis of stable government for Burke, 48

Landowners: U.S., 72